Business Power

Business Power

Creating New Wealth from IP Assets

ROBERT SHEARER AND THE MEMBERS OF
THE NATIONAL KNOWLEDGE & INTELLECTUAL
PROPERTY MANAGEMENT TASKFORCE

*Foreword by The Honorable Robert C. Cresanti
Under Secretary of Commerce for Technology
U.S. Department of Commerce*

John Wiley & Sons, Inc.

This book is printed on acid-free paper. ♾

Author Profile Caricatures: Chris Morris (chris@morrisca.com)

Published by John Wiley & Sons, Inc., Hoboken, New Jersey.

Published simultaneously in Canada.

Wiley Bicentennial Logo: Richard J. Pacifico

For general information on our other products and services, or technical support, please contact our Customer Care Department within the United States at 800-762-2974, outside the United States at 317-572-3993 or fax 317-572-4002.

Wiley also publishes its books in a variety of electronic formats. Some content that appears in print may not be available in electronic books.

For more information about Wiley products, visit our Web site at http://www.wiley.com.

Library of Congress Cataloging-in-Publication Data:

ISBN: 978-0-470-12075-0

Printed in the United States of America

10 9 8 7 6 5 4 3 2 1

A Dedication Note from the Taskforce

To the creators, inventors, and innovators who are defined by their practical needs and occasional genius to find solutions that improve the quality of our lives, one invention at a time.

Whether we are one, or one of many, it is our growing knowledge, creativity, and innovative power that define us as Americans. This indomitable spirit is nurtured by a unique freedom to invent, commercialize, and enjoy a period of protection for one's invention that is the joy of every inventor, creative team, and consumer. This is the core capability of the American dream that rewards merit and fuels prosperity.

We hope the knowledge we offer will find service in your strategy and efforts to gain new wealth from your IP assets.

Author Profiles

Dr. Cohen Pam Cohen is a behaviorist and expert in performance measurement and management, specializing in intangible valuation in complex business environments. Her work is done through unique qualitative and quantitative research design and analysis. Pam's consulting work and research focuses on behavioral economics, and in particular, on intangible valuation, developing causal business models, maximizing the utility of human capital, and devising integrated decision support systems. The results from her research and modeling work are used to develop action plans for organizational improvement initiatives. In partnership with Fleishman-Hillard, Inc. of the Omnicom Group, Predictiv has established Communications Consultants Worldwide (CCW) to provide measurement and management solutions to the communications industry.

Her publications include work on patterns of attitudinal and perceptual change. She has delivered seminars and lectures on adding rigor and reducing bias in qualitative and quantitative research analysis. Her book on intangible valuation titled, *Invisible Advantage: How Intangibles Are Driving Business Performance,* was written with co-author Jonathan Low. In addition to her published articles on the topic, her recent speaking engagements have been at ABC World News, *Forbes,* CNNfn, *Money Matters,* the *New York Times, CFO* magazine, and on a variety of radio and television programs.

Pam has a PhD in Sociology, concentrating in Social Psychology, from the University of Michigan.

Bill Coughlin Bill is the President and CEO of Ford Global Technologies, Inc. Bill has helped champion innovation at Ford by launching an Innovation Center, promoting employee ideas, and even applying his IP-based resources to initiate, create, and demonstrate new product features. He was instrumental in developing the Taskforce framework defining the power of an IP market through the securitization of IP assets.

He was formerly President of DaimlerChrysler Intellectual Capital Corporation, the Chief Patent Counsel of DaimlerChrysler Corporation, and the Director of Intellectual Property Law for DaimlerChrysler AG. Mr. Coughlin is currently on the Board of Directors for the Intellectual Property Owners Association, and he has 17 years of outside counsel experience at Harness, Dickey & Pierce PLC, 12 years of which he spent as a principal member of the firm.

Mr. Coughlin is a graduate of the University of Michigan (BSEE), Detroit College of Law at Michigan State University (JD), and the Stanford Executive Program at the Stanford University Graduate School of Business.

Bill is a founding member of the Taskforce and served as its Honorary Chairman 2000–2003.

The Honorable Robert C. Cresanti The Honorable Robert C. Cresanti was nominated by President Bush to serve as Under Secretary of Commerce for Technology on November 10, 2005. Following Senate confirmation, he was sworn into office on March 20, 2006. Mr. Cresanti directs the operations of the Commerce Department's Technology Administration, providing direction to and oversight of the Office of Technology Policy, the National Institute of Standards and Technology (NIST), and the National Technical Information Service (NTIS).

As Under Secretary, Mr. Cresanti co-chairs the President's National Science and Technology Council's (NSTC) Committee on Technology and chairs its Interagency Working Group on Manufacturing R&D. He also participates in three other NSTC committees: the Committee on

Science; the Committee on Environment and Natural Resources; and the Committee on Homeland and National Security.

The Under Secretary regularly participates in the meetings of the President's Council of Advisors on Science and Technology, a panel consisting of private-sector and academic leaders who advise the President on technology, scientific research priorities, and math and science education. Mr. Cresanti also serves as the Commerce Department's Chief Privacy Officer—the highest ranking CPO in the federal government—guiding departmental activities related to the development and implementation of federal privacy laws, policies, and practices. He also chairs the Commerce Department Radio Frequency ID Working Group.

Karl Fink Karl is the managing partner of the law firm Fitch, Even, Tabin & Flannery, and is a partner in the firm's litigation practice. He has extensive experience in commercial and tort litigation, with experience in patent, trademark, copyright, and trade secret actions. Representative cases in which Karl had primary or significant responsibility include: *Overhead v. Chamberlain,* 194 F.3d 1261 (Fed. Cir. 1999); *Greisz v. Household Bank,* 176 F.3d 1612 (7th Cir. 1999); *Energy Services Air Conditioning v. Nicor, Inc.,* 46 USPQ 2d 1639 (N.D. Ill. 1997); *Paramount Packaging Corp. v. Cello Bag Co., Inc.,* 909 F.2d 1494 (Fed Cir. 1990), *Whittaker Corp. v. UNR Industries Inc.,* 911 F.2d 709 (Fed. Cir. 1990), *Cabot Corp. v. Thai Tantalum Inc.,* 25 USPQ2d 1619 (Del. Ch. 1992), *Blanas v. Alwan,* 1995 U.S. Dist. LEXIS 9315; *Corrales v. American Cab Co.,* 524 N.E.2d 923 (Ill. App. 1988); *Reliance Ins. Co. v. Nick J. Giannini, Inc.,* 511 N.E.2d 755 (Ill. App. 1987).

Mr. Fink was admitted to the Illinois Bar (1981), the U.S. Supreme Court, the U.S. Courts of Appeals for the Federal Circuit and the Seventh Circuit, and the U.S. District Court for the Northern District of Illinois (member of Trial Bar), registered to practice before the U.S. Patent and Trademark Office (1990), member of American Bar Association, Illinois State Bar Association, and Chicago Bar Association. Karl is on the list of Leading Illinois Attorneys and is past president of the Chicago Lincoln American Inn of Court.

Education: University of Michigan (BSE 1978, magna cum laude; JD 1981, Tau Beta Pi).

Mike Geoffrey As Chief IP Counsel at USG Corporation, Mr. Geoffrey is responsible for patent, trademark, and other intellectual property matters of the Corporation and its subsidiaries worldwide. Mr. Geoffrey works with business management in developing and implementing strategic planning for the protection and licensing of the Corporation's proprietary technical innovations, trade secrets, copyrightable works, and trademarks. Mr. Geoffrey worked with clients to secure, license, and enforce intellectual property rights worldwide. In addition to his counseling practice, Mr. Geoffrey has litigated cases involving copyrights, trademarks, trade secrets, and patents.

Mr. Geoffrey is a member of the bar of the State of Illinois and the United States District Court for the Northern District of Illinois. He is also a member of the Trial Bar of the United States District Court for the Northern District of Illinois and is licensed to practice before the United States Patent and Trademark Office.

R. Mark Halligan Mark Halligan is a trial lawyer and a principal in the Chicago office of Lovells, an international business law firm, and teaches courses in advanced trade secrets law and trade secret litigation at John Marshall Law School in Chicago. He is widely recognized as the country's leading expert in trade secrets law and the Economic Espionage Act of 1996, and he has sponsored the Trade Secrets Home Page on the Internet since 1994.

Mr. Halligan has lectured and published widely in the areas of trade secrets law and the Economic Espionage Act of 1996, and has been quoted in numerous publications and broadcasts, including the *Washington Post,* the Associated Press, *Time, USA Today*, CNN, and *Crain's Chicago Business.* He has held a variety of professional positions including president of the Intellectual Property Law Association of Chicago, and he is currently serving for the second time as chair of the American Bar Association's trade secrets committee.

Mr. Halligan is the co-author of a new book entitled *Trade Secret Asset Management: An Executive's Guide to Information Asset Management,* as well as *Sarbanes-Oxley Accounting Requirements for Trade Secrets,* published in August 2006 by Aspatore Press (ISBN 1-59622-560-2). See www.rmark-halligan.com.

Dave Haug Dave Haug is CFO of SBC Knowledge Ventures. He is responsible for the finance and accounting operations of the business unit. Prior to his role with Knowledge Ventures, Mr. Haug held a similar role for SBC Internet Services and was Vice President and Controller of Prodigy Internet Services. Prior to these roles he has held various positions as Vice President of Finance for a startup company from 2000 to 2001 and a publicly registered fuel distribution and retail company from 1990 to 2000. Mr. Haug has also served as Audit Manager for a regional public accounting firm from 1982 to 1990. Mr. Haug received his BA in Accounting from New Mexico State University and is a Texas CPA.

Dr. Steve Henning Steven L. Henning, PhD, is a Partner at the accounting firm of Marks Paneth & Shron. He serves on the SEC Procedures Committee and the FASB Taskforce on Intangible Assets. He is the Taskforce program director and formerly served as the Academic Fellow in the Office of the Chief Accountant at the United States Securities and Exchange Commission. At the same time he was an Assistant Professor of Accounting in the Edwin L. Cox School of Business at Southern Methodist University. He previously held an appointment at the University of Colorado at Boulder. He received his PhD from the University of Wisconsin at Madison and an MBA from the University of Miami (FL).

Dr. Henning is the Taskforce Program Director, leading in the development of IP valuation methodologies and standards for the Taskforce in its project with the Statistics Division of the United Nations and the U.S. Department of Commerce.

Dr. Henning is a Fellow at the Center for Advanced Technologies.

Dr. Jan Jaferian is an internationally known expert in corporate and business development and in intellectual asset management. She has distinguished herself as she launched or revitalized businesses for Fortune 500 companies in the telecommunications, computer, electronics, and petrochemicals industries. Her strategic perspective and innovative analytical methods have enabled companies to collectively realize billions of dollars in revenue from licensing, strategic alliances, joint ventures, litigation settlements, spin-outs, mergers, acquisitions, and new businesses.

Dr. Jaferian was formerly president of Lucent Technologies Intellectual Property Business, where she was responsible for creating and maintaining worldwide patent and other intellectual property assets as well as generating revenue from the worldwide licensing of patents, trademarks, know-how, and copyrights. She was responsible for enforcing Lucent's IP rights through various assertion and litigation programs. She rebuilt the organization and its processes, including replenishing and refocusing the patent portfolio, revitalizing the revenue streams, rebuilding the annuity base, and increasing cash flows and profit contributions.

Dr. Jaferian has served as Vice President of Intellectual Property Operations at Xerox Corporation; served on the Board of Directors of the National Intellectual Property Law Institute since 1997 and served as its Chairman from 2000 to 2004.

Dr. Jaferian has a BS and MBA from the University of New Hampshire and her Doctor of Business Administration from Harvard Business School.

Dr. Mark Karasek Dr. Karasek is Executive Vice President of Engineering with The Chamberlain Group, Inc., a successful mid-sized company in the consumer durables industry. Dr. Karasek leads a dynamic, industry-leading organization in the area of product development, R&D, and intellectual capital management. He was instrumental in moving the company's intellectual property management effort from a narrowly focused, defensive activity to a proactive, business-focused strategic management process. Under Dr. Karasek, Chamberlain has introduced numerous industry-leading products and features covered by patents, copyrights, and/or trademarks. Dr. Karasek has also been active in study of the management and execution of innovation, serving as Chair of Strategic Development of the Kellogg Innovation Network at Northwestern University, an industry group focused on innovation best practices. Prior to joining Chamberlain, Dr. Karasek held project management and R&D positions at Illinois Tool Works and The Applied Research Laboratory at Penn State University. He is active in his community and has provided strategic planning assistance to a variety of not-for-profit organizations. Dr. Karasek has a BS in Engineering Mechanics and an MS in Mechanical Engineering from the University of Illinois in Urbana-Champaign. He has a PhD in Polymer Science from The Pennsylvania State University.

Dr. Karasek is a Fellow at the Center for Advanced Technologies.

Dr. Vassilis Keramidas Dr. Keramidas retired as the Vice President of Formative Technologies in the Applied Research Area of Telcordia Technologies (formerly Bellcore). In the 1980s and 1990s, Dr. Keramidas established the Research Division making seminal contributions in the fields of photonic and electronic materials and devices for telecommunications, fibers and fiber amplifiers, high-temperature superconducting materials, ferroelectric materials for nonvolatile memories, and magnetic materials for colossal magnetoresistance devices and energy storage. The Bellcore research activities on the energy storage front ushered the polymer battery Li-ion technology with the invention of the Bellcore Plastic Li-ion (PLiON) Technology in the late 1990s.

Dr. Keramidas formulated and carried out the commercialization of the PLiON battery technology, licensing to 22 companies worldwide. In the course of a five-year effort, Dr. Keramidas's technology commercialization efforts brought in more than $104 million to Telcordia from licensing fees, royalties, and the sale of IP. In addition, other technologies, developed primarily in his organizations, were valuated at over $60 million and were donated by Telcordia/SAIC for tax benefits.

Dr. Keramidas serves on the board of directors of two companies, continuing to provide valuable input in research, technology, and product development decisions and shaping the governance and reporting policies of these companies.

Christopher Leisner Chris is the founder of Creative IP Solutions, LLC, an intellectual property consulting firm specializing in managing and monetizing intellectual property. Chris has been an active participant in the National Knowledge and Intellectual Property Taskforce; he has made presentations at seminars and executive briefings on IP value recognition and IP value extraction techniques. He presently chairs the Taskforce IP-Finance Committee.

Chris previously served as Midwest Partner in Charge of Litigation Consulting Services and the Regional Business Line Leader for Specialty Consulting Services at BDO Seidman, LLP, where he led the litigation consulting team that was acknowledged by *Accounting Today* with its Gold Medal Award for Client Service. He serves as an expert witness on accounting malpractice, fraud, and damages and has been cited in trial and appellate decisions. Chris served as technical advisor to the American Bar Association's Legal Technology Advisory Council.

In March 2006, Chris co-authored the tenth edition revision to the Wiley *Accountant's Handbook*—Chapter 20A: "Goodwill and Other Intangible Assets—an Update."

Jonathan Low Jon is a Partner and Co-Founder of Predictiv, LLC and a joint venture partner with Omnicom's Fleishman-Hillard in Communications Consultants Worldwide, which value the impact of brand and communications on financial outcomes. His specialty is management performance and organizational effectiveness, primarily the valuation of intangibles such as strategy execution, brand, intellectual capital, innovation, alliances, and organizational transition. He and his colleagues work with clients in business, government, and the not-for-profit sector in the United States and Europe. Jon was a Senior Fellow at Cap Gemini Ernst & Young's Center for Business Innovation. Under his leadership, CGEY produced four major reports on the growing role of intangibles in the global economy. The major studies include *Measures That Matter, Success Factors in the IPO Transformation Process, Decisions That Matter,* and *The Value Creation Index*. Jon has also organized and co-hosted with *Forbes ASAP* an annual conference entitled *Measuring the Future*. His work has appeared in the *Wall Street Journal,* the

New York Times, Business Week, Forbes, and other publications. He has been a guest on ABC-TV, CBS, CNBC, CNNfn, National Public Radio, and other electronic media. He is the co-author of *Invisible Advantage.*

Mr. Low is a Fellow at the Center for Advanced Technologies.

Ed Paradise Ed is Vice President and General Manager for Cisco's Mobility, Signaling, and Control Business Unit (MSCBU) and is Site Executive for Cisco's Research Triangle Park, North Carolina campus. In his MSCBU role, Ed oversees Cisco's work with mobile operator and cable customers as they transition their networks to an Internet Protocol–based infrastructure. As Cisco's Research Triangle Park (RTP) Site Executive, Ed represents Cisco and its approximately 2,500 RTP–based employees.

As Cisco's Site Executive in RTP, Paradise represents Cisco and its approximately 2,500 RTP–based employees in the external community. Mr. Paradise works with the local business community and state and local government to ensure the existence of an environment that supports Cisco's presence in the community. He also works with other Cisco business unit/function leaders in RTP to foster the advancement of Cisco culture and teamwork on the site.

Mr. Paradise was promoted to Vice President of IBD Engineering. The IBD led Cisco to an 80 percent market share in the SNA-to-IP customer migration space. In 1999, an alliance was formed between IBM and Cisco to provide customers the best possible network solutions.

Prior to joining Cisco, Mr. Paradise worked at IBM as a senior manager at the Thomas Watson Research Center, Yorktown Heights, New York. His research projects lead to the development of several IBM communications products. Prior to joining the research team, he managed a hardware department with IBM's Biomedical Systems Business Unit. Mr. Paradise joined IBM in June 1978.

Mr. Paradise is also a founding member of the National Knowledge & Intellectual Property Management Taskforce and is Cisco's executive lead with Wake Forest University.

He is a Fellow at the Center for Advanced Technologies. He is a founding Taskforce member and served as the Taskforce Honorary Chair 1998–1999.

Steven G. Parmelee Steve is a partner at Fitch, Even, Tabin & Flannery, working out of their Chicago offices. Mr. Parmelee's work activities relate solely to intellectual property issues with a particular emphasis on patents, including portfolio management.

Mr. Parmelee worked as an intellectual property attorney in private practice for seven years prior to joining Motorola's in-house patent department, where he worked for 17 years. He served Motorola as Vice President and Director of Intellectual Property for Nascent and Emerging Technologies. Prior to that he was Vice President and Director of Portfolio Management. Mr. Parmelee has extensive experience in all facets of intellectual property practice, both in the United States and in foreign countries. While working for Motorola, Mr. Parmelee had considerable overseas exposure, including a two-year tour of duty as manager of the Motorola Patent Department office in Singapore.

He has represented clients in various patent, trademark, copyright, and trade secret matters (including portfolio reviews, defensive and enforcement studies, licensing, acquisitions and divestitures, standards bodies representation, litigation, anti-counterfeiting, and various patent acquisition and maintenance activities).

Mr. Parmelee has a JD degree from Creighton University School of Law where he graduated Magna cum Laude, and a degree in Electrical Engineering from Rose-Hulman Institute of Technology.

He is a Fellow at the Center for Advanced Technologies and a founding member of the Taskforce.

Robert Shearer Bob Shearer started the *National Knowledge & Intellectual Property Management Taskforce* to accelerate economic development through technological innovation and create an economic framework to accommodate intellectual property assets.

The Taskforce was recognized for its leadership through an invitation from the United Nations, Statistics Division, to conduct a joint research project into the effects of R&D on economic development for application in developed and developing nations. The U.S. Department of Commerce, the Bureau of Economic

Analysis, and the Office of the Under Secretary for Technology Administration have recently joined the Taskforce's initiative to put IP assets into America's mainstream economy.

Mr. Shearer is an experienced professional in executive and organizational development and has led many clients to successful solutions using staffing, organizational design, executive continuity, educational, and training strategies. He has served as an expert witness in federal court on matters pertaining to organizational behavior and market research.

Mr. Shearer was a board member of the Superconducting Super Collider, and a part of the successful grassroots $1 billion Texas referendum to finance the winning national proposal to the U.S. Department of Energy.

He earned an MBA at Southern Methodist University with honors and was recognized as the outstanding male student in the class.

Mr. Shearer is a Vietnam-era fighter pilot, serving as an air combat tactics instructor (the predecessor to the Top Gun Program) and retired as a Colonel in the Marine Corps Reserve.

Dr. Bruce Stuckman Dr. Bruce Stuckman is a partner with the Texas IP law firm, Garlick, Harrison & Markison (GHM). He has been a frequent author and speaker on topics relating to intellectual property law and technology. He has published more than 70 articles and has lectured more than 50 times at professional meetings and symposia sponsored by such organizations as the American Bar Association (ABA), the Licensing Executives Society (LES), the American Intellectual Property Law Association (AIPLA), the Association of University Technology Managers (AUTM), and the Institute of Electrical & Electronics Engineers (IEEE). He has served on the faculties of the University of Louisville and Oakland University and as a guest lecturer at the University of Michigan and the University of Texas. He is a past fellow of the U of L/BellSouth Telecommunications research center and has served as a consultant to such entities as General Motors, General Electric, British Petroleum, the U.S. Navy, and the Central Intelligence Agency. As an inventor, Bruce holds more than 30 U.S. patents.

In 1996, Bruce became the first in-house patent counsel to Ameritech Corporation, a Fortune 50 telecommunications company. In 1999, he became the chief patent counsel to the SBC Communications family of companies with the merger of SBC and Ameritech. Bruce served as an officer of several SBC subsidiaries, and in 2004 he took on the additional role of Vice President and General Counsel for SBC Knowledge Ventures, SBC's IP management and licensing subsidiary, a position he held until joining GHM in 2005.

Bruce holds a BS in Electrical Engineering (Magna cum Laude), an MS in Electrical and Computer Engineering, a PhD in Systems Engineering from Oakland University, and a JD (cum Laude) from the University of Louisville, where he graduated first in his class.

Bruce is a Fellow at the Center for Advanced Technologies.

Contents

SECTION ONE

Up Front

The Foreword: The Honorable Robert Cresanti, Under Secretary of Commerce—Technology Administration has a number of key responsibilities for our nation's prosperity. These include:

- Technological innovation and competitiveness
- Developing and promoting measures and standards
- Promoting international trade and economic growth
- Providing access to information that stimulates discovery and innovation

Mr. Cresanti's experience in banking and finance, governmental relations, and intellectual property brings a unique skill mix to this important office at a time when America is defining its "conceptual economy." In his foreword, he defines the issues and makes the case for an aggressive program of action to seize this opportunity for American-based enterprise to realize a competitive advantage. His strong commitment toward taking advantage of this opportunity to improve the prosperity for every American citizen is notable and indeed honorable. The Taskforce is fortunate to see its program's velocity accelerated by this twenty-first century pioneer who sees the linkages among technology, finance, standards, competitiveness, work force, regulation, and capital markets.

The Taskforce Program: The Taskforce program has two components and provides a blueprint for a national effort to support the operational framework of methods, measures, and metrics in the initial application of integrating business and legal pathways to corporate IP investment decisions. Other applications to follow will include R&D, M&A, and licensing. The research focus is on defining value and the corporate-level economics of IP-based commerce. The Bureau of Economic Analysis, U.S. Department of Commerce (BEA) will be the primary government relationship in this project. This project will help establish business standards for corporate managers to more effectively recognize and create new wealth from their IP-related assets.

The second component creates a national coalition of businesses to provide planning and support for the development of an inclusive industry–government effort to identify and remove barriers to IP-based transactions, and further examine the influences of regulation, accounting standards, tax, and their inhibitions on capital markets in order to create an economy that can adequately accommodate IP-based commerce. The Taskforce will follow the leadership of Under Secretary Cresanti in this part of the program.

Foreword

THE HONORABLE ROBERT C. CRESANTI
Under Secretary of Commerce for Technology
U.S. Department of Commerce

The Changing Wealth of Nations in the Age of the Conceptual-Based Economy

We have entered a new era—the Age of the Conceptual-Based Economy[1]—and the currency of the realm is ideas. One age passes when the competitive advantage and economic benefits it conferred is supplanted by the higher value offered in the next age. Each age brings with it enormous benefits—economic, political, military—and nations, institutions, and individuals must be prepared to seize the advantages of the new age, or watch as they are supplanted by others that do.

Technological, business, and political changes are rapidly reshaping the global economy and have brought unprecedented numbers of new competitors—nations, companies, and workers—into the global landscape. The availability of vastly less expensive labor, the increased education and skills of workers, the adoption of advanced information and communications technologies, and the advent of global sourcing models by multinational corporations means that commodity work can flow quickly outside our national boundaries. Clearly, the United States cannot sustain its standard of living in this new competitive environment by engaging in commoditized work. We must become a nation capable of seizing the higher-value work offered by the Conceptual-Based Economy.

The Information Age—brought about through the advent of electronic computer and communications technologies—delivered wealth to those that were able to harness the ability to generate, move, and store information.

Once scarce and tightly controlled, information is increasingly becoming a commodity. The highest value to be extracted in this Conceptual-Based Economy will accrue to those who are able to integrate information, knowledge, and insight to create and deliver new products and services to a global marketplace that is, at once, increasingly large, wealthy, and fragmented.

With ideas being the currency of the realm in the Conceptual-Based Economy, our ability to understand and value intellectual property and other intangible assets is essential to the efficient operation of markets. Today, markets have already expressed their implicit understanding of the value of intangibles. In 1982, 62 percent of the assets of U.S. corporations were physical; today, physical assets account for only about a quarter of total assets. That is to say, three-fourths of the value of companies is accounted for by intangible assets such as patents, copyrights, trademarks, trade secrets, goodwill, brand loyalty, and corporate culture—even a company's ability to connect with its customers on an emotional basis. Even more startling is the recent finding that approximately 40 percent of the average company's value can't be found anywhere on its balance sheet!

Markets need timely and reliable information to operate effectively and efficiently. Without good information, capital can be misdirected—too much flowing to companies whose intangibles are overvalued and too little to companies that are undervalued. Appropriate valuation of intangibles can accelerate innovation by enabling capital to flow to the most promising opportunities; alternatively, highly promising opportunities may be missed altogether or exploited by competitors. To illustrate the importance of the need to appropriately value intangibles, imagine offering the company's "goodwill" as the sole collateral for a bank loan. In the future, the best bankers may be able to effectively account for such an ephemeral asset and earn high returns on such investments; today, however, such a loan request would likely face quick rejection.

Along the same lines, appropriate valuation of intangibles will increase companies' effective development, management, and protection of these assets. In addition, human talent will be attracted to the development and exploitation of high-value intangible assets. Moreover, not only will the intangibles that are created become an increasingly important part of a company's value, but the company's creative talent and innovation processes will also become an increasingly important part of its intangible assets.

Extracting Value from Intellectual Property

Intellectual property (IP) is a core piece of intangible assets. Clearly, companies are able to extract value from their IP today through a variety of mechanisms. Some mechanisms are on the creative end—new products and processes, patent licensing, development of derivative intellectual property, establishing the company's reputation as a technology leader. Other mechanisms are more defensive in nature—excluding competitors, protecting against infringement lawsuits, and securing compensation from others' infringement of the IP.

In the past, many companies relegated IP protection to afterthought, all too often focusing on the high costs and uncertainties of obtaining, exploiting, and defending intellectual property rights. Those days are gone. In today's Conceptual-Based Economy, most companies understand that extracting value from intellectual property has become a business necessity. Thus, managers have shifted from simply avoiding to actively managing IP-related risks and uncertainties, with the view that in the usual case the benefits far outweigh the costs and uncertainties.

Recent changes in patent law (patent reform notwithstanding) bring IP management to the top of every corporate strategic option. Virtually every company in America now faces the real possibility of a patent (or other IP) lawsuit—not only on its products, but also on its marketing programs, customer lists, web sites, and business processes. The IP assets of a company are increasingly recognized as a significant source of value, as an additional source of high-margin profit from the sales and licensing of underutilized IP, as a means of protecting the differentiating features of a company's product and services, or as providing defense against potential assertions of IP infringement.

And we've come to know—from both theory and practical experience—IP and its protection are essential features to a functioning innovation system. Beginning with the Constitution, almost 220 years ago, the United States has placed a premium on constructing a sound institutional structure encouraging the creation and protection of IP.

The shift in companies' management of IP from one viewed as a purely legal concern to one of a pervasive and powerful business influence vital to corporate survival and prosperity has raised new challenges. Consider that

- IP strategists' work products, if not their titular authority, must provide critical input to the business and strategic interests of the enterprise.
- The growing and ever-demanding external business requirements of IP management assume executive-level skills that many IP attorneys and their companies are struggling to meet.

Some of America's most successful, advanced, and innovative companies simply pile on the IP challenges for their legal departments to handle. Other companies place the responsibility in the hands of the chief technical officer. And still others create new business units that can draw from the enterprisewide knowledge base to convert knowledge to new wealth.

The structural and accountability model that promises the most success is the one that bridges—or tears down—functional silos and integrates, corporatewide, the full array of business, legal, financial, and technical resources to appropriately manage IP assets and maximize their value.

Attention by Investor and Regulatory Communities

In an era in which there is increased demand for transparency in corporate finances, the absence of 40 percent of a company's value from its balance sheets should result in some concern. Not surprisingly, the Securities and Exchange Commission and the Financial Accounting Standards Board are seeking to make a company's management of intellectual property more transparent through periodic disclosures. They seek to ensure that IP is treated in a manner that is in compliance with reporting and controls established under the Sarbanes-Oxley Act of 2002 (also known as the Public Company Accounting Reform and Investor Protection Act of 2002).

Such efforts are appropriate and important, but must be supported by increasingly sophisticated tools for evaluating the value of intangibles, including IP, and provide insight into the type of information and data that should be collected and publicly disseminated.

Some Conclusions

Clearly, a company's ability to assert, enforce, and defend its IP rights can play a significant role in its ability to create and communicate value to potential business partners, partners for strategic alliances, and capital markets and banking relationships.

The pervasive nature of IP management means that more people need to become more sophisticated about IP and its effects on their responsibilities to the enterprise. This means senior managers must first make improvements in their own knowledge of and thinking about IP. This means focused attention by the company CEO, CFO, CTO, vice president for research and development, vice president for marketing, the controller, and the general counsel. Simply adding more to the IP counsel's workload is, at best, a short-term response, one that will not likely yield the broad corporate leadership approach that is needed to achieve or sustain global competitiveness in the Conceptual-Based Economy.

The work of the National Knowledge and Intellectual Property Management Taskforce is directed at issues whose importance is increasingly central to the nation's economic future. Its contributors offer unique perspectives, while its program seeks to establish a framework for the knowledge economy that is open to, and supportive of, business, economic, and market-based policies that can inspire a nation and catalyze a partnership between business and government to develop a leadership agenda. This is an important endeavor, and I commend their efforts to address these emerging issues that are critical to our nation's future competitive position in the global economy.

NOTE

1. Alan Greenspan used the term "conceptual-based economy" in remarks delivered to the American Council on Education on February 16, 1999 to describe the increasing importance of abstract thinking—including critical awareness and the abilities to hypothesize, to interpret, and to communicate—to successful innovation and value creation in today's economy.

Acknowledgments

The Taskforce

The Taskforce is an industry-led, industry-funded consortium of organizations focused on developing the corporate capabilities to recognize, manage, and create value from intellectual assets. Many organizations have contributed to the Taskforce program since its inception nine years ago.

Taskforce Supporting Organizations

AT&T
GWU
PMUSA
GE
EDS
SAIC
E&Y
PARC
ITAA
NASA
Kodak
Motorola
ID-NL Group
MIT
TI
Toler Shaffer
Cisco Systems
USG Group
Dow Chemical
Freddie Mac
Bell South
Dep't of Defense
NC Dep't of Commerce
Success Strategies Inst.
ADERANT
Dennemeyer
Dover Corporation
Williams Companies
DuPont Imaging
Deloitte & Touche
U. Texas at Dallas
So. Methodist U.
IP Innovations
Governor's Office (NC)
Telcordia Technologies
Cal. Auditor's Office
Ctr. Adv. Technologies
Delaware Capital Formation
Nat'l Ctr. for Mfg. Sciences
Pricewaterhouse-Coopers
Morrison & Foerster
Nat'l Technology Transfer Cir.
Pure Discovery
Predictiv
Nat'l Academy of Sciences
Chamberlain Group
Toler Larson & Abel
Chrysler

TASKFORCE SUPPORTING ORGANIZATIONS (CONTINUED)

Haynes & Boones
UN Dep't of Econ. & Social Affairs
Ford Motor Company
Ericcson
Inovo Technologies
Nortel Networks
Concurrent Technologies
Fitch Even Tabin & Flannery
Economists Inc.
Hughes/Raytheon
Creative IP Solutions
CapGemini E&Y
SkillsNET
JC Penney
Dr. Jane Armstrong
Fred Sleet & Associates
U.S. Dep't of Education
United Nations Statistics Division

Special Thanks to:

Our Honorary Chairs:

Dr. Claudine Simson, VP IP, Nortel Networks
Jane Patterson, Chair, NC Board of Science & Technology and Sr. Advisor to Governor Hunt
Ed Paradise, VP Mobile Wireless Business Unit, Cisco Systems
Bill Coughlin, President, Ford Global Technologies
Dr. Adam Drobot, CTO, Telcordia Technologies

Our Presidents:

Bob Shearer, CEO Shearer Group, Center for Advanced Technologies
Al Delorenzi, VP Strategic Planning, Nortel Networks
Rear Admiral Tom Paulsen, USN (Ret), CIO Williams Companies
Donald Mondul, Chief IP Counsel, Ericsson, now an independent IP attorney
Dr. Dennis Perry, Division Manager, Strategic Applications International Corporation
Dr. Mark Karasek, VP Engineering, Chamberlain Group Strategy
Bartlett Cleland, Center for Advanced Technologies

Our Counsel:

Ed Gray, Partner, Morrison & Foerster
Jerry Niuman, Attorney at Law
Sallie Randolph, Copyright Attorney

Fred Sleet, Sleet and Associates, Tax
Dr. Mark Karasek, VP Engineering, Chamberlain Group, Strategy

Our Fellows:

Dr. Steve Henning, Marks Paneth & Shron
Charles Goulding, Goulding Law
Dr. Mark Karasek, VP Engineering, Chamberlain Group Strategy
Jonathan Low, Founder, Predictiv
Kathy Masterson, Chief Knowledge Officer, Aderant
Damon Matteo, Vice President, IP, Palo Alto Research Center
Ed Paradise, Vice President and General Manager for Cisco's Mobility, Signaling, and Control Business Unit
Dr. Dennis Perry, Board Member, Center for Advanced Technologies
Steve Parmelee, Partner, Fitch Even Tabin & Flannery
Dr. Mike Stankosky, Professor & Co-Founder Institute for Knowledge & Innovation, GWU
Dr. Bruce Stuckman, Partner, Garlick, Harrrison & Markison
Elizabeth Thomas, President, Success Strategies Institute

Our Subject Matter Experts:

Vernon Anthony, Telcordia Technologies
Gustavo Aray, Intel Corp.
Gloria Archuleta, Fluid Innovations
Dr. Jane Armstrong, Texas A&M
Beverly Bacon, Computer Sciences Corp.
Bill Becker, Align Technologies
Carol Beckham, Bell South
Chris Bennett, NetInterests
Keith Bergelt, IP Innovation Financial Services
Johnny Berry, Center for Advanced Technologies
Dan Bolita, KM World
Jim Bramson, AOL–Time Warner
Michael Brown, SkillsNet
Alex Butler, Thomson
Gus Caballero, Hughes Training
Joe Cargioli, GE
David Clark, PMUSA

Dr. Paul Cheung, UN, Statistics Division
Dr. Pam Cohen, Predictiv
David Copps, Pure Discovery
John Dickerson, Ford
Abha Divine, President and CEO, AT&T Knowledge Ventures
Dr. Adam Drobot, Telcordia Technologies
Steve Durant, Morrison & Foerster
Joe Farrell, Hughes Training
Karl Fink, Fitch Even Tabin & Flannery
Mitch Fillet, Riderwood Group
Jim Fitzgibbon, Chamberlain Group
Harley Frost, SBC Technology Resources
Mike Geoffrey, USG Corporation
Mark Gould, Marshall & Stevens
Charles Goulding, Private Tax Consultant
Ed Gray, Morrison & Foerster
Mark Haller, PricewaterhouseCoopers
Dr. Ivo Havinga, UN, Department of Economic & Social Affairs
Dr. Steve Henning, Marks Paneth & Shron
Rodger Jackson, Ernst & Young
Dr. Jan Jaferian, Individual Contributor
Rick Jarman, Kodak
Tony Jeffs, Cisco Systems
Christine Johnson, Thomson Learning Inc.
Tracy Joltes, National Technology Transfer Center
Dr. Vassilis Keramidas, Telcordia Technologies
Bob Kirtley, Deloitte & Touche
Gary Knight, EDS
Dr. Michael Krieger, UCLA
Chris Leisner, Creative IP Solutions
Kevin Leininger, Internet Crimes Group
Tim Leixner, Holland & Knight
Jon Low, Predictiv
Jim McAndrews, Freddie Mac
Kirk McInerney, Dennemeyer
Tim Maloney, Fitch Even Tabin & Flannery
Kathy Masterson, Aderant
Elias Matsakis, Holland & Knight

Jeffrey Matsura, Alliance Law Group
Damon Matteo, PARC
Don Mondul, Attorney at Law
David Near, Dow Chemical
Son Nguyen, Dow Chemical
Nikos Nikolopoulos, Tyco Electronics
Fairfax O'Reilly, Cognistar
C.B. Owen, USG Corporation
Rear Admiral Tom Paulsen, USN (Ret)
Ed Paradise, Cisco Systems
Steve Parmelee, Fitch Even Tabin & Flannery
David Peyton, National Association of Manufacturers
Dr. Allison Rosenberg, National Academy of Sciences
Jane Smith Patterson, Chair, North Carolina Board of Science & Technology Policy & Governor's Office, North Carolina
Pam Payuk, SBC Technology Resources
Dr. Dennis Perry, Eagle Force Associates
Gordon Petrash, PricewaterhouseCoopers
David Peyton, National Association of Manufacturers
Damon Pocari, Ford
Rory Radding, Morrison & Foerster
Sallie Randolph, Attorney at Law (Copyrights)
Dr. Bruce Saari, Applied Organizational Dynamics
Ann Schaeffer, Independence Blue Cross
Dr. Larry Schmitt, Inovo Technologies
Lynne Schneider, ESSI
Dr. Nina Selz, Individual Contributor
Joe Shipley, Fitch Even Tabin & Flannery
Richard Simnett, Telcordia Technologies
Dr. Herman Smith, United Nations
Dr. Mike Stankosky, Co-Founder, KM Institute, GWU
Donna Stemmer, EDS
Chel Sromgren, SAIC
Dr. Bruce Stuckman, Garlick, Harrison & Markison
Bruce Taylor, KM World
Bitsy Thomas, Success Strategies
Jeff Toler, Toler Schaffer
John Tolomei, UOP

Steve Toton, DuPont Imaging
Dr. Paul Tukey, Telcordia Technologies
Amy Ward, Delaware Capital Formation
Dr. Larry Wasserman, Fortec Int'l
Gerard Wissing, Computer Associates
Bill White, USG Corporation
Dr. Corey Wick, EDS

The Vital "Go-To" Leaders/Visionaries:

Elizabeth Thomas, Dr. Claudine Simson, Dr. Dennis Perry, Jane Patterson, Dr. Roger Kerin, Dr. Adam Drobot, Rear Admiral Tom Paulsen, Fred Sleet, Connie Chang, Dr. Steve Henning, Mike Geoffrey, Rick Faletti, Ed Paradise, Al Delorenzi, Vice Admiral Conrad Lautenbacher, PhD, USN (Ret), Bill Coughlin, Gus Caballero, Dr. Vassilis Keramidas, Steve Parmelee, Karl Fink, Sallie Randolph, Dr. Bruce Stuckman, Kathy Masterson, Dr. George Kozmetsky, Jerry Niuman, Dr. Bruce Saari, Charles Goulding, Chris Leisner, Don Mondul, Bartlett Cleland, and Ed Gray, whose names could all be annotated with "loyalty, excellence, and performance," but in the absence of their guidance, there would be no Taskforce record of accomplishments. That record is listed below to offer more insight into the efforts of these companies and individuals.

A very special thanks to the extraordinarily talented artist, Chris Morris, at the *Las Vegas Sun,* whose portfolio can be seen at www.camorris.com.

The Road to Economic Recognition of IP Value

1. Business Practice Research—National IP Issues (1998)
2. Framework for Creating and Recognizing IP (1999)
3. Initial Conference—National Academy of Sciences (1999)
4. State Economic Development—NC Governor's Office—(2000)
5. KM Institute Established at UNC (2001)
6. Department of Defense Becomes a Strategic Partner with Focus on KM (2001)
7. State IP Asset Inventory—California Auditor's Office (2001)
8. Taskforce Teams with GWU for Education Program (2002)
9. Taskforce Presents Phase 2 Report and IAM Competencies (2002)

10. Roundtable Discussions with the SEC (2002)
11. Taskforce Develops Accelerated Licensing Program at Ford (2003)
12. Ford and Creative IP Solutions Present ALP Concept (2004)
13. IP Monetization Strategies Mapped (Capabilities-Maturity Model) (2004)
14. Photon Effect of IP Becomes Accepted (2004) (Multiple concurrent uses of IP to generate revenues)
15. Telcordia Technologies Agrees to Host Taskforce IP Modeling Lab (2004)
16. IP Decisions Research Initiated (2004)
17. AT&T Reports IP Value Extraction Business Structure at Capabilities Summit (2005)
18. Taskforce Mapping of IP Assertion & Defensive Operations in IP (2005) (business guidelines to avoid litigation)
19. Taskforce—BEA Decision Tour New York, NY; San Jose, CA; and Chicago, IL (June–December 2006)
20. Symposium with U.S. Dept of Commerce—Technology Administration and Bureau of Economic Analysis (November 2006)
21. Taskforce helps UN Statistics Division and its subordinate organizations, the Department of Economic and Social Affairs, and the System of National Accounts, and the System of National Accounts, develop a seminar on how corporate-level IP economics will support developing as well as developed nations.
22. Taskforce—work with the U.S. Department of Commerce, Technology Administration (Under Secretary, Robert Cresanti) to develop the nation's infrastructure so that it can accommodate IP-based commerce and the Bureau of Economic Analysis (Director, Dr. Steve Landefeld) to develop the measures and metrics for IP economics.

Introduction

The IP Landscape

The business world is changing and changing fast based on the innovations in IP management. Members of the Plaintiff Bar are soliciting shareholders to participate in class action suits against management and their boards of directors for failure to manage the company's IP assets effectively. Hedge funds are working "long" and "short" positions based on a company's IP portfolio and its technological trajectory. Financiers are buying companies just to acquire the IP for enforcement against deep-pocketed infringers, and companies are using the courts to establish reputational value and win damages in infringement suits. It's business, but the courts are becoming a bigger factor in IP strategies.

Let's not forget about the standards and regulatory communities, because Sarbanes-Oxley is increasingly expanding its reach into IP management. The SEC and the FASB are struggling with what rules and procedures to apply to be able to account for the approximate 70 percent of value represented by intangibles in today's enterprises. This large number is a real "stone in the shoes" of the SEC, the FASB, and the accounting community. They need to account for this value.

Meanwhile, Congress continues to look at patent reform as a legislative remedy. Many companies are moving to get more legislation to "straighten out" the IP chaos.

As you read this book, do not expect any easy answers, but do resolve to put IP management at the top of your list of priorities in your strategic plan. This cannot be done effectively without good legal counsel. Neither can it be done without an informed senior management. You will gain insights from the many experiences captured in these pages that will give you further insight into how you can best mange your company to get ahead of your competition. Your industry (every industry) will experience some dramatic shake-out based on how the IP battles are fought and won during the next two to four years. The IP landscape is moving that fast.

Your Situation

Assuming you, the reader, are a person who derives a livelihood from sitting on a board, working for a company, or one who sets the goals, objectives, and strategies for successful corporate performance—or maybe you are one who punches the clock in and out every day, regardless of your level of responsibility—IP is changing your life. Your knowledge and your and your company's ability to innovate, develop, and sustain a competitive advantage are critical to your future. In Chapter 1, Mike Geoffrey (Chief IP Counsel at USG Corporation) explains how survival and competitiveness are linked to innovation and how intellectual property is critical to your company's prosperity. Texas Instruments, Xerox, IBM, and a few others have quietly pioneered the use of IP assets, not just to build market share but to generate new revenues at virtually no cost; IP assets mean high-margin dollars, because your assets have already been expensed and cannot be recognized unless they were acquired in an acquisition or merger. Current accounting standards do not allow for valuation of internally generated assets.

Corporate America is producing new business models to extract more value from these IP assets. Spinoffs of new technologies into business ventures, joint ventures, licensing, use of the courts, and just about as many things as the "for-profit" mind can legally do—all these are making corporate managers burst with enthusiasm and excitement about getting value from these assets. IP asset value recognition and management is every bit as creative and just as pervasive as the Internet was in its innovative impact on American industry in the 1990s. American industry is the engine of economic growth— it is the foundational power to create prosperity for all—and the creation and value extraction from IP assets represents a new opportunity to create new wealth from existing assets, if you know how to identify and use them.

But we do not live alone in this competitive world. We obsess about off-shore corporations, outsourcing, and other old streams of revenue that affect our economy. It is time for business leaders to acquire the skills to at least minimally effectively interface with the IP function. The life-sustaining need to continuously innovate and create value is increasingly IP oriented. China, Brazil, France, Japan, and the rest of the world are not only emulating America's 200-year-old model of IP rights, but taking actions to ensure that IP can be acquired and strategically deployed in global commerce with an especially strong nationalistic purpose of creating competitive advantage.

This book is about helping you get a quick "take" on IP and begin to implement many of the practices described by its authors/practitioners that will alert you to many of the intricacies of IP management in its global context. We seek to alert you and provide enough foundational information that you will not be intimidated by the term *IP* and think this is all about law. It is not. It is about business and how the law affects business performance.

The winners in the twenty-first century are going to be those corporations that can develop and harness their intellectual capital, create the intellectual property to generate new wealth, and smartly assert their rights across the globe. During the very first Taskforce work sessions at the National Center for Manufacturing Sciences, one of the former TI attorneys, then working for a private law firm, reported that TI's assertion of its IP rights internationally saved the company—a big story about a big company's "bump in the road" to becoming a corporate superstar. Sooner or later, your company will be faced with IP rights issues. You need not fear such issues, but you should begin developing the capabilities to deal with this complex and chaotic new element of business. It is your quickest way to new wealth, and until you become proficient in IP management, it is your greatest vulnerability.

So here it is: your existing but unrecognized assets that have already been expensed can be used by multiple customers at the same time, and you get new revenues that mostly go to the bottom line, but you cannot put them on your balance sheet. You must develop some transactional process to create cash flows and effectively report your IP management capabilities to your investors.

So what does one need to realize that new business model? Get smart and build your company's capabilities to do what these authors suggest.

What This Book Is About

This is a book about the capabilities required to perform competitively in the knowledge economy; it draws from a unique group of people who have willingly agreed to work together over a period of eight years to define these new corporate capabilities for the benefit of others, to help define the economy for future generations of stakeholders. Each of these contributors has experience and a concern for improving individual as well as corporate performance. The focus is on the corporate level and the analysis does not get into the knowledge/skill mix that ultimately rolls up into departmental or group performance. The book is nonetheless a series of tutorials about how to immediately take action to check your company's capabilities against the events and standards offered by the authors. It is also designed to be an "enjoyable read" as well as a reference for quickly getting up to speed on IP management for the non-attorney.

Businesspeople need to know about IP, not in its legal sense—you will still need good attorneys—but rather to capture the extraordinary features about IP that make it such a critical knowledge area in every competitive organization in America, indeed in every company in every nation, as the developing world will see intellectual capital and intellectual property as the pathway to national competitive advantage. India's software strategy is a classic profile for global competitive leadership.

The capabilities analyses at the end of each chapter have been done by the writer, Bob Shearer, who is an experienced analyst and expert witness in federal court on organization behavior. The capabilities summaries, consequently, do not represent the opinion of the chapter authors unless otherwise noted. The analyses are not intended to be comprehensive; they are designed to serve as a checklist against which you can quickly measure the IP capabilities of your company. Their purpose is important as well, as it stimulates organizational development that in turn will lead to individual professional development and ultimately to the human capital resource as the primary input into an economy that can more readily support your interests: to *accelerate the transformation of knowledge to net worth.*

THE GUIDEPOSTS

This book is also designed to be placed by the side of your bed or favorite TV spot so that you can look at it during commercial breaks or before you get sleepy. Most of the chapters are short but informative and will help you solidify your own thoughts about how you might proceed to capture the value of your IP assets. Some are especially detailed so as to allow the reader to use them as reference material.

The editor has employed a set of visual cues:

- **"The key points to look for"** at the beginning of each chapter are the points that help you determine the value contribution of the chapter.
- **"Capabilities Development: Observations, Action Items for Corporate Performance Improvement"** by the "Professor" focuses on immediate implementation activities a senior manager can use to develop his own department or enterprise. (*This analysis is developed by the editor and sometimes with the help of the author and Taskforce SMEs.*)
- **Speaking of capabilities invites the question:** Capabilities for what? The only criterion guiding the content of this book is:

  The capability to create new wealth faster and with more strength of market position than your competition.
- **The formative structure** for defining the capabilities page at the end of each chapter is based on this primary objective and is focused around five key areas of corporate performance:
  1. The capability to innovate, by identifying, documenting, and evaluating IP assets across disciplines and throughout the enterprise relative to corporate goals and the competition.
  2. The capability to determine the approximate value of your IP assets.
  3. The capability to follow a disciplined, qualitative, and quantitative process to make smart decisions about how to best employ IP assets strategically.
  4. The capability to defend and assert your proprietary rights domestically and internationally consistent with your company's assessment of risk.

5. The capability to deliberately, carefully, and responsibly report the effects of corporate IP value to the capital markets to the benefit of your shareholders.

- **There are two capabilities/proficiency tables** presented for Value Extraction and Corporate Relationships that will help you visualize the next level of research and analysis being done by the Center for Advanced Technologies, managing partner of the Taskforce.

Please note that there are four more sections to this book:

1. **Section Two: Defining the Stakes.** In this section we try to paint the picture of global competitiveness and the nation's current infrastructure issues so that you know what is up and what is down. The truth is that the whole determination of IP's economic value is "topsy turvy" now with the conflicts with the EU over accounting standards, and the Supreme Court making very important rulings, while the so-called Trolls and anti-Trolls have organized to find legislative solutions. There are innovations in IP management every day. The "fast follower" may never catch up. This is a once-in-a-decade opportunity to distance yourself from the competition.
2. **Section Three: Creating the Assets.** This section states some immediate things that could be done tomorrow to help get your IP asset portfolio in place.
3. **Section Four: New Dynamics of Corporate Management.** This is a management-rich section that informs the CFO, the IP counsel, and the board about how the organization is changing and what management can be doing about those changes.
4. **Section Five: Creating New Wealth:** This bang-up, "get the cash" section offers ways to immediately recognize new value and create new wealth for your shareholders.

Commerce Technology Administration

It is with great pride and excitement that we note the contribution of the Honorable Robert Cresanti, the Under Secretary of Commerce for Technology Administration (who is responsible for America's global competitiveness). Mr. Cresanti expresses the extraordinary sense of service and vision to recognize and initiate actions to create a national economic infrastructure to support more IP-based commerce in order to improve America's economic growth and global competitiveness.

The Taskforce

The Taskforce is a member-led, member-funded program born out of the Center for Advanced Technologies, a Texas-based nonprofit corporation, in 1998. Headquartered in Dallas, Texas, the Taskforce employs a consortium business model of many companies with common interests leveraging the cost, time, and talent of its members to develop management practices that will improve the member companies' capabilities to create and sustain a competitive advantage through rapid deployment of innovations in IP management. The Taskforce has earned national recognition as one of the more influential "action-oriented" nonprofit entities in America. Companies such as Ford, Telcordia, AT&T, GE, Cisco, the Governor's Office of the State of North Carolina, the Auditor's Office of the State of California, Freddie Mac, the National Academy of Sciences, George Washington University, the National Technology Transfer Center, and many other organizations have participated as members or strategic partners in Taskforce research and operations. (See Acknowledgments for further information.)

America is fortunate to enjoy the shareholder and national-interest considerations of a generation of leaders who know that corporate economic success, upward mobility, and individual wealth accumulation are the vehicle that unites . . . or sometimes breeds corruption and conflict around the globe. This group of writers offers definitive actions that can ensure your company's survivability in the growing competition for ownership of ideas and constructs of governance in an economy that can easily become more volatile as intangible assets such as IP become more fluid and as global competitors search for ways around American standard definitions of property and wealth.

Defining the Stakes

The stakes involved in IP management are high and they are global. This is a "game" that will be won with crafty and innovative strategies to control IP in global markets. Mike Geoffrey has just applied an old performance bond technique in his IP-related business in China. It is commonplace in the construction industry, but a true innovation in more general business relationships. Whatever the technique, U.S.-based companies need to search out the opportunities for increased leverage and market presence through IP innovation.

In Chapter 1, Mike Geoffrey defines the importance of IP and business survival in the globally competitive arena. As the chief IP counsel at USG Corporation, a global building materials manufacturer, he has instituted some revolutionary ways to deal with China, but the core of Mike's message is how to get senior management focused on what IP really does for business strategy.

Ford demonstrates some extraordinary competence and leadership in its global IP strategy and execution. Bill Coughlin, the author of Chapter 2, is an innovator, helping to develop the market strategy for China and Japan. Bill is the president of Ford Global Technologies, the IP subsidiary of Ford Motor Company. He has inserted himself and his company into the R&D process at Ford, which provided funds for research and innovation that the manufacturing units could not support because of the ever-present pressures on profit margins. This is a man of courage who is the IP face of one of America's industrial icons, Ford.

IP has changed the way companies manage their R&D functions. Dr. Vassilis Keramidas's anecdotes will help you make the case for a slightly longer business threshold to realize value. Can American enterprise afford to forgo the "R" in "R&D"? Answer that for yourself after you see what this innovation warrior has to say in Chapter 3.

Confusion in the regulatory, standards, and capital market communities is something we would be reluctant to admit, but Dr. Steve Henning's unique position in the university, SEC, FASB, and on Wall Street in the past five years qualifies him as one of the nation's leading forensic accountants and consultants in trial support. He has coordinated his clients' work by interfacing with law firms, the department of Justice, FASB, and the SEC, including lead work in the Citicorp, AIG, Enron, and many other high-profile cases. Dr. Henning has been a key player in establishing the practical applications in boardroom practices, corporate governance, and accounting standards. His insight into what is happening in the economic "infrastructure" may leave you discouraged, but informed. In Chapter 4 he offers some suggestions to help you build value in the capital markets that can be implemented immediately.

CHAPTER 1

Building IP Value in the Corporation[1]

The Core of the Innovation Process

MIKE GEOFFREY

The IP process protects innovation, but the IP process itself stimulates further innovation.

KEY POINTS TO LOOK FOR

- IP supports and protects the integrity of the innovative process by enabling the company to differentiate its products and services in the global market.
- The innovative process is the sustaining capability of the enterprise, as savvy IP management stimulates more creativity and innovative R&D activity.
- IP management is no longer a specialist's job but is an integral part of business operations, requiring executive-level interaction and decision involvement.
- Companies must have a sense of how to value IP as a business (rather than a financial) asset in order to maximize the value to the company, not just in legal rights, but in regard to other intangibles—specifically reputation and market position.
- This valuation process must have quantitative as well as reliable and relevant qualitative constructs.

IP's Impact on Corporate Global Competitiveness

The ability to compete globally will define the prosperity of a nation, its people, and their institutions. America has enjoyed a hugely successful run as the world's leading economic engine, but the competitive arena is changing. Increasingly, intellectual property (IP) carries more economic weight in business decisions, and these business decisions are increasingly becoming international in scope. The ability to manage and protect innovation through the formalized rights of IP is becoming more critical to the functionality of our corporations. Our individual and collective futures will be determined by how we manage our creative and innovative processes today. Our everyday decisions are shaped by the ability to out-create, out-innovate, out-capitalize, and out-perform any competitor in the world in a civilized manner, governed by free and open markets. It is the day-to-day, seemingly mundane decisions that move us slowly but surely into patterns of thought and behavior that shape the performance of our companies. To an even greater extent that performance is shaped by the protocols of trade, agreements, financial transactions, and precedents in the courts and policies of international governing entities. Accordingly, there appears to be a need to shift the IP paradigm in corporate management from a product support role to the operational level of the corporation.

But how do companies learn to adjust from product-oriented decisions and management practices to those that can accommodate such intangibles as intellectual property?

Historically, we have left this chore in the hands of the legal function. Today, because intangibles account for so much more of corporate value, we must learn how to conduct business with the full spectrum of intellectual assets. Acquiring this new knowledge/skill/capabilities mix is especially difficult because there is no language to define value that can be used across disciplinary lines.

In business, the language is numbers, and, in spite of the fact that the SEC and FASB are struggling with writing this new language, the ability to define the language of business from the IP perspective is going to come from the corporate sector, which is exactly where it belongs!

The ability to recognize the value of IP is critical to a competitive strategy. It requires effective communication among the key executives and a flow of information that can no longer be bounded by function or title. We need to recognize that the consequences of our decisions have greater impact than ever before because we are dealing with a new and dynamic asset management process. For the product-oriented corporation this shift of thinking can pose a significant challenge. How this communication takes place is more than an education strategy for change; it is a reeducation strategy that requires integration of knowledge, adequate motives to do things differently, an easier (more user-friendly) process, typically through systems and tools and top management leadership, to redefine and refocus the definitions of performance.

The starting point is the linkage to the most fundamental principles of business. Every corporation is engaged in global commerce. To survive and prosper in the global market means that America and Americans who manage internationally based companies must continually renew themselves. Companies must create not just innovative products but new business practices as well. It is toward this end that the role of IP in the globally competitive enterprise is defined, because IP business practices and policies are the governing protocols in the current global economy, which is becoming increasingly knowledge intensive. How these practices and policies shift to accommodate new challenges is the focus of my comments.

Innovation, Differentiation, and the Avoidance of Commodification

Innovation is the creation of something new. In this context, it occurs within an enterprise—not just through technology, but also through branding, business methods, and any other operation that enables us to do things better, faster, smarter, simpler, and more efficiently. Innovation is the sustenance of long-term viability and competitiveness. Innovation leads to product differentiation and creates value.

Product differentiation is the means consumers use to gauge differences and make selections. Product differentiation means that while two or more products are useful for the same purpose, only one is distinctively superior in terms of quality, price, benefits, or customer value. Innovation creates product differentiation in a deliberate way. Differentiation is a source of value. It is a source of intellectual property, and if differentiated value is created, it needs to be protected. Differentiated value is best protected by using the protocols and structures of intellectual property law.

All companies have competitors working to guide the customer to its unique sales proposition. If product differentiation can be established, the corporation can position itself to take advantage of the differentiation and create more value through increased margins, volume, repeat sales, and greater earnings. Creating differentiation is the result of effective, sustainable innovation. Product differentiation allows companies to avoid committing commodification.

Commodification is a directed process by which products or services lose their distinction over competing products or services and, therefore, can command no premium in the marketplace. Commodification is distinguishable from commoditization, but the two terms are sometimes used interchangeably. Commodification is the process of treating a good or service as a commodity.[2] Commoditization is the process by which a good or service becomes a commodity.[3] In both contexts, a commodity is an undifferentiated good or service.[4] Commodification is, therefore, the intentional process of commoditizing a good or service.

Intellectual property provides the formal definition for innovation. It provides a means in many cases to charge more for a product, because IP can be used to exclude others from making your product and calling it by your product name. IP formalized in a patent can be used to exclude others from making, using, selling, offering to sell, or importing the product or process claimed in the patent. IP formalized in a trademark can be used to prevent others from using a confusing name for their competitive products. Copyright can be used to prevent others from copying the expression of an idea in a written form or work of art. Even trade secrets are exclusionary because we can keep this form of IP from our competitors by keeping it secret. The application of IP is a method by which we favorably position our products in the marketplace. IP itself is the body of law that governs the creation and disposition of the rights of people and entities to exploit their innovations. IP is a means to protect differentiation and, as such, IP is a corporate asset.

The process for protecting product differentiation is an important concept, and it is fundamental to sustainability and economic growth. Innovation is the driver that provides distinction, and it is IP that generates

EXHIBIT 1.1 IP AND INNOVATION

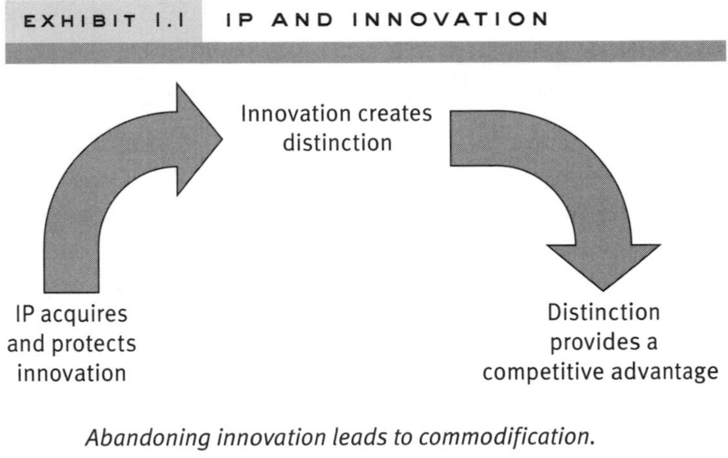

Abandoning innovation leads to commodification.

the benefits of this process and avoids commodification. The key elements of the relationships among innovation, IP, and competitive distinction are summarized in Exhibit 1.1, IP and Innovation.

One View of the Innovation Process

Business problems create a need for solution. This need drives the business and product development processes. It is in these processes that ideas are generated and become the source of intellectual property. The innovation process is cyclical in nature.

New product ideas are evaluated and value is identified with respect to those ideas. Once value has been identified, the IP process protects the innovation. But a more exciting realization about the development process is that *the IP process itself stimulates further innovation*. As the idea and its value are reviewed and placed within the formal structure of intellectual property, the innovative ideas continue to mount and to establish even greater differentiation.

IP is the product of creative endeavor. The business development process provides the framework for new IP creation as still further ideas and creative efforts spawn new value. This is the ideal situation. It is a self-sustaining process. The process is nonlinear; it drives and thrives on innovation and investment in research and development. The result of a robust R&D

process adds value to the corporation and supports a repetitive self-sustaining culture of employee enthusiasm, value creation, value extraction, continuing innovation, increased cash flows and earnings. Exhibit 1.2, Creating and Protecting Differentiation, illustrates this process graphically.

This business process is itself a valuable corporate asset, because product and service differentiation are critical to being competitive. It goes without saying that this creative, innovative energy is the source of new competing products. Intellectual property protects that differentiation and thus allows us many ways to extract value and new wealth. Unless intellectual property does something that contributes back to the corporation's business, the effort is hollow and the product is without value.

Some might question whether IP has value in a broad context. But no one would argue that being competitive adds value to the corporation, because the corporation must expand its market, sell more, and attract a broader customer base in order to realize continuing profitability and ultimate survival. The bottom line is this: *unprotected differentiation is short lived. IP protects differentiation and is critical to sustainability and profitability.*

EXHIBIT 1.2 CREATING AND PROTECTING DIFFERENTIATION

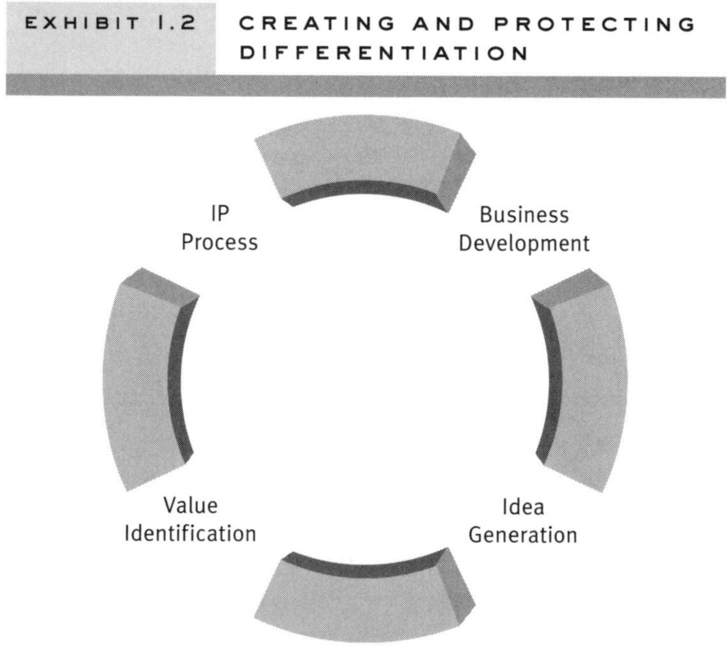

Shifting the IP Paradigm: A Simple Business Model

With the recognition of the value of innovation and the need to formalize rights to innovation in IP comes the need to manage the identification, collection, and protection of innovation within the IP process. Many different business models for managing IP have been proposed. Most of these models place IP management in one of two traditional structures: (1) the IP department reports to the research director; (2) the IP department reports to the general counsel. More recently, placing IP management in a separate IP business has been successfully used by some.[5] But the first question that should be asked is: What should IP management be?

The management of IP has two parts, one legal and one business. Too often, the two parts of IP management are merged into a single form simply called IP. Managing IP purely from the legal side tends to overlook the subtleties of the business issues that are the source of IP and that influence IP. Managing IP purely from the business side tends to overlook the subtleties of the legal issues that promote the growth of a strong IP portfolio.

IP management should be positioned to identify, collect, and protect innovation. In the corporate process, investments are made in the development of innovative products, services, and brands, which generate revenue for the corporation. Some of the revenue is invested directly into new innovation; some of the revenue goes back into the corporate assets. Of course, a part of the corporate assets are directed to corporate pursuits other than innovation. The entire process is directed towards increasing shareholder value. IP management resides both in the innovation development part of the process and in the commercialization part. This process is further illustrated in Exhibit 1.3, IP and the Innovation Process.

The legal side of IP management includes obtaining patents, protecting trade secrets, litigating or licensing out as means to enforce IP rights, drafting agreements that protect and manage IP, and educating IP owners on each of these processes.

The business side of IP management includes managing the costs of acquiring IP relative to the returns from leveraging the IP, generating income from IP through litigation or licensing, identifying the strategy that guides the acquisition and disposition of IP, and providing input into

EXHIBIT 1.3 IP AND THE INNOVATION PROCESS

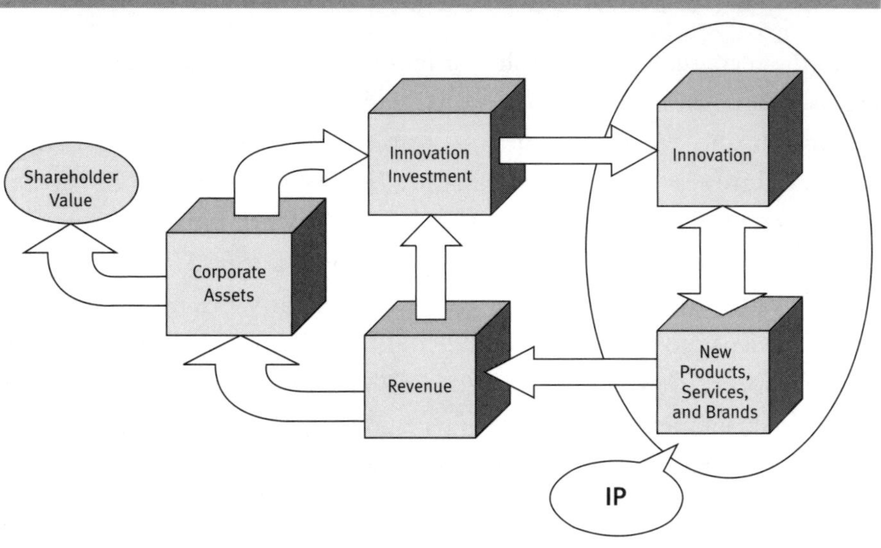

the legal side of IP management in order to accomplish the business-side goals and objectives.

Because of IP management's multidisciplinary nature requiring the integration of business, legal, and other corporate functions, it makes sense that it fits into the operational structure of the corporation. From this position, IP management communicates on an "equals" basis with the other operational functions of the corporation. IP management is positioned to contribute to and respond to corporate strategic processes. Like marketing, sales, R&D, manufacturing, and other operationa-level functions, IP management is part of the day-to-day running of the business.

If IP management is placed at the operational level, then IP itself can be fully realized as a business tool. When IP management becomes a process that operates only after the other operational inputs are considered, opportunities to identify, collect, and protect innovation are lost. For example, if IP is considered only after the product is fully designed and branded, there may very well be innovation that has occurred during the design and branding process that is lost to the corporation because it was not identified, collected, and protected under one or more of the formal IP rights. A failure to fully utilize IP is a loss of value to the corporation. Exhibit 1.4, IP at the Operational Level, illustrates this simple business model.

EXHIBIT 1.4 IP AT THE OPERATIONAL LEVEL

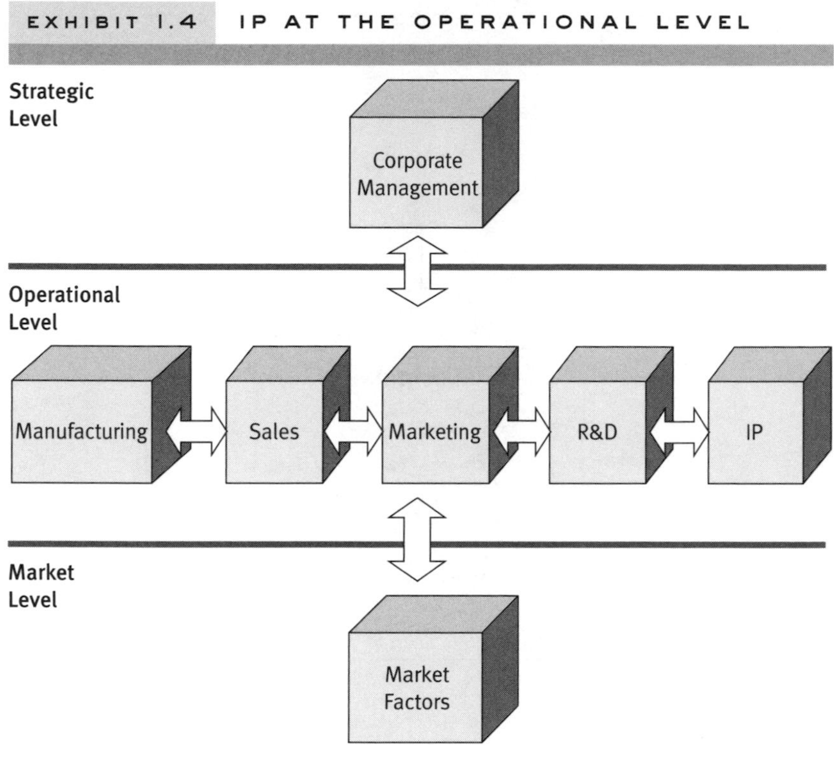

Another reason to position IP management at the operational level is because that is the level where most innovation is developed. Innovation arises within the operational functions. Referring back to Exhibit 1.2, the IP process resides within the innovation development process, and because of the "feedback loop" nature of innovation development, the IP process itself can be a significant contributor to innovation development. In fact, innovation arises at each position of the operational level as illustrated in Exhibit 1.5, Sources of Innovation.

By placing IP management within the operational level of the corporation, the IP manager is positioned at the source of innovation. This allows for a direct line of communication among the operational-level managers and places IP management where it best can identify and collect the innovation, which in turn, enhances the feedback within the innovation process. Another benefit of this structure is that the IP language will eventually become part of the operational language of the corporation. Just as sales, marketing, and manufacturing language provides the

EXHIBIT 1.5 SOURCES OF INNOVATION

communication medium for decision making in a traditional corporate structure, the addition of IP management to the operational level brings the IP language into the decision making process. IP management thus becomes more organizationally pervasive and strategic.

Ideally, the IP legal function should be distinguished from and managed separately from the IP business function. Although IP legal has the traditional role of counselor to the IP business function, it is the IP business function that communicates on the operational level with the other operational-level managers. This organizational arrangement is depicted in Exhibit 1.6, IP Management Team.

As shown, the IP manager reports to the executive management of the corporation along with the other operational-level managers. In this respect, IP management's role is to provide input, both strategic and substantive, into the management decisions that guide the corporation. With the creation of the depicted line of communication, IP issues become integrated into development and execution plans. Benefits derive not only from the contributions of IP management to executive management, but also,

EXHIBIT 1.6 IP MANAGEMENT TEAM

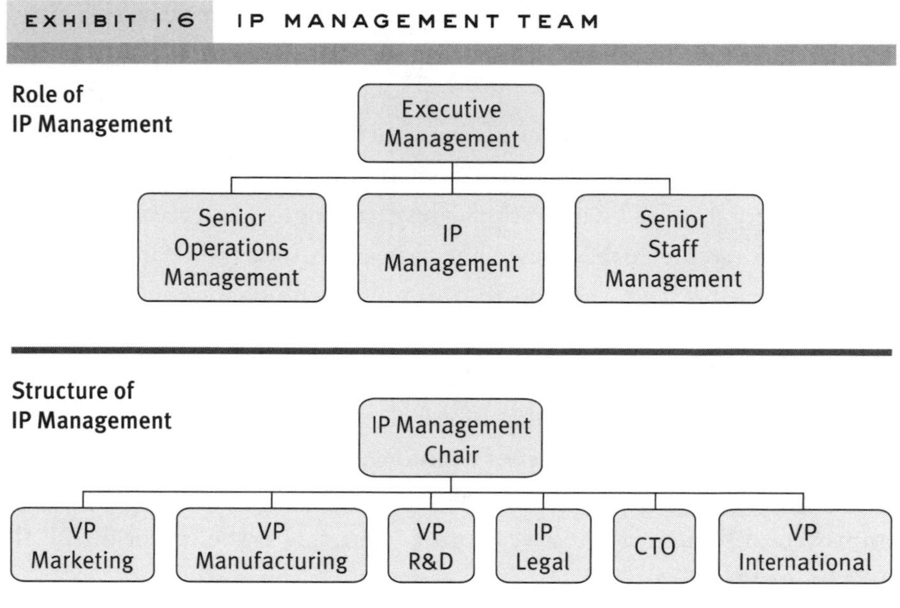

and more importantly, from the integration of corporate planning and IP planning on an operational level. Because IP issues play a strategic role in corporate planning, it is critical to corporate management that IP management has the proper functional fit within the corporation.

IP legal has a place on the IP management team, but its function is clearly distinguished from the IP business function. IP attorneys, like all attorneys, whether in-house or outside counsel, best benefit their clients when they can counsel clients within the confines of the attorney–client relationship. When an attorney–client relationship exists, communications between attorney and client on legal issues can usually be kept privileged. Furthermore, by recognizing the differences between the legal and business functions, the corporation helps the attorney keep the proper perspective while maintaining her role as legal counselor. Nonetheless, providing a place on the management team for IP legal has the advantage of allowing the lawyers to see and hear everything that the business managers see and hear and, as requested, provide legal counsel to the business managers.

The structure of the IP management team provides for input from key operational-level managers into IP decisions. In fact, this structure mimics traditional, multidisciplinary operational teams used within corporations to provide communication across the operational level. For example, marketing, R&D, and engineering managers may meet on a regular basis to ensure that they are commonly focused on responding to corporate strategic goals. Another aspect of this structure is that it provides a feedback mechanism that keeps IP management integrated in the management of the corporation. The operational-level managers collectively work to respond to strategic goals. These same managers guide the IP management process, keeping it focused on responding to the strategic goals of the corporation.

The rationale behind placing IP management at the operational level of corporate management is that it best allows the IP process to add value to the corporation. If the corporation develops new products and services, the value derived from them will be short-lived if the innovation goes unprotected. Therefore, it is economic value that is the driver of the IP management process.

A Value Proposition

Economic value drives IP management just as it drives other operational management functions of the corporation. With respect to IP, the incentive to identify, collect, and protect innovation by formalizing rights to the innovation under one or more of the intellectual property rights is purely economic. At the risk of stating the obvious, there are costs associated with the creation of innovation and the formalization of IP rights. On the balance sheet, the costs are offset by the income associated with the IP and derived from the application of the innovation. Ideally, we seek to show a positive return on the investment made in innovation and IP.

The measure of IP's value is both quantitative and qualitative. The income associated with IP may be from the sale of products that embody the innovation, from licensing the IP rights to the innovation, or from damages obtained in enforcing the IP rights that protect the innovation. Income from each of these sources is readily quantified. Additionally, there is the brand recognition that comes from a well-managed trademark, the stature achieved from being awarded patents for truly innovative technology, or the reputation gained from appropriately enforcing IP rights.

Both value categories, quantitative and qualitative, are also contextual in nature. The value of IP to one viewer is not necessarily the same to all viewers. In the licensing context, for example, the licensee of an innovative technology that is using the innovation to enhance its own technology can be expected to pay less for the license than the licensee who has no technology of its own. In the former case, the licensee has its own way of doing things and is using the innovation to improve on that way. In the latter case, the licensee is using the innovation as a means to enter a market it might not otherwise be capable of entering. The motivation for the licensor in both cases is deriving as much income as it can from licensing its innovation. The first licensee, which is already established in the market, has a price it is willing to pay that is understandably lower than the second licensee, which needs the technology to enter the market.

Exhibit 1.7, Flow of Context-Based Information, depicts the flow of information into the IP management process. As suggested subsequently, a single innovative idea possesses both qualitative and quantitative value.

Another aspect of the context-based value of innovation is the potentially synergistic effect of protecting the innovation with multiple IP rights. For example, an innovative product may be protected by patent and trademark. The process for making the product may be a trade secret. A product comprising an innovative design, such as a stylish vase, may be protected by patent, trademark, and copyright. Like the first example,

EXHIBIT 1.7 FLOW OF CONTEXT-BASED INFORMATION

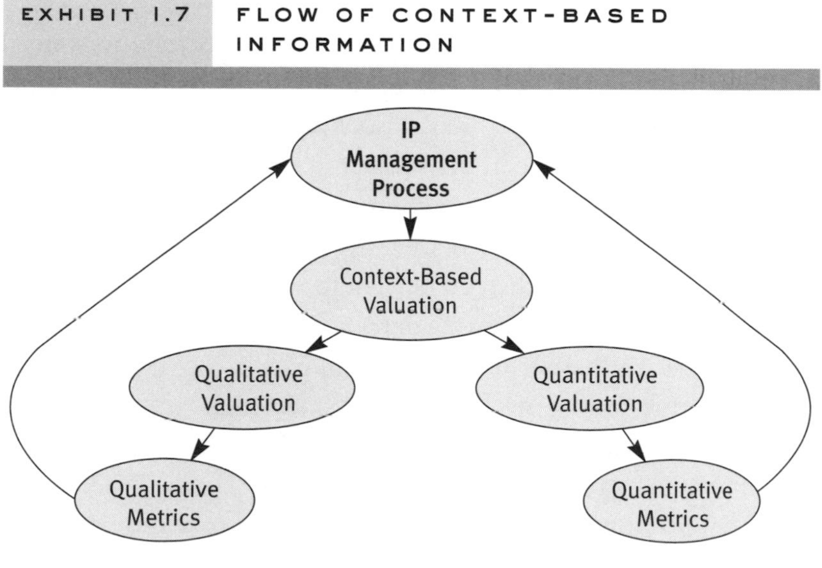

EXHIBIT 1.8 INNOVATION AND IP RIGHTS

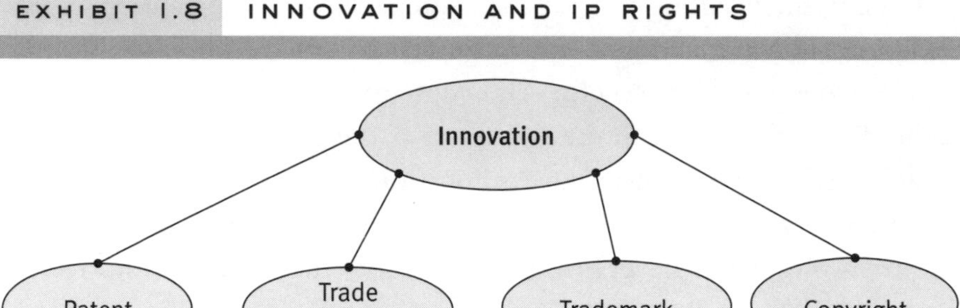

the process for making the vase may be a trade secret. As illustrated in Exhibit 1.8, Innovation and IP Rights, the idea is to protect innovation under all the formalized rights available.

The addition of each successive IP right to the protection of innovation enhances the value of the innovation because the number of opportunities to protect the innovation has increased. The value enhancement may be synergistic. Certainly the barrier to entry is made more formidable by adding successive IP rights.

Shifting the IP Paradigm: Changing Practices and Policies

To take full advantage of the value of innovation, corporations need to shift their IP practices and policies. An IP economy has been developing and has become the basis for transactions and trade. The impact of IP on our value process has been the subject of much discussion and justifiably so, because IP is a significant contributor not only to a corporation's value but to global economics as a whole. Not too recently, IP was estimated to contribute more than 20 percent to world trade.[6] More recently, it was estimated that more than 70 percent of a corporation's asset value was in its IP.[7] With these value processes in play in a competitive global economy, valuing innovation just makes good sense.

The challenge is and has been to identify and collect innovation and to leverage its value by protecting it within formal IP rights. Product differentiation comes from this process and is the means to avoid commodification.

EXHIBIT 1.9 INNOVATION AND MANAGEMENT

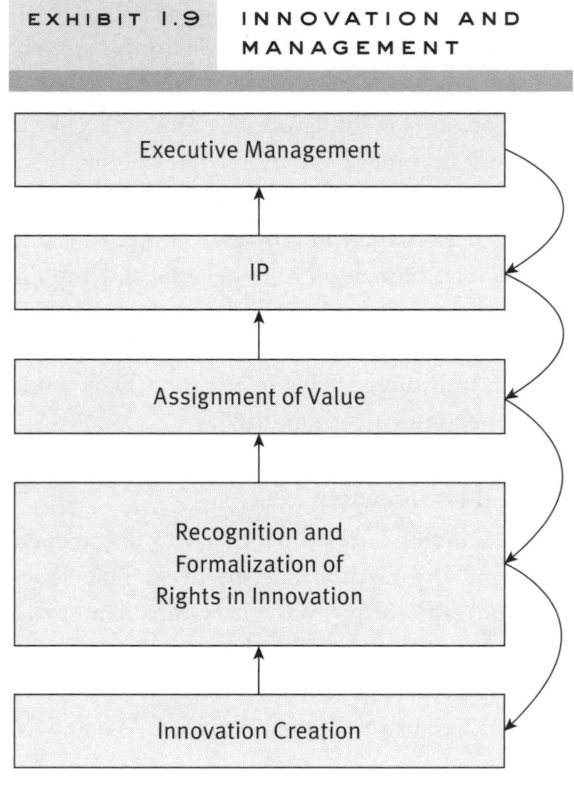

Interestingly enough, the challenge increases as technology ages. For nascent, cutting-edge technology, value is all in the innovation as defined by the IP. But for maturing technologies, differentiation becomes more difficult as the market becomes crowded with competitive products. Nonetheless, even with mature technologies, product differentiation is achievable through innovation.

Exhibit 1.9, Innovation and Management, illustrates leveraging innovation within the management process. Innovation pervades the process from the source of creation to the executive management level.

NOTES

1. The content of this chapter is solely the opinion of the author and does not reflect the opinions or practices of USG Corporation. Any and all information of a legal nature does not constitute an offer of any form of legal advice.

2. *The American Heritage Dictionary of the English Language,* Fourth Edition, Houghton Mifflin Company 2004, http://dictionary.reference.com/search?q=commodification.
3. "When a product becomes indistinguishable from others like it and consumers buy on price alone, it becomes a commodity." Investopedia.com, Investopedia Inc. 2005, http://dictionary.reference.com/search?q=commoditization.
4. "Commodity: A generic, largely unprocessed good that can be processed and resold." *Wall Street Words,* Houghton Mifflin Company, http://dictionary.reference.com/search?q=commodity. See also Investopedia.com, Investopedia Inc. 2005, http://dictionary.reference.com/search?q=commoditization ("When a product becomes indistinguishable from others like it and consumers buy on price alone, it becomes a commodity.").
5. Ford Global Technologies and IBM are noteworthy examples of companies that have successful IP businesses.
6. Gavin Clarkson, "Avoiding Suboptimal Behavior in Intellectual Asset Transactions: Economy and Organizational Perspectives on the Scale of Knowledge," Harvard Law School 2001, http://www.harvard.edu/programs/olin_center/.
7. Ashok K. Jain, "Industry Leaders Understand the Value of Leveraging Intellectual Property," Deloitte 2004; Peter J. Gerken, "Gray Matters: Protecting and Increasing the Value of Intellectual Property," Marsh & McLennan 2003.

CAPABILITIES DEVELOPMENT

Building IP Value in the Corporation

The Core of the Innovation Process

A. Observations

1. The company that tries to approach or hold IP management as a single departmental function has adopted a self-defeating policy that might be fatal in this growing aspect of the global economy.
2. The pervasive corporate impact of IP is well articulated by Mr. Geoffrey. The systems thinker gets it immediately.

B. Action Items

1. Define the company's internal economics as they are driven by international competitive (R&D, technological, and IP) strategies.
2. Create a business sense about the marketing power of IP assertion, reputation, and litigation.
3. Move the business of IP into the mainstream of corporate business thinking (e.g., IP effects on business strategy).
4. Bring the R&D operations to recognize IP value and its effect on business strategy and operations (and vice versa).
5. Create a process that returns funds from IP-based revenues to R&D to stimulate and reward effective innovation.
6. Bring IP management to the VP and board level. IP is now a pervasive function within the enterprise at every level: board to employee, top to bottom.

C. Performance Improvement

1. The CEO needs to make IP a personal interest and place it among the highest of his priorities.
2. The board and C-level executives need to better understand and begin thinking about IP as a part of their business processes as well as the technological and product innovations that drive revenues and earnings.
3. IP transactions mean high-margin dollars for assets typically expensed in prior years.

The Corporate Capabilities analysis is done by Bob Shearer and represents the analysis of the corporate performance behaviors found in the chapter, and supplemented by the Taskforce Subject Matter Experts (see Acknowledgments for a list of SMEs) over the course of related discussions and work sessions.

CHAPTER 2

Corporate IP Management in the Global Market

BILL COUGHLIN

So if you stand back and look at the way the world is changing, innovations in intellectual property management is something every company should be doing.

KEY POINTS TO LOOK FOR

- IP is the controlling factor in technological innovation and market position.
- The stakes are high as America's competitive position is being challenged in the IP arena by Japan, China, and others.
- Sarbanes-Oxley for IP is here to stay. Not everybody has figured that out yet, and hopefully the pressures will not get any worse. Today the Ford VPs at the top of the house have to certify that they've actually designed disclosure controls and procedures and, in fact, evaluated those procedures.
- The strategic principles of IP management are important at Ford; it is even more important that you develop your own critical management practices.
- The measurement of Innovation has both an internal and an external component of value that makes it an ever more critical and complex part of executive decision making.

THE AGE OF IP

I'm from Ford, and my little operation here (Ford Global Technologies) handles all of the intellectual property for Ford worldwide, so we see the entire gamut of issues and manage all aspects of it. The first point to make is that we are now in the "Age of IP." My Techno-Trends graphic (Exhibit 2.1) is a little "tongue-in-cheek" in the sense that plotting the number of patents against different economic revolutions is not the most scientific explanation of the IP age, but it communicates the magnitude of the shift in the global economy.

I am certainly not being facetious as I place intellectual property in this context for two reasons.

1. **Recognition of the Value of IP:** People are beginning to understand that intellectual property has incredible value that may not have been previously recognized. It is the controlling factor in technological innovation and market position. Over the years technologically intensive manufacturers have developed a lineage of IP, and in many cases they are a little bit lax in managing the related patents that affect a given manufacturer's core technology and operational capability. In America, we have seen creativity and innovation at work in so many unforeseen ways, but the latest example of American entrepreneurship has come from the IP community itself. Small companies now acquire patents for the sole purpose of aggressively licensing the rights to the manufacturers who depend on those patents.

EXHIBIT 2.1 TECHNO-TRENDS—THE AGE OF IP

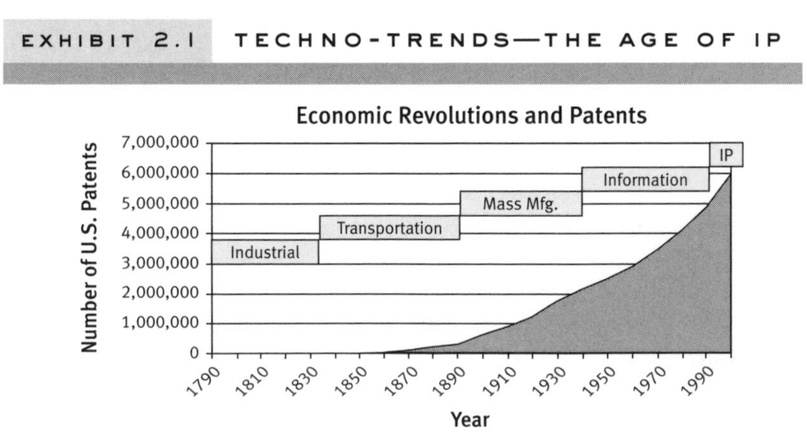

This small (but growing) number of IP owners then mount massive and indiscriminate mailing campaigns alleging infringement of their IP rights and hoping to provoke a defensive response that can be converted to cash. This practice is called "trolling," as in a fisherman's technique for luring the bigger fish to bite. Our IP fisherman is known not so affectionately as a "Troll."

The practice draws on several key factors: (1) the possible invalidity of the patent, even though granted by the USPTO; (2) the cost of litigation that provides a threshold of resistance so the accused infringer can justify a lesser amount to make the owner go away; and (3) the weight of the courts to impose injunctive relief—an action that literally shuts down production. There is a fourth factor, and that is the inability of the accused to effectively mount a fight against what many would call "gaming" the system.

One may look on these folks as either great entrepreneurs or sharp business opportunists exploiting the right to assert patent rights against potential infringers. One such company, NTT, sued BlackBerry, and there was a settlement offer of at least $450 million. (The plaintiff ultimately settled for $612 million.) And at Ford we do know (because we're on the receiving end of some of this) that this is a very expensive proposition for the competitive enterprise, not just because of the cash involved, but because the infringement allegation is disruptive and incurs an enormous opportunity expense that could otherwise be used to create new assets, improve productivity, or lower costs. By contrast, the "Troll's" only business is the prosecution of infringements against the technologically driven enterprise while increasingly exploiting the questionable quality of patents. Perhaps the most defining characteristic of the trolling operation is that the courts provide the productive (operational value extraction) function for the Troll.

2. **Global Competitive Position:** The Prime Minister of Japan said in 2002 that he wanted his nation to be built upon intellectual property. It was a shrewd observation that his nation had become a powerhouse for manufacturing. But really would that be enough in the future, particularly given the rise of manufacturing powers in China? The Prime Minister came to the conclusion that intellectual property would become the backbone of Japan's competitive position

just as it has been in the United States. Japan's economic strategy for the twenty-first century is to emulate what America has done with regard to IP—only Japan is going to do it efficiently by creating a national infrastructure to support the creation of IP-based assets. See Exhibit 2.2, Japanese Government Direction, for the precise wording.

Meanwhile, here in the United States, our Head Banker and former Chief Economist, Dr. Alan Greenspan, noted the shift in value creation at the Financial Markets Conference in April 2003. In his remarks he noted the "shift of emphasis from physical materials to ideas as the core of value creation." The more salient elements of his talk are noted in Exhibit 2.3, Alan Greenspan Speech.

IP Management and Reporting Policy at Ford

Ford is a public company, and we have to abide by the SEC rules. We do so joyfully, but until 2003 we never said a word about intellectual property in our reports. The entire statement about IP in our 2005 annual report appears in Exhibit 2.4, SEC Reporting: Ford 10K in 2005. The statement is not extensive, but it does show recognition of what we think about intellectual property. We have 11,000 active patents along with the related licensing activities. At Ford we produce one patent every single hour somewhere

EXHIBIT 2.2 JAPANESE GOVERNMENT DIRECTION

IP Policy Outline from the Strategic Counsel on IP (July 3, 2002)

As the Japanese economy remains in a severe condition social and economic revitalization by raising the international competitiveness of Japan is required. To this end it is necessary to connect the results of creativity in diverse fields such as technology and culture with the development of industry and the improvement of people's lives, thereby becoming a "nation built on intellectual property." Becoming a "nation built on intellectual property" means establishing in Japan an appreciation of the importance of invention and creation. In addition to manufacturing, by laying the industrial foundation on the creation of intangible assets, i.e., "the creation of information" of value such as technology, design, brands and the contents of music, movies, etc., this is a national policy underpinned by the vision of revitalizing Japanese economy and society.

Source: http://www.kantei.go.jp/foreign/policy/titeki/kettei/020703taikou_e.html.

EXHIBIT 2.3 ALAN GREENSPAN SPEECH

Alan Greenspan Speech

At the Financial Markets Conference on April 4, 2003

"In recent decades, for example, the fraction of the total output of our economy that is essentially conceptual rather than physical has been rising. This trend has, of necessity, shifted the emphasis in asset valuation from physical property to intellectual property and to the legal rights that inhere in the latter. Though the shift may appear glacial, its impact on legal and economic risk is only beginning to be felt.

Over the past half century, the increase in the value of raw materials has accounted for only a fraction of the overall growth of U.S. gross domestic product. The rest of that growth reflects the embodiment of ideas in products and services that consumers value. This shift of emphasis from physical materials to ideas as the core of value creation appears to have accelerated in recent decades."

around the globe. But the upshot is that it is the aggregation of these patents that is important to the business as opposed to one individual patent for an enterprise the size of Ford Motor Company.

EXHIBIT 2.4 SEC REPORTING: FORD 10K IN 2005

SEC Reporting: Ford 10K in 2005

We own, or hold liceses to use, numerous patents, copyrights and trademarks on a global basis. Our policy is to protect our competitive position by, among other methods, filing U.S. and international patent applications to protect technology and improvements that we consider important to the development of our business. As such, we have generated a large number of patents related to the operation of our business and expect this portfolio to continue to grow as we actively pursue additional technological innovation. We currently have approximately 11,000 active patents and pending patent applications globally, with an average age for patents in our active patent portfolio being 5 years. In addition to this intellectual property, we also rely on our proprietary knowledge and ongoing technological innovation to develop and maintain our competitive position. While we believe these patents, patent applications and know-how, in the aggregate, to be important to the conduct of our business, and we obtain licenses to use certain intellectual property owned by others, none is individually considered material to our business. Similarly, we own numerous trademarks and service marks that contribute to the identity and recognition of our company and its products and services globally. Certain of these marks are integral to the conduct of our business, the loss of which could have a material adverse effect on our business.

Sarbanes-Oxley for intellectual property is here to stay. Not everybody has figured that out yet, and hopefully the pressures will not get any worse. And so today the Ford VPs at the top of the house have to certify that they've actually designed disclosure controls and procedures and that, in fact, they've evaluated those procedures. See Exhibits 2.5 and 2.6, SEC Certification in Paragraphs 240.13A-14 and the definition of disclosure controls and procedures.

These controls are designed to ensure that the information required to be disclosed is recorded, processed, summarized, and reported in a timely manner. That's a reasonably tall order. If IP-related activities could be material, they must be reported.

Strategically, there are six principles I want to share with you about how Ford manages its IP. The six principles of management for Ford Global Technologies (FGTL) appear in Exhibit 2.7, Strategic IP Management at Ford.

Ford owns most of its intellectual property, so we have a stake in what happens here. We have a number of high-level reviews, including an annual profit-and-loss review with the chief financial officer, who puts us under a microscope—always a fun thing, I assure you. We participate on the operating committee for the VP of research. I have to give an annual report to the strategy and business governance committee, which consists of most of the officers of the company. And interestingly enough, one of Ford's outside directors is also a board member of Ford Global Technologies. It

EXHIBIT 2.5 SEC CERTIFICATION IN PARAGRAPHS 240.13A–14

- **Statement of Certifying Officer:**
  - (i) Designed such disclosure controls and procedures to ensure that material information relating to the issuer, including its consolidated subsidiaries, is made known to them by others within those entities, particularly during the period in which the periodic reports are being prepared;
  - (ii) Evaluated the effectiveness of the issuer's disclosure controls and procedures as of a date within 90 days prior to the filing date of the report ("Evaluation Date");
  - (iii) He or she and the other certifying officers are responsible for establishing and maintaining disclosure controls and procedures

EXHIBIT 2.6 DISCLOSURE CONTROLS AND PROCEDURES

Defined as:

> Controls and other procedures of an issuer that are designed to ensure that the information required to be disclosed by the issuer in the reports that it files or submits under the [Exchange] Act is recorded, processed, summarized and reported, within the time periods specified in the Commission's rules and forms . . . [and] is accumulated and communicated to the issuer's management, including its principal executive officer or officers and principal financial officer or officers, or persons performing similar functions, appropriate to allow timely decisions regarding required disclosure.

is crucial to have top management "in tune" with what we are doing with IP. We have our own suite for doing brainstorming and our own processes for doing that. We call it the *innovation acceleration center.* As far as we know, we're the only intellectual property team that has its own brainstorming area, and this facility has worked really well to focus on creativity and innovation.

We have reason to believe that we've been ahead of the pack in managing our IP. We developed software to help us manage this. We call it "Anaqua." We believe it's the best IP management software in the world. (Hey!

EXHIBIT 2.7 STRATEGIC IP MANAGEMENT AT FORD

Ford Global Technologies (FGTL)

1. FGTL owns most of the technical IP at Ford
2. High-level reviews are routine
   a. Annual P&L by CFO
   b. Participation on operating committee for VP research
   c. Annual strategy and business governance review by VPs
   d. Outside board member on FGTL's board
3. FGTL helps identify "white space" opportunities
4. FGTL employs a balanced scorecard aligned with Ford
5. FGTL has an Innovation Acceleration Center to facilitate creativity and invention
6. FGTL uses global processes and web-based systems

We developed it, so it must be.) But others think so too: Microsoft just dropped what they were doing and took a license to our software product, as did Coca-Cola and Kimberly-Clark, all within the past couple of months.

Intellectual property management innovations require the right tools to be able to manage these new assets effectively and efficiently. This is especially true for global companies like the ones mentioned previously that have engineering centers and brands all over the world.

Measuring IP and Why

Approaching the value of IP from a different standpoint—the determination of what should be measured and why is a critical issue for management. The market capitalization of an auto company introduces the need to differentiate between some basic external and internal factors that make a huge different in that market capitalization. Gasoline prices, for example, in recent times have had a noticeable impact on the sale of SUVs and trucks.

Internally you can measure your product mix. You obviously want a high percentage of product mix to be high margin rather than low margin. Utilization of the manufacturing capacity must be high in order to lower costs across the units produced. Anybody who is in the manufacturing game knows that without a very high utilization rate you burn through money like crazy.

Cost management is an imperative here at Ford, and we seek to make a profit with built-in quality and customer satisfaction. Exhibit 2.8, Autos: Market Cap on the Surface, lists some of the measures we use.

Ford makes a distinction between the metrics used internally and those used externally. In Exhibit 2.9, Internal versus External Metrics, internal reports are designed for management to run the business, whereas the external audience is different and needs different information that addresses their needs. There is one intangible to which I invite your attention—innovation. Author, colleague, and Taskforce Fellow, Jonathan Low, points out that innovation is one of the real value drivers of intangible asset value. Exhibit 2.10, Measure the Stream of Innovation, illustrates that you can track how much money you spend in R&D, how many staff you have, how many PhDs are on staff, and what processes you're working on in

EXHIBIT 2.8 AUTOS: MARKET CAP ON THE SURFACE

- **External Factors**
  - Auto Sales Track Consumer Confidence
  - Speed of Competitors on Your Money Trail
  - Gasoline Prices
- **Internal Measures**
  - Product Mix (a High % of High Profit Makers)
  - Plant Capacity Utilization (Number of Dealers)
  - Revenue Management (Targeted Incentives)
  - Cost Management (Make Profit on Everything)
  - Quality (More Sales + Lower Warranty Costs)

Can or Should Intangible IP Be Measured or Valued?

your pipeline. You know ultimately that IP is being created, but there must be some sort of feedback loop and a series of metrics to help you manage that business. This is an everyday problem of knowledge and business management for which a solution has yet to be found.

EXHIBIT 2.9 INTERNAL VERSUS EXTERNAL METRICS

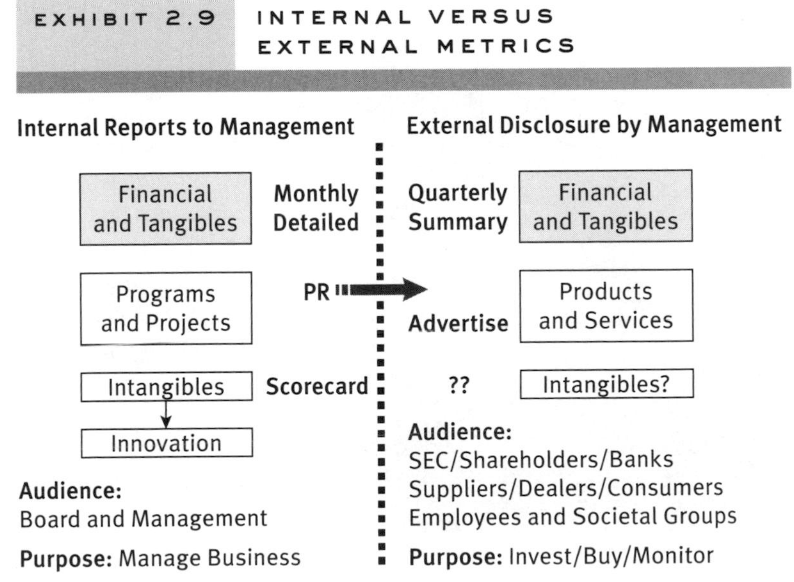

EXHIBIT 2.10 MEASURE THE STREAM OF INNOVATION

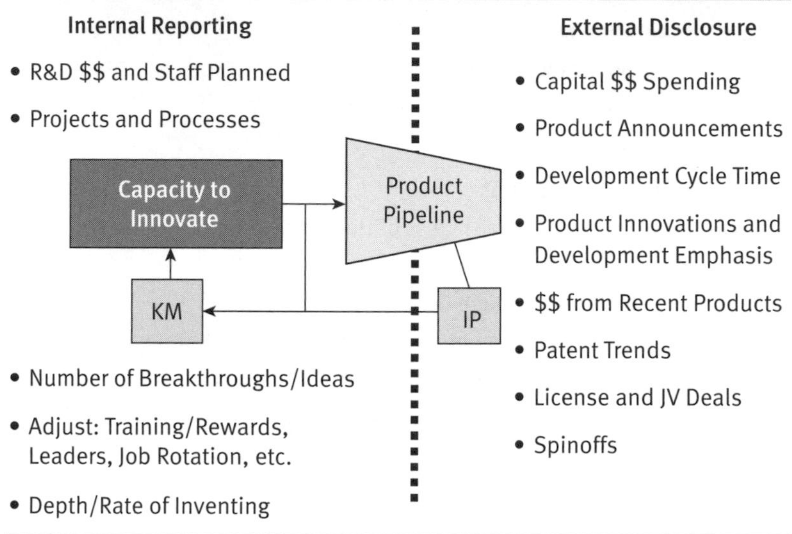

EXHIBIT 2.11 BILL FORD ON SEPTEMBER 21, 2005

From this point forward, innovation is going to be the compass by which this company sets its direction . . . . I'll invite the world to measure how the Ford Motor Company is actually setting the innovation pace.

—Bill Ford

Consequently, it makes sense for an IP group such as Ford Global Technologies to be measuring something about the invention that's going on at Ford. Are we getting breakthrough ideas? Are those ideas being serviced? How many inventions in particular areas have we had that are important to our future so that we can better allocate resources to increase our competitive position?

The competitive position includes such soft things as incentive systems, training, and job rotation, to offer a few examples.

So if you stand back and look at the way the world is changing, cutting-edge intellectual property management innovation is something every company should be doing. This is not academic for Ford. As shown in Exhibit 2.11, Bill Ford announced: "From this point forward, innovation is going to be the compass by which this company sets its direction . . . I'll invite the world to measure how the Ford Motor Company is actually setting the innovation pace."

CAPABILITIES DEVELOPMENT

Corporate IP Management in the Global Market

Observations & Action Items for Corporate Performance Improvement

A. Observations

1. The international competition regarding IP practices and policy is growing more intense.
2. Ford's IP operations are among the most innovative in the company. Those practices will eventually permeate the organization's financial performance and market position.

B. Action Items

1. Companies must track IP value relative to corporate value.
2. Technological innovation spawns IP, and IP allows a competitive distinction in global markets.
3. Companies must be able to deal with the aggressive assertion of IP rights, whether asserted by a "Troll" or by a competitor.
4. Companies must operate from a strategic global map of technologies and innovations to know where to look and what to look out for from existing and emerging competitors.
5. Companies must be able to think in terms of an economy that is based on information and knowledge creation and its commercialization.
6. Sarbanes-Oxley is reaching into the IP community, and companies must be able to comply without yielding their competitive positions.
7. Companies must develop the capabilities to measure IP value for its internal and external effects on business decisions and strategies.

C. Performance Improvement

1. The lessons from Mr. Coughlin's chapter are to innovate, believe in, and support the innovative process that begins with human capital evaluation and extends to the aggressive use of IP value extraction strategies.
2. Corporate traditions are hard to change, but the cash from innovative IP asset management begins to speak in undeniable terms at the board and investor levels.

The Corporate Capabilities analysis is done by Bob Shearer and represents the analysis of the corporate performance behaviors found in the chapter, and supplemented by the Taskforce Subject Matter Experts (see Acknowledgments for a list of SMEs) over the course of related discussions and work sessions.

CHAPTER 3

IP and Its Effects on Corporate Research and Development

DR. VASSILIS KERAMIDAS

Surprisingly, the financial people are lagging behind. They are just beginning to appreciate the hidden use of IP assets: increased liquidity, agility, dispute resolution, cash flows, and earnings.

KEY POINTS TO LOOK FOR

- R&D has now become focused on short-term ROI rather than serving the company's longer term strategic interests.
- The value creation path of innovate, create new technologies, and deploy in products and services, has been reduced from 15–20 years to 3–5 years because of short-term business driver intrusions into the R&D process.
- The typical CFO is unfamiliar and unconcerned with the opportunities and challenges of managing IP assets to create new wealth.
- The value extraction methods, while known to most, are by and large poorly executed, leaving the IP value largely ignored as the vital part of corporate business assets that it is.
- Companies can be more creative in their development of IP strategies by making more effective use of university research, innovative funding of R&D, internal valuation methods, and more aggressive and sophisticated value extraction strategies.

IP Impact on Research

I am a researcher, and consequently my comments will reflect this experience. I would like you to see my comments from that perspective. My focus is on the creation of IP and the impact of IP on the business today as compared to what it was in the past.

Examining the current landscape of IP-related issues, we all keep mentioning the fact that 75 percent—three quarters—of the total market valuation of companies is based on intangible assets, and yet we have a difficult time understanding why that is so. Why is it that we are still struggling with trying to create value from intangible assets before we convert them to tangible assets? What is the effect of IP on that process? Exhibit 3.1, Current Situation, summarizes the key components defining the state of IP in the enterprise today.

Until very recently, the creation of IP was based on what I call "old structures," because the main drivers were: (1) creating new technologies and (2) creating businesses out of those technologies that could be profitable or could help the company sustain an advantageous position in the marketplace.

Companies were generating or acquiring patents to establish a monopoly or to strengthen existing market positions (allowed by the United States Patent Office) for as long as possible. That approach to IP generation stimulated the desire and served the need to be still more innovative in order to stay ahead of the competition.

EXHIBIT 3.1 CURRENT SITUATION

1. Rapid increase in percentage of total market capitalization, driven by intangible assets, has stimulated a reassessment of how corporations view and manage IP.
2. Until very recently the creation of IP was based on "old structures."

   Main Drivers

   a. Inducement of innovation to create new technologies
   b. Acquiring patents for protection (preventing others from entering your business by establishing IP-related monopolies
   c. Acquiring patents for assertion to generate new revenues

The motives for creating IP were, in many cases, defensive in that companies "carved out" areas in which they enjoyed market dominance. Strong intellectual property practices prevented competitors from entering the company's market. There was one channel to recover the investment used to create new IP and that was through technological innovations/inventions applied in new products. New technologies and their resultant applications in products were the value driver. Today, the investment recovery is no longer an afterthought. It *is* the driver as expressed as the baseline to determine a respective ROI. This is an abrupt change in corporate thinking. Research managers feel the effects in dramatic ways, as the short-term recovery of R&D is now more focused not on recovery of cost but on suitable ROIs. Consequently, the challenge today is how to determine what should and should not be done to create and extract new revenues and earnings from the IP process.

The most pertinent question is, what areas of research do you pursue vis-à-vis your business strategy? Do you pursue areas of research that will support your present position in the marketplace? Do you want to create new businesses? Do you want to enter areas where you see others being very profitable? Software is a good example of the emergence and fast growth of intellectual property. Until recently, there weren't many software patents. They were all copyrights, but now the software patents are the favored form of IP protection. This is due, in part, to the explosive growth of software-based businesses. A contributing factor is that the holders of the older software patents are challenging the financially successful users (BlackBerry, AOL, eBay, even Microsoft) claiming infringement. This is yet another demonstration of the fact that now it is the bottom line that drives the IP creation process.

During the early stages of my career as a manger in some of America's premier R&D facilities—Bell Labs and later at Bellcore—the charter of researchers was "to broaden the horizons of science and technology." Nobody thought about business and how much money we were going to make from the inventions that might come from our research. We were just going to create intellectual property, because this was a natural consequence of pioneering research. It was the thing to do. The R&D culture was intently focused on expanding the frontiers of knowledge. The businesses that resulted from our inventions, innovations, and products were fallout from the research. Advancing the frontiers of knowledge was the main goal just 20 years ago! We were a nation of innovators, and we were upholding the tradition of invention—a tradition that extended to the nation's core capability to prosper. In many ways there was a sense of national contribution and a strong sense of duty to enable America and her citizens to prosper!

This is no longer the case. Currently, there are three parts to the IP creation process: Exhibit 3.2, The IP Creation Path, shows graphically the progression of the invention model—not in the past, but still prevailing, even today. The process remains the same and the three stages are (1) invention and innovation, (2) the generation of technology based on this invention and innovation; and (3) the creation of products or services based on the technologies with which to generate revenues.

Twenty years ago, the gap between these three stages was 15–20 years. Innovation and invention were always way ahead of the transformations into new technologies and products. Today, this gap is commonly three to five years, and sometimes in the high-tech community even less.

Examples of the Unplanned Benefits of Research

I have two fascinating stories to demonstrate how innovation and invention have always been ahead of their application (implementation of technology and product development). These cases profoundly demonstrate that when you are really doing *pioneering* work, you don't always know what the future impact of those inventions is going to be.

1. **Gallium-Aluminum-Arsenide laser:** The Gallium-Aluminum-Arsenide laser was invented in the 1960s. This laser, emitting in the infrared part of the spectrum, was originally invented with the intent of using it in telecommunications and possibly in the then-emerging field of fiber-optic communications. Later, in the 1970s, when optical fibers were beginning to be made better, we found that there was a different laser, made with different materials and emitting at longer wavelengths. These properties were much better suited for use with the emerging fibers. As a result, the optical physical properties of the competing laser technology surpassed the qualities of the

EXHIBIT 3.2 THE IP CREATION PATH

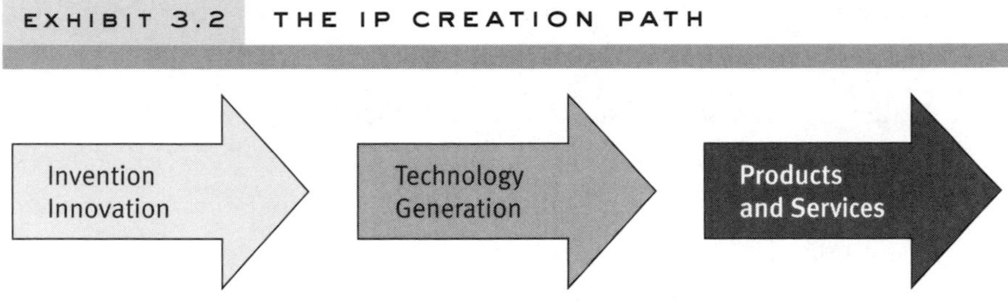

- Twenty years ago, the gap between these stages was 15–20 years.
- Today, the reduction in basic research has reduced this gap to 3–5 years.
- Research has become more and more technology oriented and business driven.

Gallium-Aluminum-Arsenide laser. It was this alternative laser that received the investment for development and was quickly converted into product because of the urgent demand. The "Cinderella to be" Gallium-Aluminum-Arsenide laser lay dormant for 15 to 20 years in spite of the fact that a massive amount of research had been done and a large number of patents had been issued to commercialize this technology.

There was no "tangible" value for the Gallium-Aluminum-Arsenide laser research and development. The investment was not on the books. It had been expensed. Then in the 1990s, along came the CD, and later the DVD, with the Gallium-Aluminum-Arsenide laser as the driving technology! Our "other" laser had finally found a "killer" commercial application. It became the underlying technology for a hugely profitable business.

Every time a CD or DVD player is used, please remember that there is a little infrared laser, the good old Gallium-Aluminum-Arsenide laser that enables the user to translate the information stored in CDs or DVDs into sound or pictures or both, in spite of the fact that that laser was invented in the 1960s for a totally different purpose.

This is a case in which most of the patents had expired before the technology found a business application. But this does offer a clear example that as much as you want to plan invention and innovation, you cannot always predict the businesses in which your inventions are going to generate a return on your investment.

2. **Caller ID:** The second story is about Caller ID. Bell Laboratories had Caller ID in 1975. It was based on light-emitting diode (LED) technology. LEDs were expensive, and they sometimes degraded too soon and caused disruptions in the displays. Those problems were corrected. Today LEDs are everywhere, including automobile brake lights.

   The Caller ID technology sat dormant until cheap display technologies became commonplace. Another "killer" application for both home and business came into existence, and the communications markets accepted and then demanded its utilization.

As these two examples demonstrate, the gap between invention and business application was once very long; the current approach is to reduce this cycle to three to five years. That time compression is a consequence of the reduction of funding in basic research. We simply do not go as far into the frontiers of science and technology as we once did. Businesses are more focused on the near-term return on investment. As a result, research today has become much more technology oriented and business driven. We are experiencing a transition within the R&D functions in most major companies as the companies adjust their strategies accordingly. This is what has happened in R&D: compressed time frames; ROI measures; and the formulation of strong, near-term business cases before the R&D investment is made.

There have been drastic changes in the way research labs such as Lucent's Bell Labs, Bellcore (now Telcordia), IBM, and others are conducting research today. Exhibit 3.3, Recent Changes in R&D, summarizes these changes over the past 10 years or so, and offers a benchmark for companies that have not yet begun to act on the impact that IP is having on them.

Some premier labs (e.g., RCA labs) are no longer in existence. The big powerhouse research laboratories responsible for the inventions and innovations that drove the telecommunications industry and created what we all enjoy and take for granted today are now drastically reduced in size, funding, and scope. Slowly, basic research has been relegated to universities, in large part because that is where the researchers who were cut by industry went when industry stopped funding basic research. This is definitely harmful to our long-term competitive interests. With the

EXHIBIT 3.3 RECENT CHANGES IN R&D

1. Basic research is now primarily relegated to universities.
2. Research in industrial laboratories is much more focused.
3. Intellectual property creation is much more structured.
   a. Patent committees include lawyers, IP management professionals, technical representatives from business units.
   b. Disclosures are scrutinized not only for novelty, but also for business relevance.
4. Financial managers are beginning to appreciate the hidden assets of IP, but still there is a long way to go.
5. Organizations, and often P&L business units, are created to focus only on extracting value from IP.

---

emergence of economies such as China and India, we absolutely need to sustain our innovative edge. This cannot happen with government-funded research and university-based efforts alone. The universities cannot be expected to take up the slack and carry the basic research forward without significant support from industry.

New Challenges to the Managing Executives

As a result of all these changes, the intellectual property generating process has also changed. It is now far more "structured" than before. Companies now have patent committees that include not only lawyers but also IP management representatives, technical representatives, and managers from the business units. As a result, patent disclosures are more closely scrutinized before the expense of filing for a patent is incurred.

Surprisingly, the financial people are still lagging behind. They are just beginning to appreciate the hidden value of IP assets: increased liquidity, agility, dispute resolution, cash flows, and earnings. Yet there is still a long way to go to get the financial community comfortable with IP value and utilization. That is another one of the issues needing the attention of contemporary CFOs.

It is the CFO's challenge to get up to speed on the value of IP and its impact on his "numbers" and his "bottom line."

The case for the CFO lies in the issue of utilization and value creation from the intellectual property already on the books. Today, there are a number of value extraction paths. Licensing is the most common form. Companies "license in" to acquire access to technologies that can be introduced as new features or new products. Most commonly companies "license out" to organizations that want to improve their competitive position and revenues by using intellectual property developed outside their own organizations at someone else's cost for the very same reason. It is a cheaper way to innovate and offers access to new markets. The desire to license to avoid litigation and all of the risks associated with infringement on another's patent(s) has generated a marked increase in revenues generated through licensing activity. The threat of litigation provides the asserting company with a big incentive to obtain licensing agreements and royalty streams. This is the so-called "stick licensing" so prevalent in today's business culture. Exhibit 3.4, Value Extraction Paths, presents a summary of the primary methods used by companies to convert their IP assets to cash flows.

EXHIBIT 3.4 VALUE EXTRACTION PATHS

1. **Licensing**
   a. Licensing In—the acquisition of IP from others to initiate new products, or improve or protect existing ones.
   b. Licensing Out—offering your IP to others for fees and royalties.
   c. Cross License—exchange of IP rights even among competitors to enhance or protect your IP.
2. **Sale**
   a. Outright sale to an interested buyer without subsequent obligation (assigning rights to buyer).
   b. Extended licensing in the sale of IP to a buyer for cash; licensing back the IP for your continuing use and assumption of a tax-deductible royalty obligation enabling and supporting the buyer to explore broader licensing opportunities and participating in those downstream licensing revenues.
3. **Equity**
   a. IP is recognized for its value as an equity input into a financial venture or spinoff.

Another value extraction option is to sell IP outright, like any other asset. The beauty of licensing is the ability to maintain the use of the asset even after it has been sold. A variation of that model is the "extended licensing program." This transaction provides cash for the acquisition of the IP asset. Ownership of the asset changes hands, but the seller is allowed to use the IP for its own businesses, for a fee, and is simultaneously allowed to participate in downstream and derivative revenues from further licensing of the IP to others by the buyer. This is a concept the Taskforce initiated in collaboration with Ford Global Technologies, Creative IP Solutions, P&G, Fitch Even Tabin & Flannery, Marks Paneth & Shron, the Center for Advanced Technologies, and a few other companies in May 2003.

Next Steps

So, considering the changes in the IP landscape what are the next steps? See Exhibit 3.5, Next Steps. What needs to be done so that we can adjust to the new circumstances and keep the innovation engine going and growing in the United States? The Taskforce is aggressively working with the Bureau of Economic Analysis, U.S. Department of Commerce to develop

EXHIBIT 3.5 NEXT STEPS

1. Selective funding of universities for research relevant to topics of interest to business units. Co-ownership of IP right-to-use and right to sub-license
2. New approaches to funding of internal R&D (in conjunction with business units) for new IP
   a. Tactical R&D—near-term product improvement
   b. Strategic R&D—long-term new product generation
3. Streamlining of the IP generation process
   a. Better management (notebooks, disclosures, filings, foreign patent filings in key geographical areas)
   b. Better coordination among technical, legal, and financial functions
   c. Better reporting to senior managers of past-present-future impact of IP assets
4. Extracting value from IP
   a. More aggressive valuation of IP and creating revenue streams via activities listed in Exhibit 3.4, value extraction paths.

the measures and metrics to define IP economics at the corporate level and also working with the Technology Administration, U.S. Department of Commerce to establish the national economic infrastructure to foster IP-based commerce.

Here are the action steps:

1. Corporations need to enhance their own reduced IP generating activities by partnering with universities and selectively funding university research that is relevant to their business but more forward looking and pragmatic than what is done in their laboratories.
2. Corporations need to have new approaches to funding of internal R&D that are well thought out and have clear paths to implementation and revenue generation. It is in this way that we can strengthen the quality of existing products and services. However, we still need to find ways for looking beyond three to five years.
3. Corporations need to further streamline their IP generating processes and their value extraction strategies. The best way to accomplish that is for our economic infrastructure to adopt business practices that make the IP class of assets more tangible and more liquid.

We also need more aggressive valuation processes. Valuation methodologies that can be found useable among the corporate, financial, and regulatory communities will contribute substantially to the transformation of IP assets from "intangible" to "tangible" definition based on protocols and standards yet to be developed. This is an important milestone, because such acceptable standards allow for asset recognitions that reach the earnings category. Furthermore, once the IP assets are appropriately "valued," they can be more aggressively marketed to create revenue streams and impact directly the "sacred" bottom line. When all these steps fall into place, creative researchers can hope that the decision makers will be stimulated to authorize the investment of new resources for future, and hopefully more forward looking, corporate R&D.

CAPABILITIES DEVELOPMENT

IP and Its Effects on Corporate Research and Development

A. Observations

1. The current R&D environment is a short-term perspective that may cause abandonment of patents that seem to have no immediate impact on revenues. Dr. Keramidas points out in his anecdotes that such short-term views would have caused his company to forfeit its income stream to others.
2. Patents need a strong technological map, but that map must be complemented by the voice of technological maturity outside of the original view of, and assumed deployment, of the invention.

B. Action Items

1. Publish a policy and plan to establish an R&D activity that serves short-term cash flows, but balances innovation and invention with a longer-term strategic view.
2. Require that your company's technology group establish policies and practices that are equal to the state of the art in your industry and that it can map and monitor those trajectories against outside industry business applications.
3. Develop university relationships, difficult as they may be to manage; still, the experience and savvy needed to employ university assets will stimulate and leverage the technical staff in your enterprise.
4. Create a sophisticated, multidisciplined group that can employ various strategies to best utilize the IP assets of the company.

C. Performance Improvement

1. Develop or acquire the tools needed to help monitor technological advances regardless of industry.
2. Keep your IP licensing team "salted" with experienced R&D personnel, either as employees or on a consultative basis.

The Corporate Capabilities analysis is done by Bob Shearer and represents the analysis of the corporate performance behaviors found in the chapter, and supplemented by the Taskforce Subject Matter Experts (see Acknowledgments for a list of SMEs) over the course of related discussions and work sessions.

CHAPTER 4

The Economic Infrastructure, Standards, Regulations, and Capital Markets

DR. STEVE HENNING

We need to understand this external landscape that not only shapes the way we do business, but also governs the way we can create and recognize new wealth.

KEY POINTS TO LOOK FOR

- **Companies must be able to measure the value of their IP assets to support internal operational decisions.**
- **Companies must know how Wall Street assesses IP value in their industry, because IP-savvy companies trade at a 30 percent premium.**
- **The recognition of IP asset value will depend upon consensus of standards and practices in the regulatory, investment, and business communities.**
- **Board members must stay apprised of the effects of IP on the company's operations and reporting.**
- **The Sarbanes-Oxley Act has sparked the acquisition of a new knowledge–skill mix that shapes the enterprise from top to bottom.**

IP Management's Two Dimensions—Internal and External

IP management traditionally refers to the practices, policies, and procedures that are used inside the enterprise to create more assets, protect them more effectively, and accelerate the value extraction from this class of assets. This is one aspect of IP management, but the other, perhaps even more critical one, is the external environment—the role the financial, investment, and regulatory communities play in shaping the management of IP and other forms of intangible assets. There is a sense of urgency in this post-Enron era to clean up corporate practices as reflected by the accounting standards, the reporting requirements, and the governance obligation to make the nation's capital markets the most reliable and transparent in the world.

What the corporation does internally is critical to its ability to attract new capital and, more importantly, to grow by way of an increasing market cap reflected through investor confidence that is in turn earned through reliable and relevant reporting. The importance of market cap growth is that this growth is the fastest way to new wealth. Consequently, we need to understand this external landscape that not only shapes the way we do business but also governs the way we can create and recognize new wealth.

The consideration of the IP landscape begins with the interface between internal and external considerations. It is our intention to bring IP and other intangible assets into a forum where the corporation, the Wall Street analyst, the investor, the standards bodies, and the regulatory communities can adopt new methodologies and standards for recognizing the new class of assets we incorrectly have labeled intangibles. We need to reconcile value definitions and the roles and relationships among the corporation, the SEC, and the FASB. It is only through the consensus of all of these stakeholders that we can begin to recognize the value of the innovative process that is so crucial to sustained competitiveness. The Taskforce is working to establish this consensus so that the new class of assets—IP-based assets—can create new wealth in the knowledge economy. If we can successfully guide this process, our economy will see a tremendous new explosion in growth, and our nation can enjoy prosperity for another generation.

The IP External Landscape

What are the effects of intangible assets on capital formation and shareholder value? Is this a domestic issue or, as some allege, is it a global issue? Inasmuch as intellectual capital and intellectual property are concerned, this is a global issue. The regulatory community is still searching for solutions regarding the reporting of intangible value, and our standards bodies are analyzing the EU's principles-based accounting versus the rules-based standards still used in the United States. Consequently, the regulatory and standards bodies are in a true state of flux. This condition does not help corporate executives to make their decisions or to be able to act with any certainty about what is expected of them from these governing bodies. In fact, it has created a firestorm of uncertainty even as the efforts to comply with Sarbanes-Oxley intensify.

This one issue is a huge obstacle and frustrates efforts to resolve what is best for America, because in a global market economy, are we not also seeing that what is good for America is fundamentally good for its trading partners? Would a new system that can accommodate creativity and innovation in a more adequate manner not accelerate transactions, ventures, and economic growth?

So as we work toward improving our ability to recognize the value in new assets, we must look to the standards bodies and regulatory community for guidance; yet there is none. The "whereases" and "what fors" abound as intellectuals pursue this value recognition problem, but we have no guidelines about how to record, manage, and report the effects of these new assets on the corporation. Consequently, the role of the regulatory environment and its influence on corporate governance issues is understood, but past efforts to facilitate a solution have eluded a successful outcome, and they serve to heighten the uncertainty associated with the reporting framework. The Taskforce believes the debate lacks the essential understanding of the economic determinants that have yet to be identified, defined, and modeled so that all communities can shape the value standards and drive our economy into the future.

Currently, public disclosures of intangible assets are perceived to lack quality and depth. There are only a few sources of information. The primary source for that public disclosure is what people will say in their annual reports, their 10-Ks, and the 20-Fs for foreign filers.

The disclosures related to investments in these strategic assets are typically generic and do not reveal much useful information. The Financial Accounting Standards Board (FASB) initiated a project several years ago when it was trying to impose a reporting structure on corporate managers that would require corporations to disclose specific information about intangibles. Ultimately, that effort did not prove useful or beneficial. In other words, FASB "tabled" its initiative—it did not feel, and still doesn't feel, that the information necessary for useful disclosures is available. FASB's conclusion was based on the opinion that the information that could be disclosed would not reveal anything useful about the underlying value of the enterprise. That is where we are today.

The Taskforce has taken it upon itself to better understand the underlying frameworks internally so that its member executives can enjoy meaningful, relevant, and reliable measures to define the effects of business strategies on value. The objective is to develop a user-friendly framework to guide disclosures of intellectual property value and its effect on total corporate value in a regulatory-friendly environment that allows the reporting and value-recognition process to evolve.

Stakeholders, including but not limited to shareholders, simply want more information. "Tell me everything I need to know and then I'll decide what's important," they say. This approach, however, creates tension in that executives want to say less—and there are a lot of good reasons for that reluctance to say much. The corporate spokesperson must be very careful about revealing vision and strategies. To do otherwise might incur legal or regulatory repercussions. There may be a "safe harbor" notion that allows forward-looking information, but as soon as the world changes, for whatever reason, the company will likely be held accountable for providing an indication of what the future might hold. The unforeseen dynamics of a market economy are far beyond anyone's control, and do not allow escape from earlier pronouncements. In such a situation, the market itself just created potential liabilities only because a corporate executive believed in his or her company's ability to execute its plan.

The legal ramifications in public disclosure are onerous and impede any progress toward discussion about anything "intangible"; after all, these are intangibles—or are they?

Intangible IP

The most definitive subset of intangibles is intellectual property. The value creation, defense, and leveraging framework for this class of intangible assets is most resident in the intellectual property rights for its use. The Taskforce has an array of databases available dealing with licensing that helps us understand the underlying economics. Similarly, there's no shortage of case law that talks about different aspects of valuation. So it's an easy place for us to start defining value, because the value definitions and decisions are already in play. To codify these practices into a framework that would serve to guide the regulatory, investment, and corporate communities would dramatically accelerate new growth, stakeholder value, and general economic prosperity.

As a result of these dynamics, we ask that you *not* presume that we are advocating the mandate of more reporting for the sake of reporting and governance. The focus is on economic growth and the ability to measure the effects of IP on total corporate value so that the enterprise itself can be more efficient in creating new wealth. It would, however, be sinfully naive to think that this might be done absent the consensus of the FASB, the SEC, and the financial communities.

There's a natural tendency, maybe as a result of an active media, to focus on areas where things have gone wrong. During the past three or four years, there has been an intense effort to make sure that all these "off–balance sheet" entities are accounted for appropriately and the information that flows into our capital markets is accurate.

Intellectual property is vastly underreported and is a missing component of any set of externally released financial statements. In fact, there haven't been many problems that have arisen out of IP management as regards financial reporting.

To bring things even closer to everyday occurrence, most executives can remember the merger or acquisition where, when the accounting was done, the deal was not recognizable. This is due to the disconnects between the reporting of financial transactions, the underlying economics of those transactions, and the accounting for the economics of those transactions. The ability to innovate in the accounting standards is one pathway toward better understanding of the basic business economics. But in many cases, the corporate economics do not allow adequate economic definition and thereby leave the accountant with no definitive basis for rules or principles to guide any change in accounting practices.

One of my close friends and accounting colleagues is adamant in his belief that current accounting practices are obsolete and cannot adequately accommodate contemporary transactions. Consequently, the successful effort to recognize IP assets means that businesses must bring the accounting community along with their own internal definition of the underlying corporate economics. Is that so different from telling a traffic cop his laws are out of date? And while we acknowledge that ridiculous illusion, we know the economics will provide the determinant set of stimuli for change, even in accounting practices.

SEC and FASB Initiatives

The SEC began a project on key performance indicators for intangible assets several years ago. It began looking at defining the internal decision making processes that executives go through in the management of their companies. The SEC examined a number of possible measures, including revenue from new product introductions, number of new patents allowed, new licensing revenue, and other things of that nature. The conclusion was that there was and would be insufficient relevant or reliable information useful for reporting, analyzing, or investing in the enterprise. The SEC project is now on hold as they monitor the work of the Taskforce.

The SEC is working to minimize any non-generally accepted accounting principles (non-GAAP). In other words, there is a strong focus on discussing business performance in the context of net income or some other intermediate number rather than using nonfinancial information. The SEC is making some accommodations, however, as foreign firms listed in the United States are insistent that they discuss the results of their operations in terms other than just net income. So the international community is exerting pressure on the SEC to expand its view to incorporate international standards.

The bottom-line impact is that the much-sought-after definitions and information are not currently available that would allow a third-party regulator to impose a reporting regime when the regulators themselves aren't sure such disclosure is appropriate. Consequently, the SEC is looking for guidance from the private sector to help it develop a framework by which more meaningful disclosure can be made.

Why Disclosure Is Important to Growth

The big question now is, "Why more disclosure?" Is it not better to "lay low" and not take the kind of risks just mentioned?

The reason for more disclosure goes against these arguments. Part of the reason is that the wealth that's contained in our intellectual assets, intangible assets, and intellectual property is increasing dramatically. There has been a tremendous growth over time in this class of assets. Exhibit 4.1, Intangible Assets and Shareholder Value, illustrates a dramatic change in the characteristics of our corporate wealth since 1982, with tangible asset value moving from approximately 62 percent of total corporate value down to approximately 26 percent, with *intangible* value now constituting about 74 percent of total corporate value based on the Standard & Poor's 500 Stock Index.

EXHIBIT 4.1 INTANGIBLE ASSETS AND SHAREHOLDER VALUE

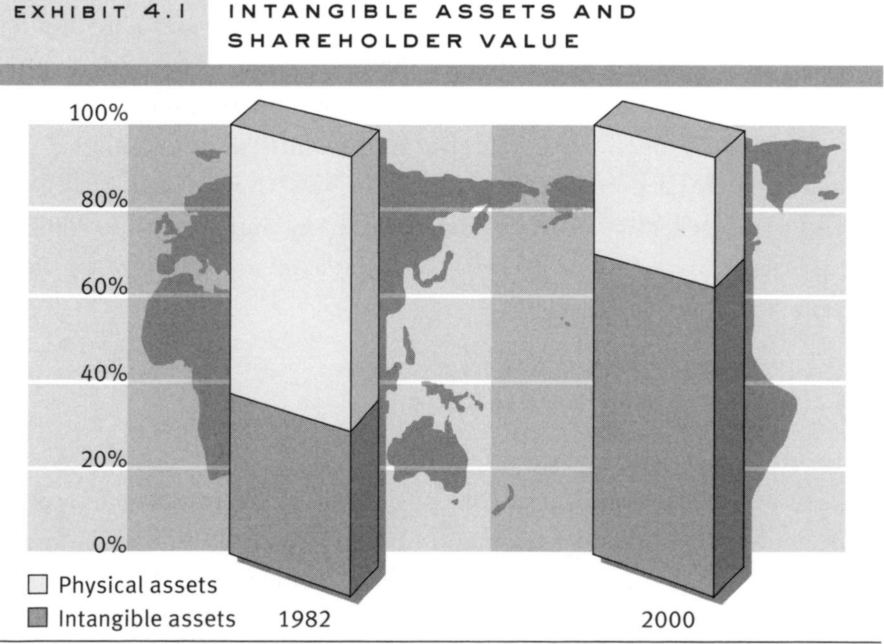

Source: Taskforce Research.

We all recognize that there are very important assets that are not reported in the financial statements. Exhibit 4.1 presents it in visual form, but you will not find it on your balance sheet.

The regulatory community with its standards-setting perspective places a lot of emphasis on making sure that all of the liabilities are reported in their financial statements. This emphasis is a detriment of the company unless ways can be found to balance the emphasis on the assets, even if they are intangible and unreported. It is my hope that we begin to think strategically about how we can develop a framework so that people can see a more revealing picture of the asset side of the balance sheet.

IP Savvy Commands a Premium on Wall Street

As we look at the creation of shareholder value from an accounting perspective, we realize that patents have a lot of value relating to competitive advantage, market position, and the company's reputation as an innovator. Smart investors perceive value in the IP competency. In fact, the Taskforce research shows that IP-savvy companies trade at a 30 percent premium. IP represents a new source of capital or certainly lower costs of capital, all other things being equal. Exhibit 4.2, Intangible Assets and Shareholder Value, is a list of items that link intangibles to value.

Shareholders are increasingly sensitive to the value of intellectual property. There have been some shareholder lawsuits filed recently against management for a perceived negligence in how they've managed their portfolio of intellectual property and failed to maximize its value. So certainly that's an issue that people are looking at as an indication of earnings potential.

Measuring Intangibles

As we move into the measurement of intangibles, the biggest obstacles to meaningful disclosures (that can positively affect stock price) are (1) the recording of intangible assets and (2) the absence of reliable and relevant measures and metrics. But corporations guard their IP dearly. Consequently, much of the corporate value goes unrecognized internally by the executive team, as well as externally where analysts and shareholders might

EXHIBIT 4.2 INTANGIBLE ASSETS AND SHAREHOLDER VALUE

1. **Recent Research Results**
   a. On average 40% of the value of U.S. and EU companies does not show up on the balance sheet.
   b. Recent survey of 284 U.S. and Japanese companies revealed that IP assets counted for 45% of the total assets.
2. **Intangible Assets**
   a. Patents sharpen competitive edge, increase sector influence, and enhance reputation as innovators.
   b. IP is a new source of capital and ingredient for success.
   c. Shareholders, sensitive to the value of IP assets, are using them as indicia of earnings potential.
   d. Positive valuation of IP is a driving force in M&A activity and business-to-business relationships.
3. **Intangible and Immeasurable**
   a. IP assets can significantly contribute to increase return to investors.
   b. According to Interbrand, trademarks for Coca-Cola, Disney, and Ford were 60% or more of their capitalization.
   c. Most corporations guard their IP closely.

---

make different decisions if they understood the underlying corporate capabilities to create, protect, and leverage this new class of asset.

New Capabilities Requirements

The reality of our current situation is that the Sarbanes-Oxley Act has sparked the acquisition of a new knowledge–skill mix that shapes the enterprise from top to bottom. SARBOX as it is sometimes called, requires the involvement of various functional areas of an organization in monitoring the intellectual property and making sure that the identification or valuation methods are updated and that information is transferred to, or made available to the CEOs and CFOs who have to certify the financial statements. Board members must stay apprised of the effects of IP on the company's operations and reporting. The CEO and CFO must know how IP is developed, the claims that have been made, alleged infringements, the portfolio's value, the company's enforcement actions, third-party claims, and the effects on the overall reporting environment as a result of the emerging influence of this new class of asset. Exhibit 4.3, Intangible Assets and the Regulatory Environment, presents a number of the basic knowledge–skill requirements (new capabilities) for easy reference by the C-level executive and the board of directors.

The disclosure of risks, to the extent that strategy or financial condition may rely on patents with a short-term, finite life, and, the absence of alternative sources of revenue are not only sound business practice, but a critical part of the intent of Sarbanes-Oxley. These risks need to be disclosed. The risks associated with patent validity (quality) today have become one of the enormous variables in today's competitive environment. The change in the dynamics of patent strategy has placed growing demands and costs on the entire system and reinforces the need to find a competitive advantage through the management of IP assets.

EXHIBIT 4.3 INTANGIBLE ASSETS AND THE REGULATORY ENVIRONMENT

1. **Sarbanes-Oxley Compliance**
   a. Involve IP counsel in the management of reporting.
   b. Ensure CEOs and CFOs are familiar with IP portfolios so they can make certifications.
   c. Update IP identification and valuation regularly.
   d. Keep the board members informed.
   e. Make accurate, comprehensive disclosures.
2. **CEOs and CFOs Must Know**
   a. How IP is developed and identified
   b. What claims are made
   c. Status of alleged infringements
   d. Enforcement actions brought by the company
   e. Third-party claims against the company
3. **Risks**
   a. IP transaction and financial risks of the deal
   b. Reliance on IP rights and licenses and their useful (revenue-generating) lives
   c. IP-related litigation—assertion and defense

IP Influence on the Private Enterprise

The implications for the private enterprise are similar to those for the publicly traded enterprise, but of course not subject to the reporting and regulatory scrutiny from the regulatory community and capital markets. But the issues are similar. A private company still contends with credit ratings as well as valuation decisions by clients, by current and potential employees, by suppliers, by lenders, and by any other entity with which a company might engage in a financial transaction; such evaluations are increasingly based on intangibles. The adequacy of GAAP measures may be challenged as a valuation measure, and also as an internal management tool. In a service economy in which the majority of value is being generated by intellectual property itself as opposed to the production of tangible assets, the inability to define the economic nature of intangibles is both a serious competitive disadvantage and a clear financial problem for every corporate competitor doing business today. The absence of a structure to provide the needed measurement guidelines is an impediment to the growth and sustainability of our economy.

What Can We Do?

After viewing this picture of the standards and regulatory communities and their effect on managing IP, one might wonder what we can really do about this situation. The answer is simple: We focus on what we can manage. We remain true to the economic practices that are based on individual creativity and corporate innovation. We develop as we drive the business practices to better measure IP and its effects on total corporate value. We develop the answers that serve our stakeholders and educate the external world as we go. In so doing, we (corporate America) can define value for our economic future.

CAPABILITIES DEVELOPMENT

The Economic Infrastructure, Standards, Regulations, and Capital Markets

A. Observations

1. The standards, regulatory, and financial communities are struggling with how to deal with "intangible assets."
2. The focus must be on patents and other forms of IP that generate cash flows until these communities can build consensus with hard data to measure the value and effect of IP assets on total corporate value.
3. Businesses must lead this new definition of value and net worth and *not* leave it to Congress or the FASB. The corporate community must drive this new value definition into consensus and practice.

B. Action Items

1. Accept that your knowledge of Sarbanes-Oxley and its implications for reporting of IP assets is both your biggest strength and your biggest liability as you push into IP asset management.
2. Develop the financial linkages among IP assets and cash flows, market share and profits.
3. Develop the willingness (and patience) to set internal policies and practices that can evolve into measures and metrics to manage IP internally.
4. Recognize and develop processes to determine what needs to be reported publicly and what needs to be kept inside the enterprise.
5. Fundamentally acquire or develop a system to identify, document, and track the value of IP assets.

C. Performance Improvement

1. Performance improvement in this context begins with a savvy CFO who takes responsibility for creating new assets and extracting value from those assets.
2. The CFO must be aggressive in national and international forums to gain information that will help shape corporate business opinion and competitiveness.
3. The CFO should actively inquire about how the capital markets use IP in their analysis and where their data are acquired.

The Corporate Capabilities analysis is done by Bob Shearer and represents the analysis of the corporate performance behaviors found in the chapter, and supplemented by the Taskforce Subject Matter Experts (see Acknowledgments for a list of SMEs) over the course of related discussions and work sessions.

SECTION THREE

Creating the Assets

Asset creation is not of much value if it cannot be recognized or converted to cash. This is the problem today—we have no way to value our IP-based assets. But let's not get distracted by valuation until we can identify, organize, and begin to manage those assets for value relative to our industry competitors. This section will help you develop those unrecognized assets.

As a nation, we seem to be less than effective in guiding our children to a pathway to economic prosperity. Avoiding math and science has become an adolescent art form, but without these skills, America puts itself at an economic disadvantage, one student, one family at a time. Ed Paradise, in Chapter 5, focuses on this problem. As the site manager for Cisco Systems at Research Triangle Park in North Carolina, Ed knows that his business in North Carolina is threatened if he and his competitors cannot find a workforce that can perform to enable his company to out-innovate the young people from France, Japan, India, and especially China. The visionary defines the problem. He leaves the solution to you and every executive in a U.S.-based enterprise.

Steve Parmelee is a unique talent. His ability to manage IP assets has become legend inside the Taskforce. But this talented IP attorney knows how to get the IP asset out of the inventor's mind—especially the inventors who are not so sure what IP is or how it is recognized and documented or even that they are actually inventors. Mr. Parmelee's process encourages the identification of existing IP assets, but pushes the enterprise toward a more definitive way to create new IP assets. In Chapter 6 he answers the question, "What can I do today to build shareholder value?"

Trade secrets are just that—secrets. How does a company manage them? How are they defined? Mark Halligan tells you what you need to know about trade secret asset management in Chapter 7.

CHAPTER 5

Human Capital: The Forsaken Resource

Ed Paradise

America has shown the rest of the world that for individual competence and capabilities to function creatively there must be a strong educational and individual value system that can grow and prosper from one generation to the next.

KEY POINTS TO LOOK FOR

- **America's future economic prosperity rests with its educational system to produce educated people.**
- **America is not producing employable people to support the nation's workforce needs; this means outsourcing to other nations must grow and immigration must continue.**
- **The United States has fallen to 16th place among the developed nations of the world in graduation rates; our nation's competitive position can be expected to follow.**
- **Only 18 out of every 100 high school graduates will complete a college curriculum within six years.**
- **IP is the substance of invention and requires creative minds to realize the promise of America—what we call the American dream.**

Forsaken Resource

Speaking about our nation's workforce as a forsaken or forgotten resource seems a bit harsh, and to many it might sound disrespectful. However, from the author's perspective, America's workforce is not just the raw material for corporate endeavor but is also the platform for a productive and happy life for everyone. Education has maturation and socialization components as adolescents struggle through the crisis years during which identity struggles are the norm in every household. These household struggles spill over into the schools, where educators and administrators are not equipped to serve as "superparents" for the students. The parental role has diminished most noticeably, and not only has this affected academic achievement, but it has also led to the failure to instill in young people the fundamental ideas about a quality of life in a free society. Will America's future be adversely affected by the education of a generation, now two, whose individual and social behaviors ignore life's most fundamental responsibilities?

Leadership at home is the framework for life's success. The educational community can only build on and reinforce responsible citizenship and create the environment for learning. It is the Taskforce's purpose to focus some attention on the need for America's corporate leaders to recognize the significance of the current educational crisis described in the next few pages. This crisis is multidimensional but must be addressed by business leaders who understand that it is not just an opportunity to help right the declining trends in America's human capital, but an urgent requirement to help reverse these trends at the very local and home level where our future leaders are born and grow up.

Key Skills for Success in the Twenty-First Century

The Partnership for Twenty-First Century Skills defined the most critical skills for future job performance as given in Exhibit 5.1, Twenty-First Century Skill Requirements.

The nation's graduates are increasingly moving away from engineering, math, physical sciences, and computer science to life sciences, which include psychology, social sciences, and biological and agricultural sciences.

EXHIBIT 5.1 TWENTY-FIRST CENTURY SKILL REQUIREMENTS

a. Internet communications used at a higher level than standard communications, but creatively and ethically to accomplish intellectual pursuits.

b. Effective communications beyond the immediate peer group and on a global level.

c. The ability to analyze complex information gathered from a multitude of sources.

d. The ability to write and present effectively.

e. The ability to develop solutions to interdisciplinary problems that have no one right answer.

f. The ability to pursue technology not as a panacea, but as a launching pad for innovation.

Exhibit 5.2, Education Trends, illustrates these trends from 1986 through 2000. These trends present a serious challenge to industry's ability to compete using homegrown resources as the base in the physical sciences, engineering, math, and computers continues its decline. This will result in either more offshore outsourcing of white-collar creative jobs or more intense recruitment of internationally developed and better-educated workers.

EXHIBIT 5.2 EDUCATION TRENDS

Worse: U.S. Degrees Don't Match Openings

Life Sciences Up . . .

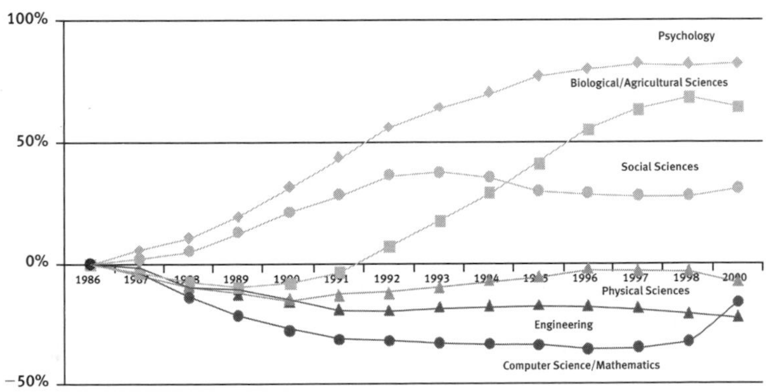

. . . Engineering, Physical Sciences, and Math Down

In North Carolina, in 2003, employers rated their high school graduates' work skills as fair or poor, even though the state spends $40 million annually on remedial education and training (see Exhibit 5.3, Skill Demand 2002–2012). The national profile is more specific. Using a baseline of 100 seniors graduating from U.S. high schools:

- Only 68 will receive a regular diploma.
- Only 40 will enroll in college immediately.
- Of those 40, 27 will stay in college until their sophomore year.
- Only 18 will graduate within six years.

Competitively, the United States has fallen to 16th among the developed nations of the world in graduation rates, and by 2010 more than 90 percent of all scientists and engineers in the world will be living in Asia. The relative performance of the United States is sadly demonstrated in Exhibit 5.4, OECD Rankings of the G8 Nations. The United States stood 24th in math, 18th in science, and 15th in reading, numbers this generation will find are not competitive in the current global economy.

The impact of these trends in economic terms is shown graphically in Exhibit 5.5, Failure to Raise Student Achievement Means Opportunity

EXHIBIT 5.3 SKILL DEMAND 2002–2012

Computer-Related Job Titles	Employment 2002	Employment 2012	% Growth
Network systems and data communications analyst	186,000	292,000	57%
Computer software engineers, applications	394,000	573,000	46%
Computer software engineers, systems software	281,000	409,000	45%
Database administrators	110,000	159,000	44%
Computer systems analysts	468,000	653,000	39%
Network and computer systems administrators	251,000	345,000	37%
Computer and information systems managers	284,000	387,000	36%

Source: Network World 8/10/05; U.S. Bureau of Labor Statistics, 2004.

EXHIBIT 5.4 OECD RANKINGS OF THE G8 NATIONS

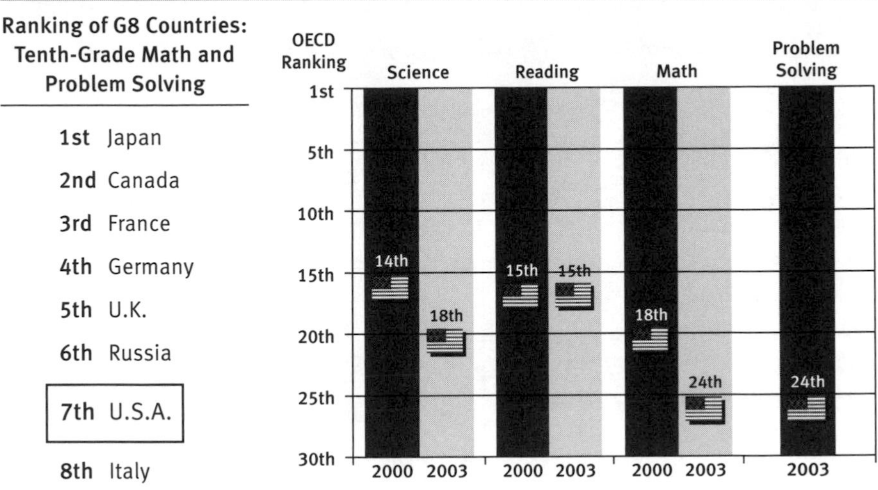

Source: PISA, 2000, 2003.

Cost. This is certainly a dramatic representation of cost and benefit; note specifically:

- A loss of $2.5 trillion in economic output between 1990 and 2002 is projected.
- A change in performance level would generate a $450 billion dividend for the national economy.
- Closing the gap would add one percent or $980 billion to the annual gross domestic product.

The Educational System

Some business leaders are aware of the impact of the current educational system and its slide to mediocrity or worse. Bill Gates, Chairman of Microsoft Corporation, commented at the National Governors' Association on February 27, 2005:

> *Today, only one-third of our students graduate from high schools ready for college, work, and citizenship. The other two-thirds, most of them low-income and minority students, are tracked into courses that*

EXHIBIT 5.5 FAILURE TO RAISE STUDENT ACHIEVEMENT MEANS OPPORTUNITY COST

- $2.5T lost economic output 1990–2002
- United States behind top performers since accountability movement
- Lost opportunity . . . pays K–12 education costs
- Closing gap 12+ years . . . adds 1% annual GDP/$980B

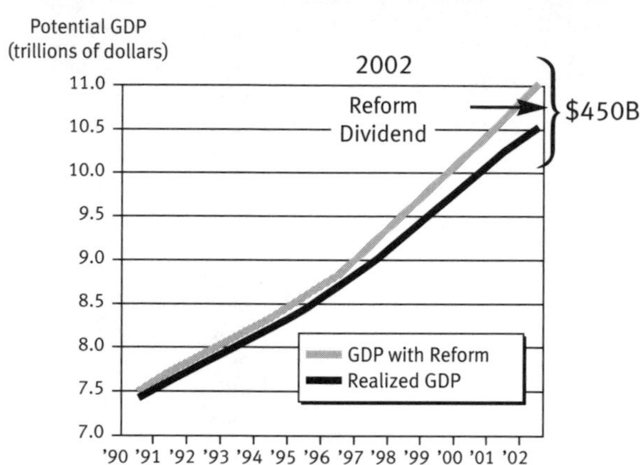

Sources: Cisco, IBSG, calculations using Congressional Budget Office data on potential GDP, January 2005; Eric Hanushek, *Lost Opportunity,* 2003.

> *won't ever get them ready for college or prepare them for a family-wage job—no matter how well the students learn or the teachers teach. This isn't an accident or flaw in the system; it is the system.*
>
> —Bill Gates, Chairman Microsoft Corporation, February 2005

America continues to work on its K–12 educational system with enormous amounts of money and intellectual power focused on improvement, but the system continues to decline. Furthermore, in a world of political correctness and social consideration, we have found ways to substitute these values for the responsibility of one generation to prepare its young for survival and success. In America's glory is found one of its most fundamental values: care for others. This value remains pervasive in every household in every city and township across America; but has it, in these recent generations, become also perverse as we refuse to look beyond the convenience of the moment and its offerings of contentment with an implied promise of success—success to be gained without the work or discipline needed to develop the capabilities for ourselves or our children?

Craig Barrett, CEO of Intel Corporation, commented on the effects of this system when he said, "The biggest ticking time bomb is the state of our K–12 education system." In a society where we forgive poor performance, we can actually impede growth and opportunity. We can actually put our children at risk—sometimes immediately and sometimes later in life. In denying the realities of global competitive economic capabilities at the individual level and at home, our nation, our corporations, and our life of prosperity and caring will become more inwardly focused and frustrated as our own inabilities to find meaning, productive energy, and quality of life lead into the morass of apathy, inaction, and indecisiveness.

America and all other nations are on their own defined trajectory to global competition. Japan and China have recently announced that intellectual property rights are the cornerstones of their twenty-first-century global strategies. Their strategies are well placed, because there is no place where intellectual property is more obvious than inside the well-educated, resourceful, and creative minds of these nations' people whose minds are focused on corporate productive endeavor in competitive environments. Economic success, whether measured in wage rate, salary, earnings, or dividends, means a quality of life full of choices, and choices generate increasing levels of freedom in most developed nations.

Although other nations have followed us in so many ways, we sometimes seem to have forgotten that America is the one that has shown the way. It has shown the rest of the world that for individual competence and capabilities to function creatively there must be a strong educational and individual value system that can grow and prosper from one generation to the next. Our education system is the primary enabling capability for this new growth—and America's future.

CAPABILITIES DEVELOPMENT

HUMAN CAPITAL: THE FORSAKEN RESOURCE

Observations & Action Items for Corporate Performance Improvement

A. Observations

The implied capabilities presented in Ed's chapter suggest that the competitive enterprise cannot afford to overlook the impact of human capital and its development on the company's future competitive capabilities.

B. Action Items

1. Companies must begin working to ensure they have access to a workforce capable of competing in a global market.
2. Jobs are no longer local; they are globally competitive, and the enterprise must be active in identifying sources of human capital.
3. One's prosperity and quality of life are linked to education and the ability to apply knowledge effectively. Can the enterprise do more than reinforce this basic truth?
4. Companies cannot intervene in a home life, but they can encourage educational programs for parents and they can recognize family accomplishments to increase the value of the family.
5. Corporate programs can foster human capital development and a significantly reduced cost of associated turnover, weak performance, and training programs in the years ahead.

C. Performance Improvement

Corporate citizenship will need to include the human resource function as companies develop outreach programs in their communities, especially for technical or engineering and math-based activities. Looking overseas is one solution, but companies can be more supportive of science fairs and become more involved in workforce issues before the student leaves school and enters the workforce.

We have to make it "cool" to stimulate interest, and that should not be too hard in view of the many new technological toys being introduced and the continuing use of the Internet's many applications.

The Corporate Capabilities analysis is done by Bob Shearer and represents the analysis of the corporate performance behaviors found in the chapter, and supplemented by the Taskforce Subject Matter Experts (see Acknowledgments for a list of SMEs) over the course of related discussions and work sessions.

CHAPTER 6

How to Turn White Space Dark for Fun and Profit

Capturing and Creating IP Assets

STEVE PARMELEE

A white space management agenda is, first and foremost, a survival activity. Done properly, however, white space inventing can also create value that leads to direct increases on the bottom line.

KEY POINTS TO LOOK FOR

- The patent portfolio should provide a comprehensive quilt of patented technologies that leaves no "white space" (holes) in the protective blanket.
- White spaces represent a vulnerability and threat to your company that, if not quickly repaired, allow a competitor to potentially disrupt your business and, in the worst case, actually create the need for you to license from the competitor.
- White space inventing is a sophisticated process that may look like brainstorming, but is much more focused and serious.
- Every company will have intellectual assets that need to be codified and protected to ensure maximum value to the inventor and the enterprise.

"White Spaces"

The IP executive (it could be the CTO, IP Counsel, or an outside law firm) must establish a portfolio of IP assets. Large and small companies need to develop their portfolio and manage it as a compilation of *business and financial assets.* Patents are business assets that often constitute some of the more challenging contents of an IP portfolio. Each patent should have a corresponding area of business coverage or influence; stray too far from that coverage and the patent no longer applies.

The ideal portfolio has no white spaces between such assets; in a perfect world the portfolio coverage extends seamlessly, from patent to patent, across the company's entire business spectrum. That seamless interface can present a competitor with a significant challenge and can greatly aid in protecting your market share, revenues, cash flow, and earnings. On the other hand, white space in the portfolio that is relevant to one's business strategy represents an opportunity that some competitive innovator might fill to your detriment. The interloper into your company's white space can have you in negotiations for licensing royalties or facing the threat of litigation.

"I Know What I Need—Sort Of"

Trying to achieve a patent portfolio having no white spaces constitutes a most challenging task. Or, perhaps more correctly, a group of challenging tasks. It can be difficult indeed to assess, analyze, and characterize one's patent portfolio to gain an understanding of what, exactly, your company has with respect to useful business coverage. Patents are sublimely subtle legal instruments that tolerate little in the way of uninformed, sloppy, or rapid consideration. Just as difficult can be the job of leveraging one's IP holdings to best effect and purpose.

But perhaps a most troubling and frustrating challenge in developing the patent portfolio can be filling identified white spaces—that is, finding and acquiring the needed assets through internal development or through an external license or acquisition opportunity.

There are various drivers and circumstances that can bring such white spaces to one's attention. Some of these drivers pertain to subject matter content. Exhibit 6.1, Patent Asset Creation Drivers, summarizes seven typical business reasons to create patent assets.

EXHIBIT 6.1 PATENT ASSET CREATION DRIVERS

1. Designing around an existing patent
2. Anticipation of, or participation in the defining of, an industry standard
3. Studying and applying technology trends to a particular field of endeavor
4. Technology breakthroughs and disruptive technologies
5. Technology mapping exercises (where, for example, an enterprise maps out the technologies that are needed going forward in order to ensure that planned product designs are executable)
6. Strategic portfolio reviews and building exercises
7. Recognition, rationalization, or monetization needs

In these and other cases, the portfolio manager has some notion of what the portfolio lacks (i.e., the white spaces in the company's portfolio). In the most dramatic case, as when dealing with a start-up situation, the entrepreneur is staring at nothing *but* white space. The portfolio manager is also, however, without the raw material, one needs to pursue development of the missing patent coverage, a conceived and enabled invention. The manager who relies solely upon a reactive approach waits hopefully for the invention to appear and then responds with alacrity, if and when this ever happens. The more proactive manager may try a bit harder. Memos may be circulated and elevator speeches shared to alert the troops to bring such an invention to the fore, if and when someone should happen to stumble across it.

The Ugly Inventing Session

There are, however, better ways to address patent portfolio white spaces. One can take steps to deliberately create the inventions needed to backfill or extend the reach of one's patent portfolio. The fundamentals are well known: gather some bright folks together, get them to think about some specific areas of interest, and take note of their deliberations. It is all just a matter of scheduling a time and place when the right group of people can get together and think their great thoughts, right?

In fact, time and experience have shown that such a process can suffer a variety of maladies and is generally inefficient and ineffective. A lot of time can be wasted as such a group meanders aimlessly down paths leading to places that lack business relevance. Hoped-for group dynamics can quickly succumb to a single alpha-innovator who takes control of the process and smothers interaction and cross-pollination of thought. In a somewhat similar but opposing role, an individual who takes it upon himself to criticize espoused ideas can quickly dampen the creative spark and bring silence down upon the room, as suddenly no one else seems to have anything to offer.

Further, even when seemingly good ideas surface, the challenges of follow-through can fully stymie any corresponding patent activity. Identifying inventorship, for example, can become a hopeless muddle. Even worse, when contacted weeks or months after such a meeting, inventors confronted with their meeting results often express confusion and ignorance regarding those inventions. "I have no idea what that concept is about. I'm not sure who the inventor might be," is not an uncommon refrain in such cases.

And so it goes. Someone calls a meeting that brings together some of the best and brightest of a given organization. It turns out to be rather fun (at least for some participants); folks get to put their feet up on the table, think big thoughts, maybe have a nice lunch or dinner, and then head back to their normal jobs. Weeks or months later, all too often, nothing has changed. The output of the meeting proves to be amorphous and ephemeral. No new invention disclosures appear in the in-box. No new patent applications are filed. No portfolio white spaces are filled. Gaps continue to remain, posing corresponding genuine risk to the enterprise.

Doing It Right—Filling the White Spaces

The white space invention session does not have to be this way. There are best practices that can turn a white space inventing activity into a potent strategic and tactical tool for the portfolio manager. The keys are those represented in Exhibit 6.2, Effective White Space Inventing Requirements, and they most conspicuously require a dedicated company champion.

Done properly, such a meeting will conclude with a graded and prioritized list of numerous guided concepts that correlate to a subject matter area of interest and that are evaluated for novelty and enablement, with

EXHIBIT 6.2 EFFECTIVE WHITE SPACE INVENTING REQUIREMENTS

1. Select a dedicated process champion.
2. Prepare for that meeting of the best and the brightest.
3. Steer and control that meeting.
4. Capture, evaluate, and filter the developed concepts.
5. Prioritize the resultant concepts.
6. Memorialize/document the prioritized results.

suggested subject matter groupings being indicated, inventorship specified, and brief descriptions captured. Also of note is that this approach can lead to a high-volume process. One can typically expect a relatively large number of high-quality and useful concepts to become available as the grist for corresponding patent applications. Done properly, one can conquer the white spaces!

Select a Dedicated Process Champion

The process champion may or may not be the portfolio manager. The process champion may or may not be the person to actually lead and facilitate the white space innovation session. The process champion may or may not have any experience with the patent system. A good process champion is, however, a person who will take responsibility for this process and work to see it through to its conclusion.

The ideal process champion is often an experienced manager who is also:

- Someone with experience and knowledge regarding the area of relevant technology
- Someone who is familiar with the enterprise and its culture, customs, ways, and means
- Someone who has at least some modicum of imagination and a bent toward creativity
- Someone with at least some sense of the business, including industry and competitor trends and behaviors

- Someone who can, and will, devote a bit of time before, during, and after the inventing session to follow up with the supporting documentation and liaison requirements of the activity

The process champion assumes responsibility, either alone or in combination with the portfolio manager and/or the session facilitator, to effect many of the steps set forth in the following text, including especially the preparation steps. These activities can be relatively modest or demanding, depending on the strengths and experience of the session leaders. In some cases, it may be necessary to use two people in order to come up with one viable champion.

Preparation

Preparation includes training, team selection, communications, concept steering pre-work, optional prior art characterization, and optional concept development, along with planning for the logistics of the session itself.

The training need not involve a deep dive into the many nuances and subtleties of patent law; instead, for the most part, such training should focus on two concepts that are genuinely important to successfully executing a white space session—novelty and enablement.

"Novelty" and "enablement" are two very critical concepts that shape the quality and quantity of the session output. Many innovators incorrectly set the technological advancement requirements bar too high because of a misunderstanding regarding these requirements for patentability. This high bar often leads to silence rather than helpful suggestions.

Simply stated, under U.S. patent law, something is "novel" if it differs in some way from any single existing thing or reference. Here is a simple example: assume every fork ever made or described in fact or in writing has two, three, four, or six tines. In such a case, a fork having *five* tines will pass the novelty test—it is, indeed, "novel." This is a relatively objective test in application and is also usually one the participants can readily grasp. Understanding this test serves two important purposes. First, the participants can use novelty as a filter when analyzing the results of their brainstorming activity (*more on this later*). Second and more importantly, understanding this test often serves as an eye-opening moment for many technologists. Many (perhaps most) people in the technology community have a considerably loftier notion of what it takes to get a patent. Returning the bar to a realistic level can actually inspire the participants to offer their suggestions more assertively and freely.

Novelty alone is not sufficient to garner a patent. In the United States, the claimed invention must also be "unobvious." This second test, however, essentially constitutes a lawyer's playground, and little good will come of trying to teach the non-legal participants much about this test; leave it to the lawyers.

The enablement requirement, however, should be addressed. Like novelty, enablement is a relatively simple concept (though numerous subtleties can and do crop up as with all topics legal) but, again like novelty, it is often misunderstood by the layperson. Fundamentally, an invention must be reduced to practice in order to qualify for patent protection. Contrary to all-too-common belief, however, this does *not* mean that the invention must have been built and tested or that the invention must be perfected and ready for the market. It really means, in practice, only that one must be able to describe, in words and pictures, *some viable way* of practicing the invention.

Consider this example: pencils are known, and erasers are known, but they have always existed as physically separate items. In a white space inventing session, someone suggests combining the two into a single instrument by using glue. That can certainly be described in a patent application without actually building it. The fact that glue is likely a poor solution and that other means of attaching the two will later prove to be a superior commercialized version of the idea is often beside the point. Such an embodiment can nevertheless serve to support a patent claim such as "A handheld writing apparatus comprising a pencil having an eraser attached thereto." As this claim contains no details regarding *how* the pencil and eraser are attached, virtually *any* way of attaching the two will suffice to infringe the claim! And therein lies the genuine power of a white space inventing session—providing the enabling grist for patent claims that can circumscribe business space of value to the enterprise, notwithstanding that the specific described invention itself may be less than commercially viable.

All session participants need to know that our patent laws *do not require* that an invention be physically brought to practice before patenting can be pursued. Neither must a commercially feasible construct be fully thought through before useful patent protection can be obtained. This, again, often stimulates and inspires session participants when they suddenly realize that the prerequisites for a patentable invention are not as imposing as they had once supposed.

Sometimes it is helpful to conduct a search for prior art that is relevant to the white space opportunity. This search can range from a modest short search using an available online database to a complete patent landscaping exercise. By one approach, prior art materials can be used to educate the innovation team to inspire their deliberations or to help avoid exploring well-plowed territory. It is possible, however, to create an overload with too much prior art.

Team Selection

The goal of a white space inventing session is to foster innovation with respect to certain areas of opportunity. The nature of that opportunity usually serves to establish the criteria for the appropriate knowledge–skill mix of participants for the innovation team. Obvious participants usually include technologists familiar with the technology area(s) at issue. The team can also include specialists and experts in other areas, as a cross-pollination of ideas and outlooks often induces a powerful creative environment. Such people can be drawn from within the enterprise, but sometimes it can be useful to reach out into the academic or consulting communities. The team makeup should also include business experience and insights as well as technological expertise. Often only a single business representative need serve in this capacity.

A typical team ranges from three to eight technologists. Less than this may result in a fewer number of hoped-for candidate concepts (though this can vary greatly with the individuals; I have seen spectacular results with only two participants—one innovator and one facilitator). At some point, too, the productivity of the sessions may be inversely related to the number of participants. Consideration should also be given to the personalities of these participants. Some people can be so unduly uncooperative in a group setting as to render their presence, on balance, unhelpful.

The participant group should include at least one facilitator and one record keeper. A good facilitator can work both tasks at the same time, sometimes to useful effect. A good facilitator can contribute in an active, rather than a passive, manner when necessary. He or she must know when to assert and lead, when and how to provoke discussion, and when to allow the flow to carry the group to its creative conclusions. The skilled facilitator can quiet a monopolizing voice, draw forth input from an overly quiet voice, and ensure that the process remains focused.

Focus and Steering

Without the constraints of goals and some bounds, a white space session can quickly and irretrievably veer off into fascinating or playful technological inquiries that yield results completely unrelated to any useful purpose of the portfolio manager. Brainstorming sessions can turn into bizarre exercises about who can find the strangest use for a given technological development. Although laughter and mirth are good for morale, such results usually offer nothing to the enterprise. Excessive constraints in this regard, however, can dampen creativity and frustrate the session. One powerful technique to control the discussion while still encouraging creativity is the use of concept seeds.

Concept seeds are nothing more than high-level suggestions or examples of innovations or innovation starting points for a particular area of interest. Concept seeds are preferably developed prior to the innovation session. This preparation creates process control bounds through two mechanisms. First, it typically identifies a number of subject matter areas where innovation may yield useful results. This in turn, acts as an agenda for structured creativity. Though simple in concept, in practice this technique alone can make or break a session. Second, two to four illustrative examples, suggested solutions, or solution directions per area of inquiry developed in the preparation stage often serve as creativity motivators and idea stimulators. Participants find themselves inclined to respond to such suggestions with useful improvements or alternatives when otherwise they might remain silent or uninspired. Such straw-man concepts are often a facilitator's ace in the hole when a participant group is struggling.

Capture the Ideas

Capturing the nuggets of creativity and inspired innovation is the key responsibility of the session facilitator. There are various ways to ensure that good ideas do not become forgotten as quickly as the next idea is uttered. Audio recording can help to maintain the pace and flow of the discussion without distraction but, in general, should not be the sole means employed. The most effective tool in this process is the facilitator and paper.

The use of flip charts and colored marking pens are critical tools for this capture process. Ideas can be quickly written down on these flip chart pages as they are uttered. A computer with a projection display can be used as a substitute, but the computer limits how much of the session output can be simultaneously displayed. A completely filled flip chart page can simply be removed from the easel and attached to a wall where it remains in full view of the session participants. Simply seeing a wall become filled with ideas is, in and of itself, inspirational and often helps induce more creativity as a session progresses.

During the innovation portion of such a session, a proposed concept should *not* be rejected as being already known in the art. This wastes innovation time, potentially quells the creative spirit as self-editing enters the picture, and further prevents such concepts from potentially sparking another thought in another participant. Evaluation of the concepts takes place later.

During one recent session, one participant, acting the wag, suggested "time travel" as a solution for a particular problem area being considered (as in, "We should just travel back in time to fix the problem before it can turn into a problem"). This earned a few laughs, but the laughter grew as I turned to the flip chart and wrote down, as the next numbered inventive concept, "Time travel facilitated intervention." Within a minute, another of the session participants opened with, "Yeah, but if we . . ." and offered what was, in fact, a very good idea about how to deal with this particular problem. This participant said later that the idea just popped up in his thinking as a reaction to the time travel exchange. My point is that critiquing does not belong in this part of the white space inventing session. Let the thoughts flow freely and without onerous restraint. Exhibit 6.3, Idea Capture, illustrates the process of recording on paper the ideas of the participants (the display on the right can take the form of a computer display that presents, for example, concept seeds as are discussed subsequently).

Identifying and accurately capturing inventorship is sometimes a particularly bedeviling aspect of a group innovation session. Under U.S. patent

EXHIBIT 6.3 IDEA CAPTURE

law, it can be risky to base inventorship simply upon the fact that a particular individual was present at a particular meeting. To meet this identification need an audio recording can be useful, but one should not rely solely upon such an approach. The dynamics of human interaction often lead to confusion regarding inventorship when relying on such a recording. I prefer the use of name cards for each participant. Then, as each idea is recorded on the flip chart, the initials of the person who espoused the idea are noted as well. This takes but a moment, does not disturb the flow of the process, and provides an excellent record of who contributed what.

One other best practice tip should be mentioned with respect to the use of flip chart sheets. Each of the innovators should be provided with a pack of Post-It notes. If and when anyone has an idea to further elaborate or improve on a previously captured concept as it appears on a flip chart sheet, she can simply write her contribution and initials on the note, walk to the posted sheet, and apply the note near the relevant concept. In this way, very useful contributions are often captured without disrupting the flow and process of the group as a whole (which now has likely moved to focus on a different aspect of the opportunity being addressed).

Sometimes the most useful of contributions are elicited through just this process. Exhibit 6.4, Flip Charts and Post-It Notes, illustrates how the charts are spread around the wall and how an inventor can add a supportive idea with a Post-It note during the creative process.

Evaluating, Filtering, and Grouping

At the conclusion of the innovation portion of the white space session, one typically has a relatively large number of invention concepts. A 60-minute innovation session, for example, will often yield between 80 and 120 such concepts. The next step is to evaluate each concept with respect to its relative novelty, enablement, and potential to be combined with other concepts. As noted previously, inventive concepts should not be criticized as being old, undoable, or even silly during the innovation portion of the process. Following the innovation portion of the session, however, old concepts that are present in the accumulated list should now be identified and expunged. Similarly, the invention concepts should be evaluated for enablement. If no one present is able to conceive of a way to actually realize a given concept in some enabled form, the likelihood of obtaining a useful patent diminishes as well. This is where, for example,

EXHIBIT 6.4 FLIP CHARTS AND POST-IT NOTES

the time travel inventions are struck. This filtering process often reduces the list of concepts by five to ten percent.

The grouping concept permits related concepts (regardless of how, when, or by whom those concepts were offered during the session) to be collected together to present a more comprehensive, broader, or better enabled overall inventive concept. This in turn can yield a patent of improved scope and viability and hence represents a useful and important exercise. To facilitate the grouping process, it is helpful to provide each concept with a sequentially increasing number during the course of the innovation portion of the session. By this approach, for example, the first idea raised will be denoted as "1" while the fourth concept espoused will be denoted as "4," and so forth. This in turn, makes it easy to simply express grouping thoughts. To illustrate with a simple example, one can now note on the flip charts that concept 14 can be grouped with concepts 73 and 3.

These evaluation, filtering, and grouping activities are preferably organized into an individual session and a group session. Using different colored markers (to help identify who made what contribution), each participant can note any instance where he or she believes that the novelty or enablement requirements present a problem for a given concept (as when a given concept is, in fact, already a known concept or where there doesn't seem to be any viable way to describe how to practice such a concept). The participants also can individually indicate suggested groupings of two or more related or relatable concepts.

The participants of the white space inventing session then, as a group, once more quickly review all of the concepts with respect to these same criteria. Old or undoable concepts are confirmed as such and are dropped. Similarly, proposed groupings of two or more concepts that make sense are formed into approved groupings (the idea being that such a grouping will now be treated as a single invention for the purposes of moving forward with patenting activities).

Prioritization

The inventing activities often yield a relatively large number of worthy concepts. By this point in the process, some ideas will have lost their luster as being old or undoable, and some independent concepts will have been grouped together to form a single concept. Nevertheless, the number of remaining inventive concepts will often commonly exceed the resources of the sponsor—that is, it will usually not be practical to simply file a patent application for each and every one of the surviving inventive concepts.

The list of surviving concepts is therefore next reviewed on a basis of business impact and priority; in other words, one now determines whether a resultant patent for a given concept will likely constitute a valuable IP asset. This prioritization emphasizes the business asset side of things and reflects the perceived business value of a patent for the concept rather than the degree to which the concept is, or is not, a technological wonder. Significant technological advances *can* emerge from such a session, but the real point of the process is to build business assets. This is why it is important to have business folks present at such a session.

Any internal business process to define priorities can serve this element of the process, but a relatively simple three-tier rating scale, for example, works well. An "A" or a "1" rating can serve to identify an idea that appears to offer a solid business advantage; a "B" or a "2" rating can identify an idea having some business potential; and a "C" or a "3" rating can serve to denote ideas that are more neutral in this regard. Patenting activities can then be more rationally focused on the higher-rated concepts.

Memorializing and Documentation

The session will serve no useful purpose if the ideas produced become lost, forgotten, or misconstrued. To prevent this from occurring, the next step is to capture the ideas in more detail. This is accomplished in one or two paragraphs elaborating on the basic concept title. When relevant, drawings are also useful.

This activity is rarely popular. Nevertheless, it needs doing. Intuitively, one can simply assign each idea to a key contributor to prepare the disclosure statement. Sometimes, however, one or more participants will discover themselves as being key contributors to a disproportionate number of concepts. This in turn, can lead to something of a logjam in that these particular people will be overly taxed to provide a written description for each contribution. A solution often arises in the form of the previously mentioned grouping practice in which grouped concepts often contain a corresponding group of contributors who can share the documentation and disclosure tasks. Exhibit 6.5, White Space Invention Disclosure Form, provides a work simplification format designed to ease the burden of documentation.

The basic information important to the inventor and the enterprise is captured from the flip charts or recordings. In some cases it may be necessary that further information be provided, such as contact information, identification of any known prior art, identification of known business value, and so forth.

This style of white space inventing session works well using only half of a typical business day. Exhibit 6.6, The Time Management Chart, provides a realistic time frame for the relevant activities.

Many managers are often surprised (even distressed) that only one hour of such a session is recommended for use as the actual brainstorming time. More time can be allocated if desired, but there are some basic needs and truths being observed in this process. First, most people simply cannot stay on task in such a manner in an effective and useful way for a long unbroken period of time. Simply extending the time generally does not serve to proportionately increase the volume or quality of the results.

EXHIBIT 6.5 WHITE SPACE INVENTION DISCLOSURE FORM

Concept No(s): ______________________________

Concept Title: ______________________________

Concept Description: ______________________________

____

____

Inventor (print name and date and sign as well):

____

____

EXHIBIT 6.6 THE TIME MANAGEMENT CHART

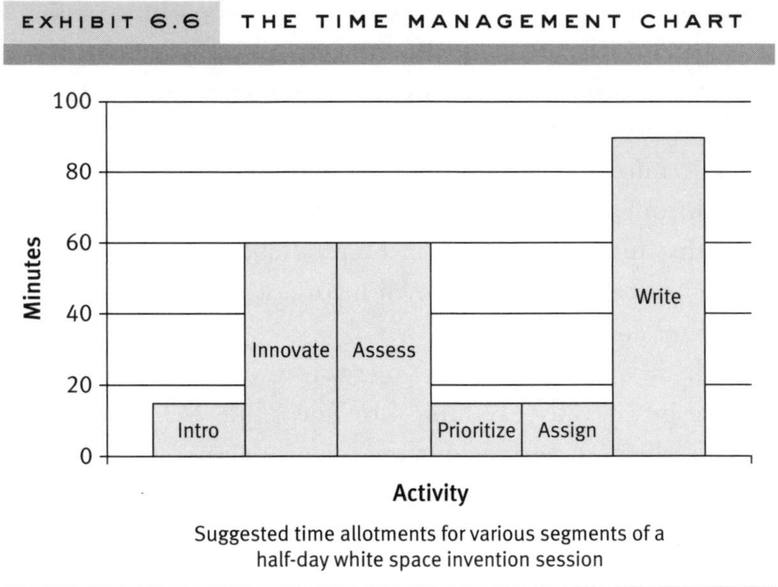

Suggested time allotments for various segments of a half-day white space invention session

Further, great thoughts alone are not enough; the other described activities are critical and are what help bring true value to the overall exercise.

That said, a session host anxious to explore more opportunities than such a session can accommodate can certainly pursue parallel sessions with multiple groups of participants or can pursue consecutive sessions using some or all of the same participants. In the latter case, however, it will usually be good to separate such sessions with some activity such as a dining experience or reconvening the following day to give the participants some time to recharge their mental batteries. Managed properly, as many as three sessions per day can be successfully carried out if desired.

Conclusion

This white space inventing process can reliably yield a graded and prioritized list of guided concepts that correlate highly to a subject matter area of interest to the company. These concepts are evaluated for novelty and enablement and have their inventorship reliably captured. Useful groupings of related concepts are also provided that can lead to stronger, broader patent assets. The briefly written disclosure statements ensure that the substance and gist of each concept is preserved for future reference and use. Such tangible and reproducible results contrast sharply with so-called brainstorming sessions that leave almost nothing in their wake except a general recollection of congenial fellowship and an amorphous sense of something interesting having happened, but with little or no substantive follow-up or deliverable resulting from the activity.

Whether your white space opportunity is small or large, bounded on all sides by an existing portfolio or open to a strategically unlimited future, this white space inventing process can help create new IP assets relevant and useful to the company's business strategy and its efforts to increase market share and net worth.

The stakes are high. White spaces in your patent portfolio represent opportunity. The real question, however, becomes, an opportunity for whom? Many companies have discovered that the white spaces in their portfolios were the proverbial chinks in their armor. A white space management agenda is, first and foremost, a survival activity. Done properly, however, white space inventing can also create value that leads to direct increases of the bottom line.

CAPABILITIES DEVELOPMENT

How to Turn White Space Dark for Fun and Profit

Observations & Action Items for Corporate Performance Improvement

A. Observations

1. Mr. Parmelee provides the initial activity to recognize or create new IP assets; it is an easy process and applies to trade secrets as well.
2. This process enables the company to immediately (within hours) recognize some of its more salient IP assets.

B. Action Items

1. The company should identify the people most effective in identifying potential IP within the company.
2. The company must view its technology in context with its competitors in the industry, but it should also have a view to other applications in other industries.
3. The white space facilitator requires extraordinary communications and technological skills to be effective in multidisciplinary environments.
4. The white space inventing effort should be formalized, and it requires follow-up action within a specified period of time.
5. The white space inventing participants should show some ability to transition from abstract to structured, purposeful action items.

C. Performance Improvement

The company should establish a normative process to capture new ideas and inventions, beginning with a series of such inventing sessions with each identifiable technology and each product produced by the company.

The Corporate Capabilities analysis is done by Bob Shearer and represents the analysis of the corporate performance behaviors found in the chapter and supplemented by the Taskforce Subject Matter Experts (see Acknowledgments for a list of SMEs) over the course of related discussions and work sessions.

CHAPTER 7

Capturing the Value of Trade Secrets

R. Mark Halligan, Esq.

Trade secret assets are information assets from which companies derive economic value from the secrecy of such assets. Trade secret assets can be identified and monetized.

KEY POINTS TO LOOK FOR

- **Trade secret protection is broader than patent protection and need not meet the patent requirements of being novel, useful, and nonobvious.**
- **Trade secrets must be inventoried and managed as business assets.**
- **Trade secret valuation requires sophistication, especially following a merger or acquisition, as SFAS 141 and 142 require annual review for impairment.**

Trade Secrets

Trade secret protection applies to any information that is sufficiently valuable to provide the owner with an actual or potential competitive advantage in the marketplace. The scope of trade secret protection is thus broader than patent protection, as trade secrets need not meet the patent requirements of being novel, useful, and nonobvious. Also unlike patents, trade secrets need not be disclosed and do not revert to the public domain after a finite term.

Trade secrets that first come to mind for most companies are those that relate directly to the design and manufacture of the company's products. Research, development, and engineering trade secrets may include the results of laboratory tests, the design of product and manufacturing equipment prototypes, and the company's testing and evaluation processes. Manufacturing trade secrets may include the manufacturing processes, raw materials and proportions, and supplier names and contract terms.

But trade secrets exist in other areas of the company as well. Marketing trade secrets may include the results of customer or consumer surveys, plans for advertising campaigns, discount structures, and market analyses and projections. Sales trade secrets may include the structure of sales incentive plans, contact information for targeted or key customers, and customer vetting processes for sales promotions or special treatment. Financial and accounting trade secrets may include financing plans for new facilities, quarterly financial projections, and prerelease quarterly results.

Trade secrets can also include information about what does not work, called "negative know-how." If the company has tried 40 formulations for a new process, all of which failed, before succeeding with the forty-first formulation, all 41 formulations may be trade secrets. The relevant issue here is that a competitor would economically benefit from knowing that those 40 formulations did not work, saving it the time and expense of trying all of those formulations in developing its own process. If reasonable measures are taken to maintain the secrecy of these failed formulations, they qualify as trade secrets under the definition.

Novelty is not required for trade secret protection, and in fact trade secrets are often combinations of known art. It is well established that a trade secret can exist in a combination of known elements that together afford a competitive advantage. The fundamental test is the economic value, actual or potential, derived from the secrecy of the information vis-à-vis competitors. The idea or information need not be complicated. It may be intrinsically simple but nevertheless qualify as a trade secret unless it is generally known in the trade or readily accessible from a public or well-known source in the trade.

Inventory of Potential Trade Secrets

The first step in accounting for any group of assets is to take an inventory of the assets. The company must have a list of what the assets are before any further steps such as classification, valuation, and reporting, can be taken. Inventorying trade secrets is difficult, because information assets seldom have a physical presence. They are being continuously created and destroyed—classified, reclassified, and declassified—in the normal business operations of the company. As trade secrets are seldom purchased, there is no record of invoices that can be used to generate a list of trade secrets. There is no physical location that can be inventoried for trade secrets. The company's entire trade secret portfolio is an amorphous, intangible, and inchoate cloud of information stored on paper, in computer drives, and in the minds of employees.

The key to the "trade secret portfolio construction" is that any trade secret used in the normal course of business—any information that derives value from being secret—is generally known to some employee of the company. The employees, as a group, know what the company's trade secrets are; more precisely, they know all the information that may qualify as a trade secret. The employees often do not know what does in fact qualify as a trade secret under the law, but the information itself is known to the employees who use it in the company's business operations.

Development of a trade secret inventory requires an evaluation of the six factors from § 757 of the *Restatement (First) of Torts.* These factors define the trade secrets shown in Exhibit 7.1, Defining Factors of the Trade Secret Inventory.

Trade secret asset information should be captured on a department-by-department basis using capture methods that are best suited to each department or division in the company. For example, many companies have procedures in the R&D department for reporting inventions on invention disclosure statements. Because every patent starts out as a trade secret, similar forms can be designed or modified for trade secret disclosures. In other departments, where weekly status reports are prepared and circulated on a need-to-know basis, procedures can be established for the extraction of trade secret information from these weekly reports. At a more sophisticated level, keyword lists can be created for extraction of trade

EXHIBIT 7.1 DEFINING FACTORS OF THE TRADE SECRET INVENTORY

1. The extent to which the information is known outside the plaintiff's business
2. The extent to which the information is known by employees and others involved in the plaintiff's business
3. The measures taken by the plaintiff to guard the secrecy of the information
4. The value of the information to the plaintiff's business and to its competitors
5. The amount of time, effort, and money expended by plaintiff in developing the information
6. The ease or difficulty with which the information could be properly acquired by others

secret information from e-mail traffic and other electronic information flows within the corporation.

A Trade Secret Control Group should be created in every company. Participants selected to be in this group should include key officers in the company. It must have a liaison to the general counsel's office so the activities of the Trade Secret Control Group that involve legal evaluations can be protected by the attorney–client privilege. Another option is to establish a Trade Secret Officer position that reports to the general counsel's office.

Categorization of Potential Trade Secrets

Once an inventory of potential trade secrets is in hand, it is necessary to organize it into categories for efficient use. This is similar to the organization of items in a physical inventory, which may include the categories of real estate, vehicles, furniture, manufacturing equipment, office equipment, and the like. With trade secrets, the design of a system of categories is complicated by the tremendous variety of information that may qualify for trade secret protection within a single company, as well as by the differences in this information from company to company.

Trade secret assets most efficiently fall into a categorization system based on "<Subject><Format> for <Product>," such as "Manufacturing

Process for Disk Drives," "Marketing Business Case for Cola Beverages," "Sales Forecast for Lawn Furniture," or "Engineering Specification for Transmission." These categories of trade secrets are called SFPs. All of the possible SFPs form a three-dimensional trade secret space of the company, into which all of the trade secrets fit.

The SFP categorization method provides a manageable number of "buckets" for large numbers of trade secrets. For example, a company that has 10 departments, for which 30 different information formats are meaningful, and which produces 20 different products, has a total of 6,000 SFPs available as trade secret categories, into which tens or hundreds of thousands of trade secrets can be efficiently sorted. No employee training is required to use these 6,000 categories, since everyone already knows what constitutes an "Advertising Plan for Snack Products" or a "Packaging Design for Laundry Detergent."

The categorization of the company's trade secret inventory into SFPs can also be accomplished during the inventory collection process. The department in which the trade secret is created or used, or that has immediate control of the trade secret, is likely to be the proper Subject, whereas the proper Format and Product are known to the employee submitting the trade secret to the inventory. If the SFPs are collected during the trade secret inventory, redundancy elimination needs to be performed only within each SFP, simplifying the collation process as well.

Information Classification Systems

An information classification system can be divided into four categories of information. First, public or nonclassified information relates to publicly available information. This information does not qualify for trade secret protection. The next tier relates to what is called "internal" information. An example of "internal" information is an internal telephone list or an internal organizational chart. This is the bottom level of trade secrets within a typical company. The third category defines "confidential" information. The bulk of a company's trade secret assets resides in this classification. Finally, some companies have a superconfidential designation for their most closely guarded trade secret assets, where unauthorized disclosure would cause immediate and catastrophic consequences. The most well-known example of this category of information is the formula for Coca Cola that is kept locked in a secret bank vault with access by only two living persons at any one point in time. These classification categories are summarized in tabular form in Exhibit 7.2, Information Classification System.

Access and Tracking Systems

Trade secret assets should be restricted on a need-to-know basis. This is the best way to protect trade secrets. Only those persons with a "need to know" a trade secret should have access to the trade secret. But controlling "access" to trade secret assets does not address all of the security issues. Trade secrets in motion must be tracked to prevent unauthorized disclosure or use after initial access.

Valuation Methods for Trade Secrets

Since 2002, valuation for trade secrets and other intangible assets acquired in a merger or acquisition has been covered under SFAS 141 and 142. Previously carried in the aggregate on the books as goodwill and amortized over 40 years, some acquired intangible assets must now be accounted for individually, including a determination of the fair value and useful life of the asset. These valuation determinations must be conducted or reviewed

EXHIBIT 7.2 INFORMATION CLASSIFICATION SYSTEM

Classification Standard	Type of Information Included
1. Public Information	Openly available to the public—does not qualify for trade secret protection
2. Internal Information	Information important to the company's operations that might cause the loss of a tactical or competitive advantage if disclosed
3. Confidential Information	Information that is critical to the business's competitive position that, if compromised, would result in a serious loss to the company's competitive position

by a valuation expert, independent of the company or its auditors. SFAS 141 and 142 offer flexibility in how fair market values are determined, but express a preference for valuation using discounted cash flows as in the preceding discussion for internal trade secrets.

Several accepted methods exist for the valuation of a property. Depreciated cost, replacement cost, fair market value, and net present value of future cash flows are all proper measures in specific circumstances. For intellectual property, however, depreciated cost is not appropriate. The direct acquisition cost of intellectual property may be insignificant, as when the intellectual property results from a flash of insight. However, that same insight may result from the sudden emergence of an idea after years of study in the field and years of experimentation in the laboratory. Which, then, is the true cost—the negligible cost of a moment's insight or the sum total cost of the education and experience of a lifetime?

Similarly, replacement cost is problematical. How does one replace a flash of insight? By what means can one predict the machinery of invention? For patents, trademarks and copyrights, injunctive relief is true replacement—that is, the restoration of the exclusive use of the intellectual property. But trade secrets, once lost in the public domain, are lost forever. The bell cannot be "unrung." How then can a replacement cost even be conceptualized, much less determined?

As for fair market value, there may be no marketplace for the intellectual property in question. An advance in the method of manufacturing a proprietary product, a unique corporate organizational structure or compensation plan, negative know-how (knowledge about what doesn't work)—none of these intellectual properties has a marketplace from which a fair market value may be obtained.

What we are left with, then, for trade secrets is the net present value of future cash flows. This is a particularly appropriate measure for trade secrets, because the very essence of a trade secret anticipates future cash flows. A trade secret is any information not generally known in the trade, which the owner has made appropriate efforts to keep secret and which confers a competitive advantage from being kept secret. The net present value of future cash flows resulting from that competitive advantage is an appropriate method for placing a dollar amount on the current value of a trade secret asset.

Net present value of a future cash flow requires an evaluation of three factors:

1. The total amount of future cash flow
2. The discounted basis of that future cash flow as a present value
3. The probability of the future cash flow's occurring

The total amount of the future cash flow is the total amount of income over time that will be derived from keeping the information secret as compared with the expected income over time if the information was in the public domain. This is analogous to the valuation of patents, where the economic value of the patent is the value of the exclusive use of the invention as compared to the situation in which the invention is available for use by all.

The second factor in the trade secret valuation model, the discounted basis of a future cash flow, is that percentage of the future cash flow that must be invested now as principal to realize the calculated future cash flows over the expected life cycle of the trade secret. This is a traditional accounting method for the calculation of the present value of a future income stream.

The last factor in the trade secret valuation model is the probability of future cash flows derived from the trade secret asset, which can be calculated by evaluating and determining the probability of prevailing in a civil lawsuit to defend the trade secret asset. Implementation of the measures outlined in this chapter will secure a very high probability of success.

Trade Secrets and Sarbanes-Oxley

The Sarbanes-Oxley Act does not specifically mention intellectual property assets, nor does it mention trade secret assets. However, the Sarbanes-Oxley Act also does not mention property assets, motor vehicle assets, plant and equipment assets, or any other specific asset class. Sarbanes-Oxley does require that financial reports "fairly present in all material respects the financial condition and results of operations," that a "report does not contain any untrue statement of a material fact or omit to state a material fact," and that officers signing the reports "have designed such internal controls to ensure that material information relating to the issuer and its consolidated subsidiaries is made known to such officers by others within those entities." These requirements transcend any specific asset class and relate to the financial condition of the corporation as a whole.

Conclusion

Trade secret assets are information assets from which companies derive economic value from the secrecy of such assets. Trade secret assets can be identified and monetized. The steps toward monetization of trade secrets require identification, classification, protection, and valuation. The outstanding importance of this brief chapter is that trade secrets exist in every business. The process to identify these assets is simple but disciplined, and it will take the company toward defining the value linkages among human creativity, business process innovation, and the capture of new wealth. Not every trade secret is a financial asset, but it is a business asset that may well become a financial asset through the application of the procedures outlined in this chapter.

CAPABILTIES DEVELOPMENT

Capturing the Value of Trade Secrets

A. Observations

Trade Secrets are an immediately recognizable asset group, and every competitive company needs to begin documenting these assets. It is the first step to recognizing new value.

B. Action Items

1. Develop a disciplined methodology to identify trade secrets.
2. Establish a Trade Secret Control Group to develop policy and practice consistency across all functional lines.
3. Establish a value and asset tracking system linking trade secrets to cash flows, market share, and earnings.
4. Develop valuation methodologies to support internal decision making. Even basic do-it-yourself methods will prove helpful until such time as you may choose a more sophisticated external valuation methodology. The point is, do not let consulting fees stymie your initiative.
5. Require the Trade Secret Control Group to begin reporting trade secret portfolio values and changes in portfolio value to the corporate executive team.
6. Require the Trade Secret Control Group to begin developing value extraction strategies.

C. Performance Improvement

The action items are all focused on performance improvement, and the procedures for developing the trade secret inventory will quickly lead to a new appreciation of IP assets.

The Corporate Capabilities analysis is done by Bob Shearer and represents the analysis of the corporate performance behaviors found in the chapter, and supplemented by the Taskforce Subject Matter Experts (see Acknowledgments for a list of SMEs) over the course of related discussions and work sessions.

SECTION FOUR

New Dynamics of Corporate Management

Just like the Internet, IP is not a fad. It is the basis for new business, new revenues, and new wealth. The challenge outside most of the Fortune 100 is getting ahead of the "IP management wave of innovation." Changes to meet this challenge are worth every reasonable and focused effort to turn your company into one that can create revenue streams from technologies and patents as well as products from *existing assets.*

The demands of IP management are defined in Chapter 8 by Bob Shearer and Dr. Bruce Stuckman. Here you will learn how to organize your business opportunities and begin to develop your own framework for getting more out of your IP assets. These guys not only tell you what is going on in the world of IP but offer a capabilities–proficiency benchmark in sufficient detail to allow you to know what your company's needs are before you close the book.

Dave Haug is a CFO who has developed some effective valuation criteria and stringent decision gates used by AT&T Knowledge Ventures to extract value from AT&T's portfolios of IP assets. Dave's comments in Chapter 9 may seem routine, but they are basic and well tuned to the financial community. Do not be too quick to pass over them. What he does not and cannot tell us are the criteria and specific methodology used by his company. One thing we do know: these are criteria set by businesspeople from multiple disciplines who have guided AT&T Knowledge Ventures to an exemplary role in creating new wealth with IP assets in the nation's economy.

For the person charged with setting up an IP-based business, there is no better procedural map than what Dr. Jan Jaferian offers in Chapter 10. Take the time to study this. It will anchor your understanding of IP management in a way that can place you in the (estimated) 75th percentile of IP-competent executives. The study required to understand the graphics and constructs could pay big dividends within just a few days.

Dr. Mark Karasek is the understated guru of IP management. As the vice president of engineering at a high-tech company, Chamberlain Group, Mark has directed his company to a dominant position in his industry. How he did it is explained in Chapter 11. It is noteworthy that Mark is the VP of engineering, not the VP of IP. Chapter 11 talks about the mid-market company, but Mark and Chamberlain are big-league IP managers.

The revolution is taking place in the CFO's office, but many CFOs do not yet know it. Chris Leisner offers counsel to the CFO as well as the controller and the IP counsel in how to go about recognizing IP value inside the enterprise. Chapter 12 is a must-read for every CEO and CFO.

CHAPTER 8

Intellectual Property Drives Corporate Changes to Create New Wealth

Bob Shearer and
Bruce Stuckman

KEY POINTS TO LOOK FOR

- IP value is driving changes in the way companies must manage their businesses and are increasingly expected to communicate their capabilities to manage the IP class of assets to financial and capital markets.
- The external business requirements of IP demand leadership skills that many IP attorneys cannot find time to develop because of the increased burden of "doing" rather than "managing" the workload.

(continues)

KEY POINTS TO LOOK FOR (CONTINUED)

- **Chief IP counsel need to adjust to the increased prominence of their role in value creation, recognition, and reporting within the corporation.**
- **Most companies react to fast-moving IP changes by simply demanding more from their IP counsel, when what is needed is help in the form of increased resource allocation.**
- **The pervasive nature of IP management means that more people need to be more sophisticated about IP and its effects on their responsibilities in the enterprise.**

The Increasing Influence of Intellectual Property (IP)

There was a time when, apart from a few patent-focused industries, IP laws and practices were relegated to the backwaters of a company's R&D program. More often than not, patents were accumulated to demonstrate the technological prowess of the company or to protect against perceived, sometimes vague defensive threats in response to competitors generating patents of their own. Even in industries that considered themselves IP savvy, with few exceptions, the patent wars that many companies feared materialized only as occasional skirmishes. Most companies preferred to sit on their rights or settle their differences with broad cross-licensing programs rather than risking an all-out war. Most business leaders persisted in the belief in their ability to compete in the marketplace, leaving the IP function as a commonly suppressed reality that has become the current framework for business strategy and global competitive position.

The business of intellectual property in America has changed. Beginning in 1982 with the formation of the Court of Appeals for the Federal Circuit, patent laws became stronger and damages awarded became larger. This began a trend of increased patenting and increasing litigiousness that continues today. In particular, the annual filing rate of patents in the United States nearly doubled between 1994 and 2004.[1] As one might surmise, the number of patent lawsuits filed in federal district court nearly doubled during this same period of time. At the same time, the *value* of patent actions also increased. In the past, nine-figure patent damages awards were a rarity. However, in a study of 34 cases in the 21 years between 1984 and 2004 that yielded $100 million-plus patent license payments and/or damages awards, more than half of these cases occurred within the five-year period from 2000 to 2004.[2] Companies have begun selling underutilized IP assets in regular auctions,[3] as a further indication of the increasing recognition of IP value.

Changes in patent laws have allowed business-method patents to be issued in traditionally underpatented areas such as banking, insurance, and other service industries. Although patents were once thought of as being restricted to the high-tech sector, virtually every company in America now faces the real possibility of a patent lawsuit based not only on its products, but also on its marketing programs, web sites, and business processes. Dozens of holding companies have been formed, solely for the purpose of accumulating, licensing, and enforcing patents.

There are very few corporations of significant size that have not faced at least one patent lawsuit or aggressive licensing overture within the past few years. The cost of defending these lawsuits, along with potential settlements, significant damage awards, and the risk of possible injunctions, has raised the awareness of IP issues for most companies in the most alarming of ways.

What has happened in the not-so-quiet world of IP is that IP management has dramatically shifted from a purely legal concern to a pervasive business interest that is vital to corporate survival and prosperity. IP strategists sit near the top of the corporate enterprise. Companies are quickly adapting to this need for operational and strategic IP leadership. The external business requirements of IP demand executive-level skills that many IP attorneys cannot "find time" to assume or develop because of the increased burden of "doing" rather than "managing" the IP workload. Today this reality presents a serious challenge, one that is increasingly being met through the multidisciplinary corporate team. This business-focused approach has been managed very effectively by a number of organizations that have placed businesspeople in charge of the business aspects of IP.

Value Drivers from the External Economic Infrastructure

The investment and regulatory communities have observed these changes in the corporate structure and are beginning to find ways (1) to seek more disclosures from the corporation regarding IP management; and (2) to make sure that the corporation's IP is in compliance with reporting and controls as defined in Sarbanes-Oxley. The Financial Accounting Standards Board (FASB) as well as the Securities and Exchange Commission (SEC) are awakening to the effects of IP on business value and searching for prudent mandates that might be imposed on the publicly traded enterprise. The investor community is becoming more sophisticated and interested in how well a company complies with the "best practices" in managing IP assets. The ability of the company to enforce and defend its IP rights can play a significant role in the company's ability to create and communicate value to strategic alliances: bankers, investors, and the capital markets. Exhibit 8.1, External Intersections with Corporate IP Management, provides the constructs that define the external influences driving changes in corporate IP management.

The intersections offer the definition of the new organizational IP performance requirements with the external world. Each intersection defines the relationship between the IP function and the many "communities" that influence wealth creation and management in the twenty-first century.

Each summary statement in Exhibit 8.1 is backed up by more definitive performance and proficiency statements to facilitate a self-assessment or needs analysis by the CEO. No one way is the only way, but the successful companies have one thing in common: they address the problem of developing a competitive IP knowledge–skills mix that will serve the enterprise's needs for innovation, cash flows, and earnings as well as competitive position. The more advanced company will recognize the opportunity to create distinction in each of these relationships (i.e., intersections).

IP value management has redefined the business landscape globally. The IP assets of a company are increasingly being recognized as a greater source of value, not just in terms of protecting the differentiating features of a company's products and services and providing a defensive position

EXHIBIT 8.1 EXTERNAL INTERSECTIONS WITH CORPORATE IP MANAGEMENT

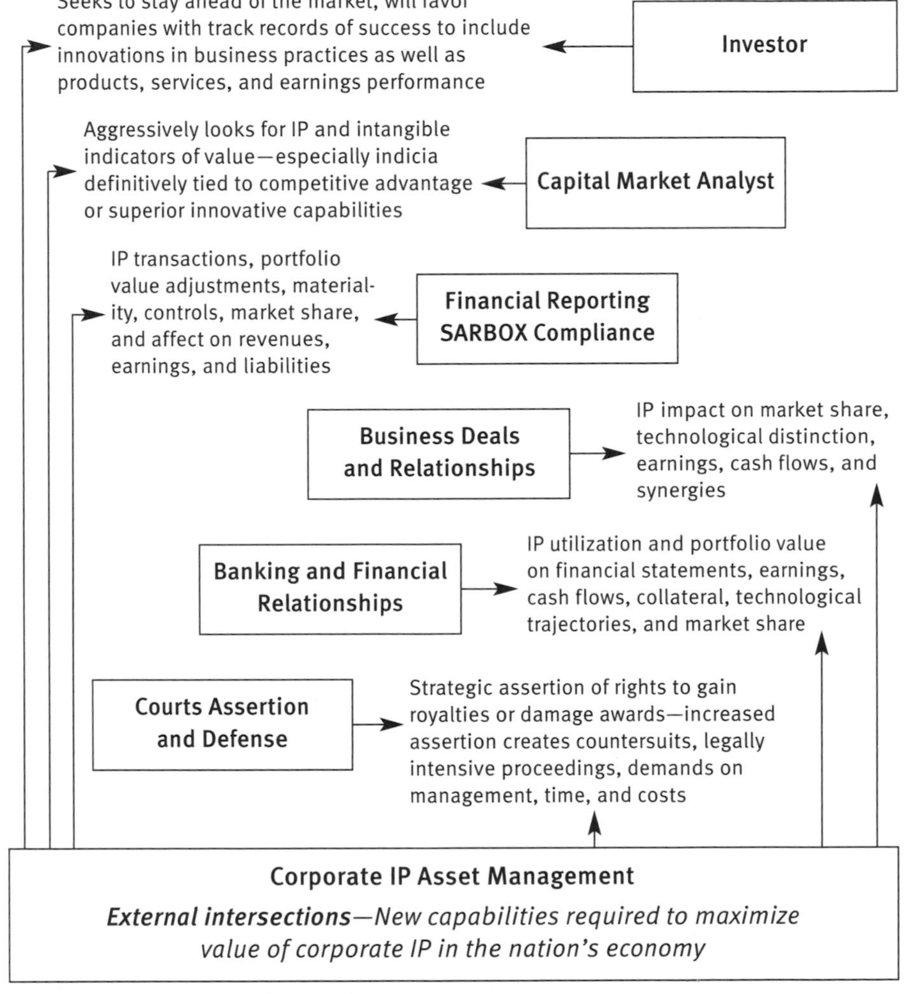

The "Points of Intersection" provide a summary-level definition of new corporate requirements. These are corporate capability requirements regardless of who performs the tasks. More definitive performance statements can effectively lead to determination of education, training, and staffing objectives required to meet the demands of the external IP communities.

Source: Robert Shearer, "Intersections," a white paper #0522BS for the National Knowledge & Intellectual Property Management Taskforce, April 2006.

against potential IP assertions, but also as an additional source of high-margin profit from the sales and licensing of underutilized IP. The net result is that more companies are viewing IP as strategic assets that can affect the bottom line and forming internal organizations to take a more active role in managing these assets. For many companies, this also means allowing the *business of IP* to take a critical seat at the executive level of corporate leadership.

The Changing Role of Corporate IP Leaders

The changing role of IP in American business has been accompanied by a change in what is expected from its IP leaders. IP counsel have always needed strong technical and IP experience. However, IP management organizations are increasingly becoming multidisciplinary teams that include expertise in finance, marketing, business case development, negotiation, licensing, enforcement, defense, portfolio management, and the valuation of IP assets. Attorneys in an IP leadership role might need stronger business skills to adapt to the increasing business focus and business attention surrounding IP issues. The IP counsel can quickly find him- or herself faced with the challenge of managing many outside law firms that are required to pick up the additional burdens of managing IP: the prosecution, defense, assertions, and litigation.

Chief IP counsel also need to adjust to the increased prominence of their role within the corporation. With the increasing frequency of IP issues reaching a company's senior management, IP leaders require the ability to effectively operate at this level. For many companies, this means a shift of IP leaders from middle management to top management responsibilities. The sample behavioral patterns outlined in Exhibit 8.2, The Management Pyramid and Focus, reflect the effects of such a shift.

The process of elevating anyone from mid-level responsibility in a specialty field to senior-level functionality with the executive team is a colossal step because of behavioral norms and corporate culture. Due to a lack of knowledge of IP issues, many senior managers find that IP counsel "speak a different language," even from the other lawyers in the company. The knowledge and skill mix required to operate at the *top management level* in the organization is not something every IP attorney can manage without additional support, education, and training. One CTO

EXHIBIT 8.2 THE MANAGEMENT PYRAMID AND FOCUS

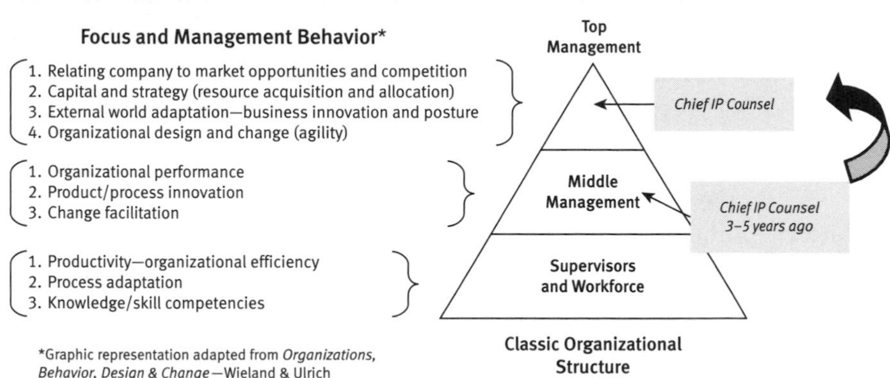

Portrayal of the jump in the managerial focus required of both the organization and the IP counsel

Source: Robert Shearer, "Intersections," a white paper #0522BS for the National Knowledge & Intellectual Property Management Taskforce, April 2006.

noted that the mid-level specialist is not immediately functional at the top management level in the enterprise where detail is assumed and the "so what" of the issue is immediately and effectively communicated. The intrapersonal capabilities of the IP counsel, along with the counsel's skill and knowledge mix, are the determinants of the counsel's effectiveness in participating in executive-level decisions. Typically, mid-managers and specialists have not had opportunity to acquire the more demanding skills required of top management and need executive development, top-level support, and coaching (from internal or external coaches—preferably both) through a deliberately planned, behaviorally anchored and executed transition period.

New Demands Mean New Internal (Corporate) Functionality

For many companies the growth in IP issues and workload demand more from their IP counsel. The IP counsel must still perform the basics of IP portfolio management, handle enforcement and defensive issues, and support IP aspects of transactions such as procurement, sales, and M&A transactions, as well as licensing, but these functions can now be important components of everyday decisions in the executive levels of the enterprise. As these demands on the IP counsel have grown in complexity and pervasiveness, time consumed, and workload, many organizational structures lag in their ability to make the necessary adjustments for corporate IP functionality. Management of the outside legal resources is a serious challenge to many companies. The shortage of IP attorneys means the inside counsel job can be more demanding than that of the practicing attorney in a leading law firm.

The corporation that effectively manages this disruptive nature of IP is one that focuses on bringing other departments up to a working knowledge of the critical effects of IP on business. Simply adding more to the IP counsel's workload is a short-term and ultimately self-defeating action likely resulting in the loss of competent leadership. Instead, senior managers must first make adjustments in their own knowledge of and thinking about IP.

The pervasive nature of IP management means that more people need to be more sophisticated about IP and its effects on their responsibilities in the enterprise. Key among these are the board of directors, CEO, CFO, CTO, VP R&D, VP marketing, controller, and general counsel. The successful enterprise will bring together these points of intersection where the necessary IP knowledge and skills become inherent in the functionality of each department.

The Internal Change Dynamics

Few things in corporate America are more difficult than bringing about changes within the enterprise. There is rarely motivation to change practices, policies, or behaviors, especially when things are perceived to be working well. People who seek new and innovative ways rarely have viable strategies for effecting new practices—it is not something for which many have been trained. It is risky business to ask others to do things differently, especially within their own functional area.

The intersections described in Exhibit 8.3 should help the IP counsel or executive leader focus in on the primary corporate skills for the people (functions) involved. The intersections are one-on-one capabilities that must be established for the organization to excel in the knowledge economy. From these intersections, the IP counsel can develop a change strategy;

the intersections define the critical elements of knowledge and skill that *each player* needs to become proficient so that the company can become more competitive.

EXHIBIT 8.3 INTERNAL INTERSECTIONS WITH IP COUNSEL

Internal Intersections with IP Counsel and Other Leaders in the Corporation

(Roles and Responsibilities Requiring IP Integration into Other Functional Processes and Their Effects on Total Corporate Value)

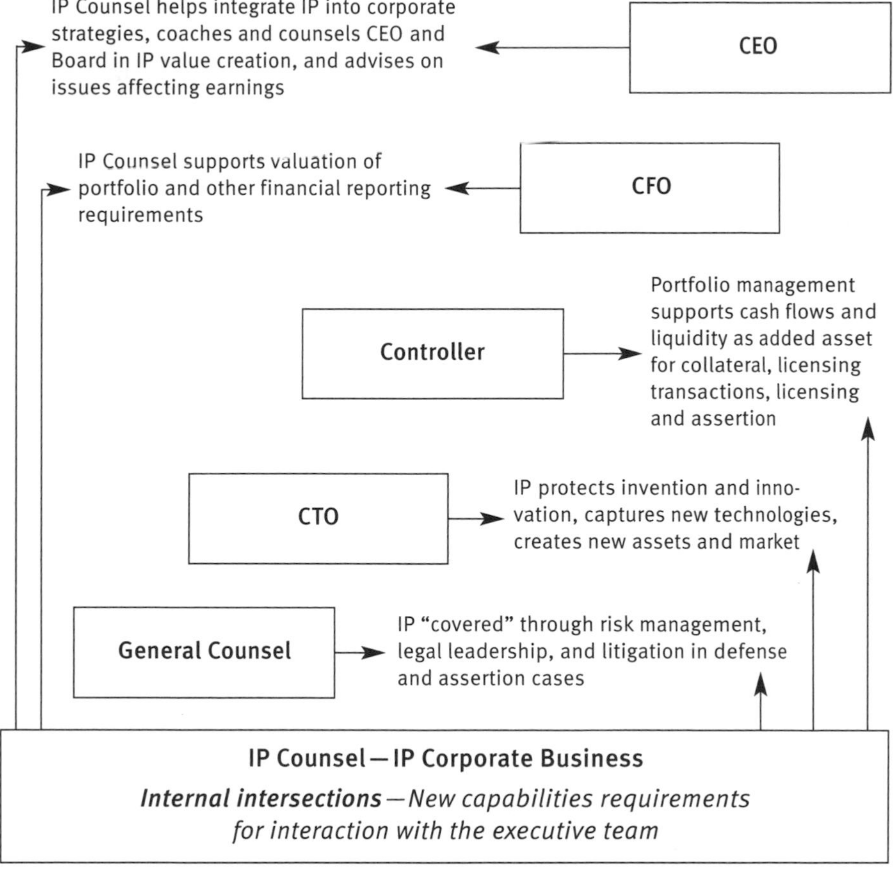

The "Points of Intersection" provide a summary-level definition of new corporate requirements. These are corporate capability requirements regardless of who performs the tasks. More definitive performance statements can effectively lead to determination of education, training, and staffing objectives required to meet the demands of the external IP communities.

Source: Robert Shearer, "Intersections," a white paper #0522BS for the National Knowledge & Intellectual Property Management Taskforce, April 2006.

Implementation Strategies

The complexities of organizational change make it a completely unique discipline in most universities and in many organizations. It is called organization development and supports executive leadership development as a fundamental element of corporate performance. The biggest obstacle to innovation in most organizations is simply the fear of exposure that one experiences when faced with the need to do something differently. But doing something differently requires a road map to minimize risk and maximize success. This know-how is a new dimension for American enterprise because it is about business strategy and execution. The change does not start with an increasing workload on the IP counsel, but at the board where IP must be recognized as the driving force in creating new wealth in the knowledge economy.

Summary and Implementation Plan

1. Help your IP counsel make the transition to top management.
2. Increase awareness of and education in IP issues on the part of other executives.
3. Develop a capability to incorporate IP issues in decision making.
4. Use consortia, associations, and other such organizations to help address external needs.
5. Take action to create a competitive distinction in capital markets.
6. Educate your board.

Notes

1. William Atkins, Bruce Stuckman, Sue Halverson, and Seth Brown, "IP Litigation 101: Financing and Budgeting," *10th Annual ABA–IP Law Conferences,* April 15, 2005.
2. Based on the author's review of 34 publicly reported patent licenses, settlements, and damages awards valued at $100 million or more, unadjusted for inflation, between 1984 and 2004.
3. Michael Kanellos, "Patent Auction Pays More in the End," *CNET News,* May 10, 2006.

CAPABILITIES DEVELOPMENT

Intellectual Property Drives Corporate Changes to Create New Wealth

A. Observations

1. The internal and external dynamics of IP management provide only a sketch of how these relationships have evolved and continue to evolve.
2. Developing the competitive proficiencies is one serious challenge that management must meet to survive the ongoing IP revolution.

B. Action Items

1. Management should require revisions in the corporation's job descriptions and performance evaluation criteria that begin to address the new levels of capability.
2. Such revisions can realistically begin only after a baseline capabilities evaluation.
3. Management should support aggressive professional and organizational development activities to reach levels of increasing proficiency.
4. To say it another way, corporate management should make a serious investment in leapfrogging even these capabilities as defined.

C. Performance Improvement

1. The capabilities proficiency table that follows enables you to develop a baseline analysis of your firm's present capabilities. You will be surprised at how quickly you can determine your company's needs.
2. Take the time in your next staff meeting to go through this quick analysis to develop your own baseline and then begin working to improve. See the Capabilities/Proficiency Levels columns.

The Corporate Capabilities analysis is done by Bob Shearer and Dr. Bruce Stuckman and represents the analysis of the corporate performance behaviors found in the chapter. This particular analysis lists proficiency levels that have not yet been reviewed by the Taskforce SMEs. Proficiency levels are the next step in defining performance capabilities. Consequently, this analysis page offers an advanced insight into the Taskforce's work to help organizations define and develop the capabilities to compete in the knowledge economy. This analysis presents the Taskforce methodology to provide benchmarks based on levels of proficiency so that the senior executive can measure his or her company's proficiency, determine developmental needs, and focus on strengths and weaknesses.

CAPABILITIES—PROFICIENCY LEVEL CHECKLIST

Capabilities	Proficiency Levels
1. Stand responsible under Sarbanes-Oxley rules for accountability on IP-related matters	(1) Talks to CFO when changes are obvious (2) Works with CFO to define effect of IP on financial reports (3) Routinely monitors and measures effect of IP on corporate performance
2. Provide valuation guidance on M&A due diligence to cover potential future impairment charges (SFAS 141 and 142)	(1) Reacts to the controller's assessment of value (2) Applies a rigorous review of the accounting of IP and goodwill (3) Plans for impairment contingencies and prevents write-downs or charges against corporate value.
3. Provide input and counsel in all IP value determinations for M&A due diligence	(1) Calls on consultants to define portfolio value estimates (2) Provides in-house IP measurement and valuation process (3) Integrates IP with financial analyses to define impact of IP on value
4. Provide innovation vitality index for each business unit	(1) Asks CTO and VP marketing about features and functions in order to impute financial IP impact—no metrics (2) Develops corporate IP landscape to determine IP impact (3) Coordinates IP value determinations by integrating C-Level inputs
5. Provide strategic assessments of licensing in versus investment in R&D	(1) Surveys IP landscape to identify licensors to determine make-or-buy decision (2) Utilizes IP resources to provide cross-licensing cost savings (3) Looks to next-generation derivative IP to assess make-or-buy decisions
6. Provide market share analysis to support IP strategic decisions	(1) Market share is approached according to a purely defensive mode (2) Market share is viewed as a vehicle to gain additional IP assets to create competitive advantage

CAPABILITIES—PROFICIENCY LEVEL CHECKLIST

Capabilities	Proficiency Levels
6. Provide market share analysis to support IP strategic decisions *(Continued)*	(3) Market share is the product of a dynamic among IP, technology, and law that tolerates no infringements—globally
7. Provide cost–benefit analyses on assertion	(1) Imputes value based on experience (2) Performs disciplined cost and risk assessment (quantitative terms) (3) Performs breakdown of costs, risk, and benefits in qualitative and quantitative terms that have been developed with the CFO
8. Provide cost–benefit analyses for defense	(1) Imputes value based on experience (2) Performs disciplined cost and risk assessment (quantitative terms) (3) Performs breakdown of costs, risk, and benefits in qualitative and quantitative terms that have been developed with the CFO
9. Provide IP-related competitive analyses to support opportunity identification for market share growth	(1) Reacts to ideas of convergent value propositions (2) Knows licensing and IP landscape to be able to react to opportunities (3) Systematically covers the IP landscape of IP users and prospective users to create initiatives for convergent business operations

Taskforce Proposed Value Rating Scale: Capabilities Statements (1–3) are used to rate (scale) the company's capability. Generally speaking, the capabilities statements above:

(1) *Statements that signify early stages of capability development*

(2) *Statements that signify where most competitive companies function*

(3) *Statements that signify advanced competitive capability*

CHAPTER 9

Valuing Intellectual Property

DAVE HAUG

We're at a point where traditional valuation models are being applied to intangible assets that are very difficult to value. And in the process of doing so, the benefit for all of us is that we can have a better understanding about what value is attached to certain intangible assets. This takes us to a deeper level of understanding, knowledge, and business application. We're getting closer to a standard-setting perspective.

KEY POINTS TO LOOK FOR

- Intangible assets are responsible for an increasing level of value in the competitive enterprise.
- The financial and regulatory communities are concerned about this increasing and undocumented value, but the enterprise should focus on its own internal capabilities to evaluate and value its IP assets. This is the next level of maturity in IP asset management.
- Value must be determined on at least three levels: (1) cash flow to the operating business unit, (2) cash flow to the IP business, and (3) non–cash value benefits to the total business.
- Creative work done for us at our request will continue to be our property, and we hold the intellectual property rights to that work.

The Increasing Responsibility of the CFO

AT&T Knowledge Ventures is a business unit within AT&T Communications. Its primary responsibility is to manage the intellectual property and intellectual assets of AT&T. Knowledge Ventures has developed its own methodology for valuing its intellectual property, and it is my job to direct, manage, and continually improve that process.

Exhibit 9.1, Why Focus on IP Now?, shows in rather dramatic fashion why the role of CFO is increasing. The graphic illustrates the value of IP and intangibles in the nation's capital markets. The relationship between intangible and tangible value contribution has definitely shown a shift that demonstrates that the knowledge economy has arrived. Market cap is the fastest way to new wealth, and the use of IP assets does not interrupt the normal productization of IP to create new revenues, cash flows, and earnings. IP revenues and licensing complement (rather than preempt) the traditional means of capturing value from new technologies and from new products.

This graph is based on a study by the Brookings Institution. It shows that in 1982, the value of market capitalization was reflected based on tangible assets versus intangible assets, and how during the past 20 years, the

EXHIBIT 9.1 WHY FOCUS ON IP NOW?

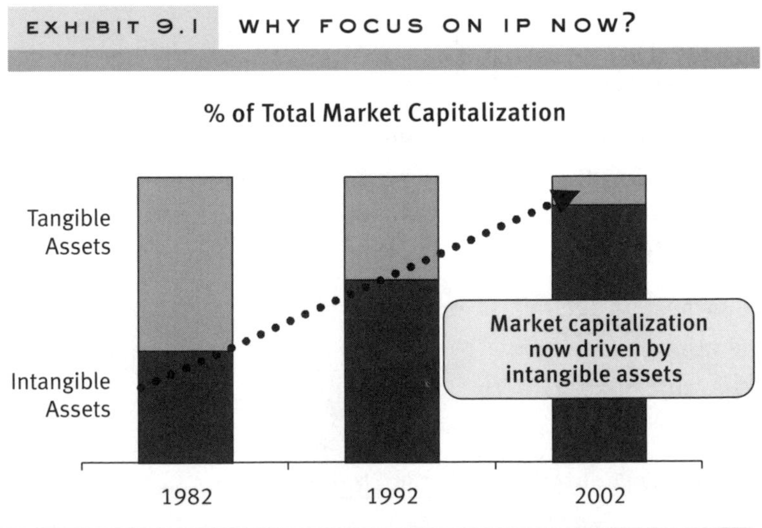

Source: Brookings Institution.

contribution of intangible assets to the total market capitalization has increased dramatically. There has been a big shift in how firms are driving their market value.

We learned through our benchmarking study that more than 50 percent of the Fortune 500 firms are now taking a more proactive approach to managing their intellectual property assets in an effort to create greater value.

One of the aspects of what we do at AT&T Knowledge Ventures is to consider how intellectual property can be used to influence business results, especially in terms of value creation. This is encompassed in our processes aimed at creating new cash flow streams for the AT&T family of companies. We examine the cash flow impact on the core business. We also look at the benefit of a non-cash business to the core business. This can be, but is not limited to, licensing of our intellectual assets. Exhibit 9.2, Sources of Value, provides a visual flow diagram depicting the AT&T process of transforming knowledge-based assets to cash, cost reduction, and earnings.

AT&T also looks at cash flows from revenue growth and cost reduction perspectives. Typically, the view is to look at new IP-related revenue

EXHIBIT 9.2 SOURCES OF VALUE

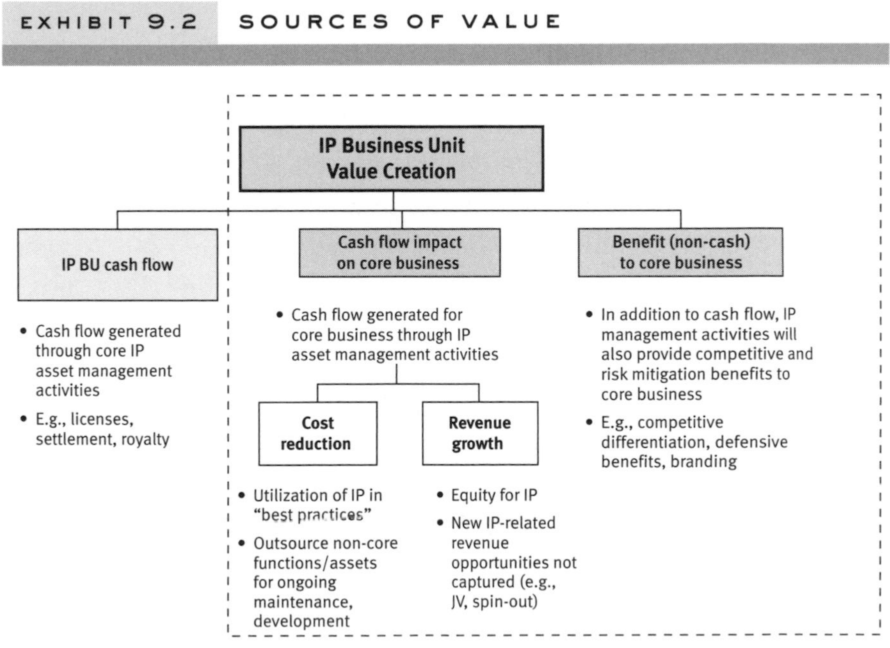

opportunities, which may include a joint venture or spin-out, and "equity for IP" opportunities as well as opportunities for cost reduction. These opportunities can come through utilization of IP in "best practices" as well. The analysis of benefits that are non-cash to the core business looks for a way to provide competitive and risk-mitigation benefits, for example, competitive differentiation.

FASB Requirements

The FASB's Financial Accounting Standard 142 was issued several years back. This standard indicated how companies are to deal with the valuation of acquired goodwill and other intellectual assets. SFAS 142, while primarily focused on goodwill, requires an annual evaluation of all intangible assets. Intellectual property is, of course, only one type of intellectual asset that might be on the books of a company, but there are other intellectual property/intellectual assets that may not be reflected on the books, such as "know-how."

Valuation Approaches

We establish value for our intellectual property through various approaches, including the traditional financial models—the cost approach, the income or discounted cash flow approach, and the market comparables or fair market value approach. In each of these approaches, we try to identify which one works best for the specific type of asset we are trying to value.

A software licensing opportunity, for example, would be assessed with a cost approach. The outcome would be to determine the cost savings of getting a license versus the cost of developing a solution—the classic "make-or-buy" decision analysis.

Income and discounted cash flows methods are used to evaluate patent licensing and can also be used to value litigation that may be involved in an effort to defend patents. The same principle applies to trademark licensing as well.

The market approach is applied for both patent and trademark licensing assessments.

As we go through a valuation on a patent, not only would we look at the discounted cash flow approach, we would also look to the market comparables or fair market value in an effort to triangulate a value range that helps us better identify the value of that asset. Exhibit 9.3, Valuation Process, provides a condensed summary.

Valuation Factors

The valuation process uses several factors: (1) patent duration or the age of the assets (how many years were left on the patent, what stage is it from when it was issued); (2) in software, the stage of the technology, which is an important factor; (3) the market position of the asset; (4) royalty rates or discount rate that we would be using in applying our valuation.

One other thing we do is to look at what a theoretical ceiling could represent, assuming that a licensee would be willing to pay the ceiling.

The final step is a risk analysis on each one of the valuations performed typically using a Monte Carlo and/or a decision tree analysis.

This is the process we use to help each business unit that is ultimately responsible for creating the asset and finding value for its use.

Business activity that generates a licensing opportunity that will create revenue and/or a contractual relationship that would require disclosure, which of course is reflected in the financials of the Knowledge Venture business unit that rolls up into the financials of AT&T.

EXHIBIT 9.3 VALUATION PROCESS

1. **Valuation Approaches**
   a. Cost approach
   b. Income/discounted cash flows
   c. Market comparables
2. **Factors to Consider**
   a. Patent duration/age of asset
   b. Stage of technology
   c. Royalty rates/discount rates
3. **Risk Adjustment**
   a. Monte Carlo analysis
   b. Decision tree analysis

Communication outside of the company will be limited to revenue and expense presentation in the financials and footnote disclosure if a materiality threshold is met or required. One relationship item that we have identified is that we try to protect our intellectual property when we engage a third party to do work for us. We strongly feel that the creative work done for us at our request will continue to be our property and that we hold the intellectual property rights to that work.

The AT&T Knowledge Ventures approach to valuation considers an overall estimate of the portfolio value in total. The valuation process just described, however, is not applied to every asset. We identify what we feel are opportunities that we can pursue within a marketplace, rank those opportunities, and identify the valuation as we go through the process. The AT&T process is pretty evolved with specific stages and stage–gate decisions. Those decision criteria typically are used to evaluate the overall asset value, for market value assessment, and, ultimately, to arrive at a pricing level for determining monetization options.

Knowledge Ventures is an organization established to do just what we're doing, and that is monetizing and protecting the intellectual property of our company. So far we have done pretty well. The Taskforce selected us as the Innovator of the Year for our performance, and that's a good benchmark as it puts us in the company of GE, Ford, and USG, all leaders in their industries.

We're at a point where traditional valuation models are being applied to intangible assets that are very difficult to value. And in the process of doing so, the benefit for all of us is that we can have a better understanding about what value is attached to certain intangible assets. This takes us to a deeper level of understanding, knowledge, and business application. We're getting closer to a standard-setting perspective. And until we can separately identify and then value these assets, it's difficult to talk about a framework by which disclosure of these processes ought to be made.

Once we are able to reach some consensus in practice, then the market for IP assets will expand, deals will become more efficient, and corporate as well as national economic growth will follow.

CAPABILITIES DEVELOPMENT

Valuing Intellectual Property

Observations & Action Items for Corporate Performance Improvement

A. Observations

1. Mr. Haug's extraordinarily high level of professionalism, competency, and modest temperament create an understated view of the importance of the role of the CFO in this chapter.
2. One of his secrets is not only the multimethod valuation discipline but also the establishment of "stage–gate" decisions using specific financial criteria to manage the value extractions process.

These processes are unique to his company, just as yours are to your own company.

B. Action Items

1. Develop an internal methodology (actually, multiple methodologies) for valuing IP assets that goes into the value extraction strategy process.
2. Develop a conceptual linkage between IP and market cap; make sure the linkage is repeatable and easily understood.
3. Treat IP as an asset that can be used by many players at the same time.
4. If you are engaged in an IP management operation, be sure to link cash flows from IP assets to the core business units. Managing the revenues can create some serious internal accountability or performance problems.
5. Develop a methodology to link IP to business performance (using cash and non-cash criteria).
6. Develop a cost and revenue tracking system for IP.
7. Develop a risk management process useful for internal decision analyses.
8. Develop the marketing capabilities to assess the relevant IP markets.
9. Develop internal "decision–stage gate" criteria suitable for application and industry.

C. Performance Improvement

1. Putting the CFO into the IP process begins to drive the process that results in performance and shareholder value.

(continues)

CAPABILITIES DEVELOPMENT

Valuing Intellectual Property

C. Performance Improvement *(Continued)*

2. **Consider the organizational structure to support asset creation as well as asset value extraction and, most importantly, how to handle the "ownership" of the new revenue streams.**

The Corporate Capabilities analysis is done by Bob Shearer and represents the analysis of the corporate performance behaviors found in the chapter, and supplemented by the Taskforce Subject Matter Experts (see Acknowledgments for a list of SMEs) over the course of related discussions and work sessions.

CHAPTER 10

Competitive Power through Integrated IP Strategy

DR. JAN JAFERIAN

The message is clear: develop and manage your IP portfolio—it's a matter of survival and a means for growth. IP strategy development is an evolutionary process commensurate with the needs, aspirations, and resources of the organization.

KEY POINTS TO LOOK FOR

- **IP influence running "silent and deep" for a decade is now one of the most urgent issues for the competitive enterprise to master.**
- **The portfolio is the focus of the IP resource management, but it must be aligned with business and technology (R&D) strategies.**
- **Comprehensive IP portfolio management requires consideration of five strategic thrusts: creation, calibration, defense, assertion, and leverage.**
- **Each strategic thrust is supported by operational infrastructures that include role assignments, operational processes, deliverables, and databases.**
- **Organizations need to develop multifunctional intellectual asset management (IAM) capabilities, which requires the incorporation of IP business management and analytical skills to augment traditional legal skills.**

The Impact of IP on Today's Enterprise

Today's business environment could be considered in Dickensian terms as "the best of times and the worst of times," depending on whether your company is an intellectual asset "have," a "have not," or simply a "have less" as compared with your competitors. Despite the fact that patents continue to be filed in prodigious quantities worldwide, piracy and counterfeiting proliferate. IP matters are creating havoc in international markets and are fully disruptive of what were once "normal corporate operations" for the board and executive team. Disputes regarding patent, trademark, copyright, or trade secret misappropriation increasingly dominate headlines, courtrooms, and board meetings. While such misuses could be considered backhanded recognition of the value potential of the intellectual assets, they are serious offenses that erode the asset owners' return on their investments in R&D as well as the development, production, and marketing of the owners' legitimate products and services.

On the positive side, intellectual assets are increasingly a means of knowledge transfer and wealth generation through judicious licensing, strategic alliance, joint venture, and spin-off transactions. These revenue-producing activities can be vehicles for fostering further innovation and marketplace growth as well as nurturing productive relationships between companies, universities, government labs, and private research institutions. But most importantly, as a company begins to recognize the power of IP, it finds that a well-conceived and coordinated corporate strategy stimulates further creativity and innovation throughout the enterprise. The IP-enabled enterprise begins to teem with new ideas that propel it to the front of technological and business innovations that serve to keep the competition off balance and struggling to catch up.

Companies Are Increasingly Reliant on Their Intellectual Assets

More and more, companies are using their intellectual assets to

- Enhance their ROI on R&D investments
- Protect product revenue streams
- Provide collateral for loans

- Enhance cash flows and earnings
- Improve analysts' perceptions and stockholder value

Some CTOs use the size and growth rates of their patent portfolios to demonstrate the strength of their leadership and the efficacy of their technology development strategies. CFOs are using the patent portfolio as collateral for debt financing to obtain more favorable interest rates. As royalty revenues grow and become more predictable, financial institutions embrace this cash flow as the basis for structuring nonrecourse financing instruments. CEOs proudly report the enhancement of shareholder value by the significant profit contribution from their intellectual property portfolios.

Traditionally, patents and other intellectual property assets are utilized to protect and augment the commercialization of innovative products and services. They are used to enhance brand value and increase market share through various licensing or alliance arrangements. Such beneficial uses not only leverage technology investments for the licensor, but also strengthen the internal resource base to shorten development cycles, reduce costs, and improve time-to-market for the licensee or product launch.

The management of these assets has become a competitive imperative. CEOs, CFOs, and CTOs and their departmental teams or staff are increasingly expected to demonstrate responsible management of both tangible and intangible assets. Analysts, boards of directors, and shareholders expect that investments will yield returns that improve the company's total performance and market cap. As cost and competitive pressures increase, no entity can afford idle or underutilized assets of any type.

The "what to" and "how to" of designing and managing IP organizations—not just for value maximization, but also for competitive advantage in the global economy—are complex, especially where the business rules are much more uncertain. Your company can create a competitive advantage and help shape the global business landscape if it takes a proactive approach to IP management. If it lags or is a "fast follower," it may well miss unique opportunities attendant to these times and critical to its future. Tomorrow's leaders are those executives who know how to make the best of times from today's opportunities as IP reshapes the way of creating new wealth.

Strategic Context and Alignment

Corporate performance depends on astute strategic planning and meticulous operational execution. Technology roadmaps, R&D objectives, product development, and market penetration strategies are the contextual foundation for an IP capability and infrastructure that has been running silent and deep in the world's more IP-innovative companies during the past decade. It has now surfaced and forces the integration of strategic thinking and operational execution. Resource requirements, priorities, schedules, and deliverables from R&D and manufacturing are calibrated to create a vibrant, agile, and sophisticated corporate money-making machine. This is a highly interdependent, continuous process of anticipation, assessment, adjustment and execution. In Exhibit 10.1, Aligning Business, Technology, and Patent-Filing Strategies, a generic three-phased strategic process illustrates the complexity and sophistication inherent in deriving a patent-filing strategy from the alignment of business and technology strategies.

Phase 1

The business strategy is linked to and aligned with both product specifications and schedule requirements. The business units define the mix of products needed by their customers in various market segments. In Exhibit 10.1, products are designated by the letters A, B, C, D, E, and F. Each product embodies a set of features, functionalities, and performance characteristics that correspond to the market research data about customer requirements in the market segments denoted by the letters X, Y, and Z.

Some products, such as B and C, address generalized needs in multiple market segments. Other products, such as A, D, E, and F, are more specialized for particular market segments. For example, Product A is needed by Market Segment X only, whereas Products D, E, and F are required solely for Market Segment Y. Product managers and technical specialists translate the multifaceted customer requirements into detailed product specifications. These specifications, along with their expected market introduction or launch dates, become the context for the development of technology strategies in Phase 2 of the strategic planning process.

EXHIBIT 10.1 ALIGNING BUSINESS, TECHNOLOGY, AND PATENT-FILING STRATEGIES

	BUSINESS STRATEGY		
	MARKET SEGMENTS		
PRODUCTS	X	Y	Z
A	A		
B	B		B
C	C	C	C
D		D	
E		E	
F		F	

	PRODUCT/TECHNOLOGY STRATEGY					
	PRODUCTS					
TECHNOLOGY	A	B	C	D	E	F
In-Ш	In-Ш	In-Ш	In-Ш	In-Ш	In-Ш	In-Ш
In-Ø		In-Ø	In-Ø	In-Ø	In-Ø	In-Ø
In-ђ			In-ђ			In-ђ
In-Ω					In-Ω	In-Ω
In-β			In-β	In-β	In-β	In-β
Bk-Ю					Bk-Ю	Bk-Ю
Bk-Ж					Bk-Ж	Bk-Ж

Phase 1: Business Units assess customer requirements to develop product specifications and determine the product mix needed for each market segment.

Phase 2: R&D determines which technological improvements (In-) or breakthroughs (Bk-) are needed to meet Business Units' product specifications and product launch plans.

Phase 3: Through dialogue and trade-offs, the business and technology strategies are adjusted and aligned into a coherent corporate strategy, including determining a protective patent filing strategy.

	TECHNOLOGY STRATEGY		BUSINESS STRATEGY: *Develop Innovative Products—Grow Market Share*									PATENTING STRATEGY
			Market Segment X			Market Segment Y				Market Segment Z		
	Technology	$M	Product A	Product B	Product C	Product D	Product E	Product F	Product C	Product B	Product C	Filing Quotas
INCREMENTAL IMPROVEMENTS	In-Ш	$89	In-Ш	In-Ш	In-Ш	In-Ш	In-Ш	In-Ш	In-Ш	In-Ш	In-Ш	12
	In-Ø	$45		In-Ø	In-Ø	In-Ø	In-Ø	In-Ø	In-Ø	In-Ø	In-Ø	11
	In-ђ	$8			In-ђ			In-ђ	In-ђ		In-ђ	7
	In-Ω	$24					In-Ω	In-Ω				4
	In-β	$48			In-β	In-β	In-β	In-β	In-β		In-β	9
INNOVATIVE BREAKTHROUGHS	Bk-Ю	$150					Bk-Ю	Bk-Ю				34
	Bk-Ж	$136					Bk-Ж	Bk-Ж				23

Phase 2

Products are linked to and aligned with technology. R&D uses the product specifications to define the scope of development plans. The more general the specifications, the more likely that incremental improvements to existing technologies can be made to meet the requirements. However, more specialized specifications may present significant challenges that can be met only through innovative technological breakthroughs. In this generalized example, the five *incremental improvement technologies* are represented by the symbols In-Ш, In-Ø, In-Ћ, In-Ω, and In-ß while the two *breakthrough technologies* are designated by the symbols Bk-Ю and Bk-Ж. These technologies will be utilized as follows in the various products under development:

For the incremental improvement technologies:

In-Ш will be incorporated in all of the products;

In-Ø will be used in Products B, C, D, and F;

In-Ћ will be embedded only in Products C and F;

In-Ω will be limited to Products E and F; and

In-ß will be broadly used in Products C, D, E, and F.

For the breakthrough technologies:

Bk-Ю will be used in Products E and F; and

Bk-Ж will be incorporated only in Product F.

Phase 3

The focus is on innovation and asset creation, which requires more detailed analysis of R&D expense budgets and patent filing objectives. The In-Ш, In-Ø, In-Ћ, In-Ω, and In-ß technology projects are budgeted at $89M, $45M, $8M, $24M, and $48M, respectively, for a total budget of $214M for incremental improvements. The budgets for the two breakthrough innovations, Bk-Ю and Bk-Ж, are set much higher—$150M and $136M, for a total of $286M.

When setting patent filing quotas, several factors must be taken into consideration, such as the degree of innovation, the expected competitive advantage to be derived from the technologies, and the need to create a barrier to entry for competitors. The higher the degree of innovation for competitive advantage or the greater the need for protection from competitive threat, the more patents are required to protect the R&D investments. In this illustration, the patent quota for the five incremental improvement technologies is set at 47. Technology In-Ш will be covered by 12 patents; In-Ø by 11; In-Ћ by 7; In-Ω by 4, and In-ß by 9. In contrast, the patent filing quota for the two breakthrough technologies is set at 57, with 34 to cover technology Bk-Ю and 23 to cover technology Bk-Ж.

To more fully utilize intellectual property assets, organizations need to develop a multifunctional intellectual asset management (IAM) capability. Exploiting their IAM capabilities will enable organizations to enhance their competitiveness and more fully realize their wealth-generation potential. IAM requires strategic vision. It also requires streamlined processes and infrastructure. Strategic analyses, highly skilled IP specialists, and multi-discipline teams are critical to the implementation and executions of IP strategies. This interdependent, interdisciplinary team approach is a departure from the days and ways when legal staffs dominated the creation and protection of intellectual property assets.

As new ways to use IP assets have emerged, new IAM competencies are needed to pursue expansive and multifaceted business objectives. Examples of the new skill sets include:

- The ability to search and sort through massive patent databases to categorize one's own organization's assets and to characterize competitors' portfolios
- Analytical and financial knowledge to develop value propositions for licenses, litigation settlements, strategic alliances, joint ventures, spin-outs, mergers, acquisitions; licensee audits; and alternative financial structures such as securitization and lease-back arrangements
- Deal structuring knowledge to posit alternative ways to formulate terms and conditions
- Technical analytical skills to investigate possible infringements, identify prior art, develop test methodologies to acquire evidence to support infringement allegations; and ways to characterize the cost and performance advantages others could realize through the authorized use of the organization's IP

- Multidimensional negotiation skills to handle the range of technical, legal, business, and contractual deliberations to consummate multifaceted and multicultural deals
- Computer literacy to develop and utilize web-based tools and databases needed for various analytical and administrative purposes

The management processes are so intensive and the skill requirements so extensive that many companies create subsidiaries or holding companies to focus on creating new wealth from existing assets—assets that have typically been expensed in years past but now have recognizable value. Most folks call that "found money," and it is present in most mid-sized and large companies. Regardless of organizational structure, developing IAM capabilities has become the primary means by which organizations harness the potential value in their intellectual property treasure troves. Effective IAM can revitalize both individual companies and national economies.

Companies that wish to truly capitalize on the wealth-generation potential of the patent assets need to develop more refined, deliberate, and systemic strategies for building the IP inventory and for effectively disposing of the assets in that inventory. In Exhibit 10.2, Comprehensive Alignment of Business, Technology, and Intellectual Property Strategies, a comprehensive intellectual property strategy includes a set of *Intellectual Property Inventory Strategies* that address the *creation* and *calibration* of the portfolio. The comprehensive strategy also includes a set of *Intellectual Property Disposition Strategies* that focus on other uses for the patents beyond incorporation into the organization's own products.

Disposition falls into two categories: responsive and proactive. When a third party with allegations of infringement attacks the organization, the organization must *defend* itself against the allegations. Alternatively, the organization may choose to adopt a proactive set of strategies. It could *assert* its patents against infringers or it could *leverage* its patents to enhance the competitiveness or business performance of other organizations through licensing and technology transfer arrangements with them. This latter strategy is not altruistic. It assumes that encouraging others to use the organization's patents will yield benefits such as market expansion, brand recognition, the establishment of standards based on the organization's patents, and, of course, revenue from licensing fees and additional product sales.

EXHIBIT 10.2 COMPREHENSIVE ALIGNMENT OF BUSINESS, TECHNOLOGY, AND INTELLECTUAL PROPERTY STRATEGIES

Comprehensive Strategic Alignment

			BUSINESS STRATEGY: *Develop Innovative Products—Grow Market Share*									
	TECHNOLOGY STRATEGY		Market Segment X			Market Segment Y				Market Segment Z		PATENTING STRATEGY
	Technology	$M	Product A	Product B	Product C	Product D	Product E	Product F	Product C	Product B	Product C	Filing Quotas
INCREMENTAL IMPROVEMENTS	In-Ш	$89	In-Ш	In-Ш	In-Ш	In-Ш	In-Ш	In-Ш	In-Ш	In-Ш	In-Ш	12
	In-Φ	$45		In-Ø	In-Ø	In-Ø	In-Ø	In-Ø	In-Ø	In-Ø	In-Ø	11
	In-ђ	$8			In-ђ			In-ђ	In-ђ		In-ђ	7
	In-Ω	$24					In-Ω	In-Ω				4
	In-β	$48			In-β	In-β	In-β	In-β	In-β		In-β	9
INNOVATIVE BREAKTHROUGHS	Bk-Ю	$150					Bk-Ю	Bk-Ю				34
	Bk-Ж	$136					Bk-Ж	Bk-Ж				23

CREATE AND CALIBRATE

IP INVENTORY STRATEGY

ENFORCE/LEVERAGE

IP DISPOSITION STRATEGY

DEFEND

Building New Wealth

Just as a product sitting in inventory is nonproductive, so too are underutilized or unused intellectual property assets. While the prospect of generating significant incremental revenue and other value from the IP portfolio is growing exponentially, there is a corresponding downside. As more companies and individual patent holders enter the lucrative—albeit risky—fray of patent assertion and litigation, there is mounting consternation about the threat of attack and the subsequent erosive impact this could have on revenue streams and stock value. Of primary concern is whether products and services are sufficiently protected to provide adequate freedom to operate. A corresponding concern is whether the company might soon be under siege from others alleging misappropriation of trademarks or infringement of patents. A third concern is whether or not someone might be infringing on their company's IP assets. Such a condition could be transformed into potential stick licensing revenues or low risk litigation, which is increasingly analyzed as a normal course of business investment decision. Litigate or not, "let's do the math and assess the risk" is the norm in most IP-savvy companies today.

The message is clear: develop and manage your IP portfolio—it's a matter of survival and a means for growth. IP strategy development is an evolutionary process commensurate with the needs, aspirations, and resources of the organization. An intellectual property portfolio is constructed over time and requires periodic culling as well as replenishment. It is an asset that requires thoughtful and continuous management from both strategic and operational perspectives. Having a portfolio enables possibilities for its disposition. Astute exploitation converts that potential into value-maximizing realities.

The IP portfolio is the focus of the transformation of knowledge to net worth. This process has five distinct strategic thrusts supported by operational infrastructures. These thrusts and infrastructures are here presented in template form followed by additional discussion. These five strategic thrusts are creating, calibrating, defending, asserting, and leveraging the IP portfolio. The operational infrastructures include role assignments; investigative, business, and legal processes; deliverables; and databases.

1. Creating the Patent Portfolio

Building a valuable portfolio is the result of purposeful decisions and actions. It is a continuous process reflecting the vision, innovativeness, determination, and interdisciplinary collaboration of the organization (see Exhibit 10.3, Creating Strategic Thrust and Related Operational Infrastructure). These cultural characteristics, supported by financial resources, are the critical success factors needed to create and refine a competitive patent portfolio.

Portfolio creation is dependent on an innovative culture. Such a culture is nurtured first and foremost by funding research and development staffs, labs, and projects. Funding is made possible by the revenues and profits derived from the business—the more successful the business, the more funding available for R&D. This highlights the symbiotic relationship between technology development and business deployment and is the basis for their alignment. Business requirements provide the context for the R&D agenda. Ensuring that R&D embraces the organization's business strategies provides both focus and impetus to the R&D team's work. Together,

EXHIBIT 10.3 CREATING STRATEGIC THRUST AND RELATED OPERATIONAL INFRASTRUCTURE

STRATEGIC THRUST:
CREATE **the patent portfolio and use it to**
PROTECT **the organization's revenue streams and freedom to operate.**

Operational Infrastructure

Assignments	Processes	Deliverables	Databases
Cross-Functional Teams (*Legal, Technical, and Business*) review and score invention disclosures and potential patent applications. **Patent Attorneys** draft and prosecute patent applications on behalf of **Inventors.**	Invention Disclosures Generation Invention Disclosure Review and Scoring Patentability Assessment and Scoring Maintenance Reviews	Invention Disclosures Trade Secret Designations Invention Disclosure Scores Patentability Scores Patent Applications Renewals and Abandonments	Invention Disclosure Scoring Trade Secret Log Patentability Scoring Patent Docket Prosecution History Inventor Reward and Recognition Patent Portfolio Patent Keepers List

they express the inventive prowess of R&D and establish a shield for the business.

The patent portfolio upon which to base an intellectual property business depends on invention disclosures and the patents that may result from them. Throughout the lifetime of each project, there is urgency to document inventions in real time. This is necessary so that essential ideas are not missed in the pressure to meet multifaceted project deadlines. Given the "first-to-file" versus "first-to-invent" criteria for granting IP rights, the criterion used for national and international filings date is important in gaining the protection to exercise the use of the invention.

To fuel the patenting engine, inventors must document their research results in invention disclosures that capture the essence of their unique contributions. These disclosures are precursors of patent applications. They are used to determine which inventions are patentable. Invention disclosures generally include:

- The plain-language descriptions of the purpose of the invention, such as the problem solved, the improvement achieved, or the material invented
- The perceived novelty of the invention
- Any prior art known to the inventor
- The distinct advantages the invention provides over existing known technologies or solutions
- Drawings, flow charts, and methods of practice to more fully explain the functional design and operational use of the invention:

Streamlined methods to capture IP opportunities and disclosure submission are a critical element of asset creation. Efficient and effective invention disclosure processes and tools include:

- User-friendly invention disclosure submission form (capturing the information noted previously)
- Identification of a central repository to which invention disclosures can be sent
- Development of web-based tools for quick and easy submission and logging of invention disclosures
- Establishment of technical review teams that can meet frequently to assess the merits of the disclosures in a timely manner
- Establishment of criteria to be used by the review teams to assess or score disclosures objectively
- Deployment of training to the technical staff to ensure they know how and why to write and submit disclosures
- Clear linkage to the legal department so that they know what and how much is in the disclosure pipeline, enabling them to be prepared to process the disclosures chosen to become patent applications efficiently and effectively
- Feedback to the inventors to obtain missing or additional information and to report the status of their disclosure

Most companies practice some form of filtering or scoring to sort through the disclosures to determine what is patentable, what is best kept as trade secret, and what can be left unprotected. Unlike invention disclosure reviews that are generally conducted by technical teams focusing on the technical merits of the invention, patent reviews are conducted by multidisciplinary teams that consider a broader range of selection criteria. The selection criteria they use include such considerations as:

- **Strength of the technical concept**—the breadth of applicability to the business and competitive advantage it could achieve, with special recognition or scoring for a breakthrough concept or technology that could enable a paradigm shift
- **Degree of product support**—the extensiveness of new features or performance enhancements
- **Licensing potential**—an assessment of revenue potential based on the scope of applicability to other companies' businesses and the depth of the markets in which they operate
- **Strategic fit**—the degree of alignment with the business objectives of the company
- **Workaround barrier**—the degree of difficultly and cost to develop alternatives
- **Detectability**—a measure of the difficulty and cost of detecting the use of the concept in other companies' products and the resulting ease or difficulty in enforcing a patent based on the concept
- **Geography**—what country-specific coverage is needed to protect locations where products are made or sold
- **Trade secrets**—which concepts or technologies should be kept as trade secrets rather than disclosed in patent applications

Preparing and submitting patent applications is the distinctive competency and contribution of the legal staff. The quality of the patent depends on the staff's ability to capture the fine details and nuances of the invention in the claims they draft. They must be able to comprehend the technical concepts and translate them into detailed structural and operational descriptions. Language is critical; the patent examiners will analyze each word. Later, if the patent is used in an assertion, every aspect of the patent will be scrutinized, including its prosecution history, specification, claims, and drawings. Each asserted claim will require compelling explanation and evidentiary support to defend its validity and alleged infringement. Having a portfolio of carefully crafted patents is of immense value to the company.

Like their technical and business counterparts, patent attorneys also face pressures to speed up their processes. At the same time, they are expected to provide quality drafting and prosecution of patent applications. Because in-house legal staffs are also subject to pressures to meet a multiplicity of demands on their time, most corporate staffs are augmented through the use of outside counsel. It is imperative that in-house counsel carefully manage their outside counterparts to ensure timeliness, cost effectiveness, and, especially, quality. This last challenge—quality—can be daunting. The more complex or unique the innovation, the more specialized and skilled the patent attorney must be to ensure that the nuances of the innovation are fully stated in the claims. As more companies are becoming reliant on outside counsel to handle a larger portion of their patenting quotas, it is increasingly likely that inexperienced or overworked attorneys may be used to handle the expanded workload.

The various deliverables of these processes, such as invention disclosures, patent filing recommendations, and patent applications, should be retained in searchable databases for record keeping and future reference. Examples of useful databases include inventory of invention disclosures, disclosure scoring log, trade secret log, patent application scoring, patent prosecution dockets, prosecution history, and inventor rewards and recognition. The users of these databases are primarily those involved in the review and prosecution processes, or as will be discussed subsequently, in defense, leverage, or assertion processes. Given the confidential nature of much of the information contained in these databases, use of them should be controlled, with access permission granted on a need-to-know basis under explicit confidentiality requirements.

Patent creation has many components. The result of these many efforts is a treasure trove of valuable patents that protect the company's product investments. These assets can also become the foundation for an intellectual property business that further rewards the company with significant high-margin revenues. Creating a portfolio is an ongoing process, but it requires calibration to remain competitive and cost effective.

2. Calibrating the Patent Portfolio

Creation is an additive process designed for the accumulation of patents. But mere accumulation can become a burden on the company. Patenting is expensive and time consuming. If the patents are being used and are returning value to the company, then the cost of building and maintaining the portfolio can be justified. However, without periodic review of the portfolio, it is difficult to determine how and to what extent the portfolio is actually being used. Another concern is the status and evolution of competitors' portfolios. Are they patenting more intensively in fields aligned with your business, poising themselves to exploit gaps or weaknesses in your portfolio? Have they discovered new areas of advantage that could threaten your business? If the answer to these questions is "yes," then it's a clear signal that the value of your portfolio is at risk.

In order to maintain the robustness of the portfolio and to maximize its overall value, it is essential to calibrate it. Calibration is an adjustment process by which patents are added to or deleted from the portfolio to ensure strategic alignment, cost effectiveness, and competitiveness (see Exhibit 10.4, Calibrating the Strategic Thrust and Operational Infrastructure). Profiling and maintenance reviews are two ways to make informed decisions for calibrating the portfolio.

Before profiling competitors' portfolios, it is necessary to profile your own to establish a baseline for comparison. A profile is a characterization or representation of the portfolio by various criteria, such as technology coverage or age. The methods for profiling your portfolio and those of your competitors should be the same so that comparisons can be made. There is a common denominator that makes profiling possible. All patents are assigned an International Patent Classification (IPC) by the patent office upon issuance. Consequently, IPCs provide a convenient and uniform means of gathering and sorting patent data for any company. Some useful ways to develop the profile include:

- Distribution of patents into all of the IPCs assigned to the company's patents
- Rank ordering IPCs by the number of patents in them
- Age of the patents based on when they were filed
- Useful life of the patents, based on how much time is left before they expire
- Number of patents issued per year, in either the entire portfolio or in particular IPCs

EXHIBIT 10.4 CALIBRATING THE STRATEGIC THRUST AND OPERATIONAL INFRASTRUCTURE

STRATEGIC THRUST:
***CALIBRATE* the patent portfolio for cost effectiveness and competitiveness.**

Operational Infrastructure

Assignments	Processes	Deliverables	Databases
Technical and IP Business conduct maintenance reviews; make renewal/ abandonment decisions. **IP Business with Technical** profile competitors' portfolios; assess competitiveness of own and others' portfolios.	Maintenance Reviews Comparative Analyses	Renewals Abandonments Replenishment Recommendations Investment Recommendations Competitive Analyses and Profiles Filing Recommendations	Maintenance Data and Decisions Patent Keeper's List Company Profiles

The range or number of IPCs into which a company's patents are distributed indicates the breadth of technologies they use. The number of patents in particular IPCs demonstrates the depth of their technology coverage. Their age or useful life can be a measure of increasing or diminishing value or threat. Finally, the rate of issuance per year can indicate the pace of investment in R&D overall or in specific areas of technology. Based on this information, an assessment can be made of how well the portfolio aligns with the company's strategies. For example, the breadth and depth of patent coverage should correspond to the types of products being sold and to the protection they require. With these insights, competitive opportunities or concerns can also be identified. A paucity of patents in a technology area well covered by a competitor can indicate a gap or weakness in the portfolio that needs to be augmented by additional patent filing.

By analyzing profile data, informed decisions can be made to calibrate the portfolio to address concerns or to enhance strengths. However, there is one limitation with this type of data—it is retrospective; it is based on issued patents. The invention or its underlying technology is not visible for two to three years or more from the time a patent is applied for until it is issued. While historic filing is no guarantee of future filing, the trends are indicative and the form of the data—patent counts—is the same for all companies. In the absence of a crystal ball or insider information, this data is a common platform for understanding the composition of portfolios. It is available to the public, and intellectual asset managers use it worldwide. It provides a common basis for answering questions such as:

- How many patents do companies have in technology areas of importance to your business?
- What are the filing rates in these areas?
- How well are related technology areas being covered?
- Who has what advantages?
- Who poses what threats?
- What new technologies are being pursued or are covered by competitors' patents?

These questions are being asked and answered daily around the world by technology-driven companies. Any company that hopes to survive and thrive in such an intensely competitive environment needs to be able to create and calibrate its IP portfolio in a timely and cost-effective manner. An important way to manage cost is through maintenance reviews. Given the ongoing and rising costs of maintaining patents, it is not only prudent but also necessary to periodically audit, cull, and adjust the portfolio, determining which patents should be abandoned and which renewed. Several questions need to be answered when making renewal decisions, such as:

- Is the patent necessary now or will it be in the foreseeable future to protect products?
- Is the patent used or expected to be used to generate licensing revenue?
- Is the patent currently or soon to be involved in litigation?
- Does the patent cover an area of competitive advantage for the organization?
- What is the likelihood that this patent is being infringed by others?

- Is this a strong patent, with clear and detectable claims?
- Has the patent been reexamined, reissued, or opposed?
- Is this patent cited by others in their patents?
- Is the patent already on the keeper list?

A "yes" answer to any of these questions means that the patent should be renewed and placed on a keeper list. In addition, if a competitor poses a current or potential threat in a particular area where there is current patent coverage, then those patents should be preserved for defensive purposes, regardless of whether they are involved in current products, licensing programs, or litigation. Finally, if patents are truly unused or unuseful, abandon them and use the cost savings to invest in new R&D programs and patents. Effective operation of this process can result in substantial cost savings as well as provide insurance that valuable patents are not being overlooked or forsaken.

Developing and refreshing searchable databases of maintenance reviews and competitive analyses is as important for the calibration thrust as it was for the creation. The patent keepers list, a log of patents being used or contemplated for use in licenses or litigation, is particularly important to retain so that these valuable patents are not inadvertently lost by neglecting to pay their maintenance fees or by assigning them to others. The comparative portfolio profiles and assessments provide critical information to guide technology, business development, and patent-filing decisions. These profiles are also useful for making adjustments to strategies on the basis of competitive insights. Access to and use of such information should be monitored to ensure confidentiality of sensitive information.

3. Defending the Patent Portfolio

Defense is a responsive strategy activated when others accuse the company of infringement. While the strategic thrusts of creation and calibration are chosen by the organization, the defense strategic thrust is imposed from outside. Attack can come at any time from a multiplicity of sources (see Exhibit 10.5, Defending Strategic Thrust and Related Operational Infrastructure). Any patent holder of any size can assert against anyone they have some reason to believe is practicing their patent without permission. In today's litigious environment, these allegations are as likely to come

EXHIBIT 10.5 DEFENDING STRATEGIC THRUST AND RELATED OPERATIONAL INFRASTRUCTURE

STRATEGIC THRUST:
DEFEND **the patent portfolio when attacked to preserve both freedom to operate and product/service revenue streams.**
DEFEND **the patent portfolio when asserted against by others to protect freedom to operate and revenue streams.**

Operational Infrastructure

Assignments	Processes	Deliverables	Databases
Patent Attorneys review claims and prior art/assess legal merits/ coordinate discovery/negotiate legal portion of settlements. **Technical staff** investigates products; provides data to attorneys. **IP Business** analyzes potential exposures and develops business negotiation strategy; negotiates business portion of settlements.	Infringement Analysis Invalidity Analysis Prior Art Investigation Business Risks and Revenue Exposures	Defense Value Proposition Defense Claims Charts Rebuttals Defense Business Case Defense Disposition Strategy Defense Negotiation Strategy Defense Litigation Strategy Response Correspondence	Defense Archives/Prior Art Repository Defense Investigation Results Defense Proof Packages Defense Correspondence

from attorneys representing private patent holders as from other companies, both large and small.

Defense strategies have two purposes: (1) to preserve the company's freedom to operate and (2) to minimize the risks of reducing or eliminating the company's revenue streams by adverse settlements. Having a patent portfolio does not immunize the organization from attacks. It does, however, provide a defensive arsenal upon which to draw for possible rebuttals or settlements. With both patenting and asserting becoming increasingly popular means of conducting business, organizations should view the threat of attack as ominous and imminent. The consequences of successful assertion can be severe, ranging from substantial royalty payments to court-ordered injunctive relief. In order to maximize its defensive potential, the company needs to be as prepared for attack as its resources allow. Preparation, however, is no guarantee of success.

As in sports, defense is a team effort. Lawyers, technologists, and IP business executives all play important roles. The cornerstone of defense is the legal staff. They are expected to prepare and present the cogent arguments needed to dispel the asserted claims or to support counterclaims. This requires that they be adept at claims construction, file history analysis, and the application of current case law. They must be also able to comprehend quantities of technical data about how the accused products conform to or deviate from the asserted claims. In addition, they must be effective in both corporate and courtroom settings, as either or both may be the venue for deliberations. Supporting the lawyers must be a creative and tenacious technical staff. They provide detailed product investigation and test data as well as relevant product prior art to the attorneys. The third components of the defense team are the intellectual property business managers. One of their roles is to scope the extent of possible damages. This includes valuation of historical and projected revenues derived from the accused products as well as assessment of the risk and impact of injunction. Other roles are the development of alternative deal structures and, with the lawyers, the negotiation of business settlements.

To be most productive, negotiations should be fact based and objective, not conjectural and emotional. It is possible that the companies may find creative grounds for settlement, such as future joint marketing or product development collaboration, thereby converting adversaries into partners. However, it is more likely that a clear distinction is sought between a winner and a loser. A distinct win for the accused is to be cleared of the accusations, with no payment of damages to the accuser. The opposite, of course, is true for the accuser, who wants payment—and usually large payment—for having been aggrieved by the misappropriation. It is difficult, though not impossible, to bridge such a gap of desired outcomes. Unlike sports, there can be more than one winner. There can also be more than one loser.

If negotiations fail, litigation may ensue. Litigation is a multiphased process encompassing claims construction, infringement and invalidity arguments, and damages assessments. These are spread across the time-consuming course of discovery, judgments, and appeals. The analysis of data and the collection of evidence needed to support litigation are broader and deeper in analytical scope than that which is used for the negotiated or prelitigation defense described previously. Many of the legal, technical, and business skills and much of the data required for litigation may be resident in the company. However, given the demanding nature of litigation and the stakes involved, these in-house functions are usually augmented by outside counsel and their technical and financial subject-matter experts. With each of the parties engaging teams of legal, technical, and financial specialists, litigation is extraordinarily expensive. It is also fraught with uncertainty. In the end, both parties may lose vast sums of money as well as impair reputations and marketplace momentum. It's like a sports team not only losing the championship, but also losing its uniforms, its stadium, and its fans.

Whether defense is negotiated or litigated, the company needs to provide its defense investigative and analytical capabilities with databases to support its position. Databases should include products and documentation archives, prior art repositories, defense investigation results logs, defense proof packages (composed of claim charts and related supporting evidence), and defense-related correspondence. The contents of these databases are highly sensitive.

Defensive capabilities are essential to protect the company's financial interests. These capabilities, spread across many functional disciplines, must be honed and harnessed. By working collaboratively and in real time, members of the defense team maximize their efficiency and effectiveness. To strengthen their responsiveness they share data, knowledge, insights, and perspectives. Their defense, however, may not shield or yield a "slam dunk." In the end, they may or may not prevail, no matter how comprehensive and compelling their defense. Best efforts do not always get best outcomes.

The foundation for an intellectual property business is the calibrated inventory of patent assets. The inventory can be used to commercialize those assets beyond their traditional use in products, services, or standards. There are two modes of proactive commercialization. One is *assertion,* which is a recovery-oriented strategy intended to obtain redress and recompense from the misuse of the company's IP assets by another. The other is *leverage,* an offer-based sharing strategy intended to financially reward both the company, as intellectual property licensor, and its licensees, as authorized users.

An organization may elect to pursue assertion, leverage, or both as its strategic thrust. The choice is dependent on the alignment of the strategic thrust that is adopted with the overall business objectives of the company and on the expected level returns the thrust may yield. Calculus of risk may also influence the strategic choice. Engaging in enforcement often invites retaliation. Some organizations would prefer to base their intellectual property business on the less inflammatory strategy of leverage, the sharing of the company's intellectual property for mutual business enhancement. Both strategies can be value maximizing. Each requires a diverse and slightly different mix of skills. Relatively speaking, enforcement programs require more depth of technical and legal analysis than leverage licensing programs, which require more business assessment and marketing and relationship management.

4. Asserting the Patent Portfolio

Patents consist of rights that only the owner can grant. Practicing these rights, either knowingly or inadvertently, without being authorized by the owner, is an infringement of those rights. The burden of proving infringement is on the owner of the rights. The challenge is to identify those who are misappropriating the company's rights and to prove such misuse in a sufficiently compelling manner that the misuser agrees to either stop its unauthorized use or to compensate the owner for the right to continue practicing (see Exhibit 10.6, Asserting Strategic Thrust and Related Operational Infrastructure). Of course the owner could file a suit against the alleged misuser, thereby entering into litigation. But since litigation is costly, risky, and time consuming, it is preferable to try to resolve assertion matters through investigation and negotiation. The *assertion* process is based on three investigative tracks—products, patents, and business impact. Negotiation scope and settlement terms are based on the results of these investigations.

EXHIBIT 10.6 ASSERTING STRATEGIC THRUST AND RELATED OPERATIONAL INFRASTRUCTURE

STRATEGIC THRUST:
ASSERT: **Enforce portfolio by *ASSERTING* patents to generate revenue and return on technology and patent investments.**

Operational Infrastructure

Assignments	Processes	Deliverables	Databases
Technical analyzes targets' products and publicly available documents/ conduct teardowns and tests. **Legal** interprets claims and confirms/prepares and presents proof packages utilization. **IP Business** develops business case; issues notice; conducts settlement negotiations.	Target Identification Product Investigations Claims Analysis and Interpretation Business Assessment	Assertion Investigation Results Assertion Proof Packages Assertion Correspondence Assertion Value Propositions	Assertion Investigation Results Assertion Proof Packages Assertion Correspondence Contract Database Encumbrances Database Contract Database

Product investigations are conducted by technical subject matter experts. Their studies begin with the compilation of charts of other companies' product offerings, highlighting three aspects: (1) when the products were introduced into the market, (2) which market segments they are in, and (3) what features, capabilities, or technologies may be covered by the company's patents. Initially the investigations focus on the study of publicly available documentation to gain insight into the design features, performance parameters, and operation of specific products that have been identified as targets. Examples of documentation include user guides, maintenance manuals, marketing literature, trade journals, and conference proceedings.

Documentation alone may not be sufficiently substantive and compelling to fully support the infringement allegations. Detailed investigations, including product teardowns and material decompositions, may be needed to test for operations, features, or characteristics that conform precisely to all elements of assertable patent claims. The development of test methods can be both challenging and creative. Obvious design features can be physically observed. Other performance characteristics must be tested or monitored while the product is being operated, such as electrical signatures of sensors or the movement of parts in particular ways to achieve certain results. The composition of substances, such as chemicals, may need to be tested in external laboratories that have specialized equipment not available within the company. Both test methods and test results become evidence that can be used to substantiate the infringement allegations.

Patent investigations are conducted by lawyers in parallel with the technical product investigations. Focus is on the identification of specific claims within patents that relate to (i.e., are practiced by) the targeted products. They need to determine whether all elements of the claims are used in the product in precise accordance with the language of the claim. Remember the earlier comment in the section regarding creation of the patent portfolio—that drafting is a distinctive competency? This is where those skills get tested, and where their interpretation capabilities come into play. To prove infringement it is not necessary that all claims within a patent be practiced by the target product. It is necessary only that each element of the asserted claims be shown to be used as stated in those particular claims and as may have been amended by any limitations or clarifications in the patent specifications or file wrappers. Interpreting the claim language, element by element, and demonstrating applicability to the target product form the basis for proving infringement. Interpretations, or constructions, are compiled into claim charts in which each claim is decomposed into its constituent elements. Each element is then cross-referenced to correlate to interpretations and evidentiary support. This composite chart and its supporting evidence constitute the *proof package* that will be presented to the accused company.

Product investigations and claims construction are interdependent tasks requiring a high degree of collaboration between the technical subject-matter experts and the lawyers. As the investigations evolve from exploration to evidentiary substantiation, it is critical that perceptions about both technical findings and claims interpretations be shared, correlated, and integrated. Conducting cross-functional reviews as mock assertion presentations enables the lawyers to present and refine their interpretations. During these mock sessions they can get feedback from their legal and technical colleagues about the reasonableness of their arguments. These sessions also provide an opportunity for the technical subject-matter experts to present their supporting documentary and operational evidence, testing for precise conformance to all elements of the claims to be asserted. Several iterations of these review sessions may be required to attain convergence of interpretation and evidence. At the conclusion of these reviews, the attorneys finalize the proof packages, incorporating modifications to the claim charts and supporting evidence based on the recommendations of their cross-functional colleagues.

Business impact constitutes a third track of investigation. Both historical and projected sales data are compiled for each accused product sold wherever there is patent coverage. This data is the foundation for constructing settlement alternatives. Other factors may also be taken into consideration, such as exchanging some portion of expected royalty revenue for access to some of the accused company's patents. Another option may be obtaining favorable pricing considerations on other products or services from the accused company that may be of benefit to one's own company. A further alternative may be charging a higher price for granting broader access to one's own patents. Limiting or expanding the field of use for the patents in dispute may provide a rationale for other price adjustments. The aggregation of impacted revenues and deal alternatives constitutes the *value propositions* for settlement. Other useful insights can be gleaned from profiling the target's patent portfolio to understanding its composition and evolution. From newspaper and trade press articles it may be possible to learn how the accused company responds to assertions—whether it is likely to settle or to litigate.

Exercising the assertion strategic thrust engenders a special risk—the threat of counter-assertion. Legal and business assessments of this threat can be scoped in general as a means of preparation. Once an actual counter-assertion has been made, the detailed product, patent, and business investigations can be conducted to formulate a defensive response.

The tripartite cross-functional investigations, analyses, and deliberations lead to a decision point regarding whether and how to formally pursue the target company. The lead lawyer in the case is usually responsible for recommending the legal premise for the decision, based on the quality of the claims construction and supporting usage evidence. The intellectual property business manager is responsible for making the final go or no-go decision, taking into further consideration the value propositions and the likelihood of prevailing.

If the decision is to proceed, then the remaining major steps in the assertion process include:

- Issuing formal notification to the accused company, identifying the accused products and the allegedly infringed patent claims
- Determining, through communication exchanges with the accused company, the procedures and protocol for negotiations, such as venue, schedule, and directionality (i.e., lateral, based solely on the accuser's asserted patents or bilateral, based on both the accuser's assertions and the accused's counter-assertions)
- Conducting patent discussions focused on claims construction and evidentiary support
- Negotiating settlement focused on license scope, value propositions, and other contractual terms and conditions

In the event that the parties are unable to reach consensus about the alleged infringement or settlement terms, the patent owner must decide whether further action is warranted and what costs and risks he or she is willing to assume to proceed further. If the accuser and the accused have been unable to achieve resolution through negotiation and do not view withdrawal as a viable option, the next step is some other form of formal unilateral or bilateral dispute resolution, such as mediation, arbitration, or litigation. Intellectual property business managers and their corporate senior management must fully understand that, despite the efficacy of efforts in trying to achieve resolution amicably, there is a likelihood that the assertion negotiations may be replaced by litigation. If this happens, *the strategy shifts to defense.*

The assertion processes, deliverables, and databases are analogous to those used in the defense strategic thrust. Interpretations, tangible supporting evidence, and value propositions are the foundation on which settlements are based. It is critical that all of the highly sensitive and confidential materials associated with the assertion strategic thrust be captured and maintained for both current use and future reference. Examples of relevant databases and archives include assertion product investigation results, patent investigation results, claim charts, inventory of test methods and results, proof packages, and correspondence. As with defense, access to and use of the assertion databases and materials should be controlled on a need-to-know basis.

Assertion is a labor-intensive and analytically oriented method of business. It is potentially risky and correspondingly potentially rewarding. Companies that are most successful at assertion have strong, easily detectable patents. They employ the multidisciplinary investigative and settlement approaches discussed in this chapter. If you have the patents, the team, and the resolve, you too can be successful at assertion. When you prevail, your C-suite executives and shareholders will be delighted with the results, but they should also understand that not every assertion case would be decided in their favor. A more risk-averse or genteel strategic thrust is leveraging. Unlike defense or assertion, which may have winners and losers, in leveraging there are many winners.

5. Leveraging the Patent Portfolio

Leverage is a technology-driven and customer-focused strategy adopted by the licensor to generate incremental revenue (see Exhibit 10.7, Leveraging Strategic Thrust and Related Operational Infrastructure). It is intended to provide business performance advantages to the licensee, such as decreasing time-to-market, reducing production costs, adding product features, improving product performance, or enabling entry into new markets, thereby increasing his revenues, profits, or market share. When any of these objectives is obtained, the revenue streams returned to the licensor can be very favorable.

The challenges to developing and implementing leverage-based strategies are multifaceted. They include:

- Identification of licensable intellectual property
- Identification and qualification of potential licensees
- Development of mutually advantageous value propositions and deal structures

EXHIBIT 10.7 LEVERAGING STRATEGIC THRUST AND RELATED OPERATIONAL INFRASTRUCTURE

STRATEGIC THRUST:
LEVERAGE **the portfolio through licensing and technology transfer programs to generate revenue and return on technology investments, to protect freedom to operate and revenue streams.**

Operational Infrastructure

Assignments	Processes	Deliverables	Databases
IP Business identifies and qualifies market opportunities for licenses, strategic alliances, or joint venture partners; develops marketing materials, value propositions, and deal structures; conducts negotiations. **Technical** mines portfolio; refines the scope/depth of benefits provided by the IP.	Portfolio Mining to Find and Assess Licensable Technologies, Patents, Copyrights, and Trademarks Business Case Development Target Identification Marketing Programs	Leverage Value Propositions IP Offerings Target Qualification Marketing Collaterals Deal Structures Negotiation Strategies Strategic Alliances	Licensable IP Taxonomies Portfolio Mining Results Lead Generation Contact Records Contract Database Encumbrances Database

- Gaining a market presence and reputation as a beneficent technology and intellectual property provider
- Development and deployment of marketing materials
- Overcoming internal objections to sharing intellectual property with others, especially competitors

The inventory to supply the leverage business is derived in part from the patent portfolio. In addition, there often is a plethora of other intellectual property scattered throughout the organization in such forms as know-how, prototypes, production procedures, architectures, and source code. This abundance must be identified and then correlated with potential market opportunities. The process by which this is done is *portfolio mining*—a comprehensive, intellectually demanding, time-consuming, and creative search, sort, and score process. It requires knowledge of both the technology-push and market-pull dynamics impacting producers and consumers.

Cross-functional teams composed of technical and marketing subject-matter experts initially sort the patent portfolio and other sources of IP by various criteria such as level of innovativeness, competitive advantage, and degree of potential benefit to a licensee. As patents and other intellectual property are sorted and scored, the rationales and results should be captured in a database. This information will be useful for designing promotional materials to market the intellectual property and for developing value propositions to structure licensing and technology transfer deals. Mining is followed by the identification and qualification of prospects (i.e., potential customers), based on broad searches for financially viable companies interested in and capable of incorporating multisourced technology into their products.

The effectiveness of the leverage business in generating value for the organization requires articulation of the relevance and value of the intellectual property to others; in other words, it's "selling." Relevance and value are customer-oriented parameters that require explanation, substantiation, and promotion in order to attract positive attention. Consequently, the effectiveness of the leveraging strategy requires both promotional marketing and a combination of value and affordability-based value propositions.

Two types of promotional marketing are required—image-based and product-based. People are more likely to deal with companies that are known for the quality of their innovations and the integrity of their conduct in business transactions and relationships. Reputation may open a door, but it is the actual feasibility and functionality of the product offering that leads to an invitation to enter. Promotional marketing drives the business. Marketing collaterals used for promotion take many forms. Particularly effective are web sites (especially those linking the corporate and intellectual property business sites); hardcopy targeted marketing, including pictures and performance specifications, useful for mailing campaigns and negotiation support; and active participation in targeted tradeshows at which relevant intellectual property can be showcased. The content must be benefits-oriented and focused on solving specific problems that the potential licensee faces. The more concrete your knowledge of the prospects' business concerns and opportunities and the more compelling your marketing data and messages, the better able you will be to formulate offerings valuable enough to convert prospects into paying customers.

Leverage negotiations, like most negotiations, are multiphased. The first phase of engagement is focused on the feasibility and advantages of the intellectual property. Does it work? Are there measurable advantages to using it? How much more needs to be added, technically and financially, to commercialize it? The second phase focuses on price, shifting the agenda of the meetings from knowledge sharing to compensation. The challenge during this phase of the negotiations is to derive a mutually satisfactory balance between the licensor's constructs of value and the licensee's sense of affordability. There is usually elasticity in both positions, especially if there is a viable market for the intellectual property–enhanced product. In that case, both benefit. The licensee will be enabled to generate enough profit to compensate for his expenses, including a reasonable royalty to the licensor. Once the contract is signed the parties often enter into an implementation phase during which technology and know-how are transferred. This often involves consulting or training support. Relationship management is especially required on the part of leveraging-based businesses to ensure effective implementation, revenue generation, and repeat business.

As the business grows, contract management becomes increasingly important. Licensing contracts memorialize the rights conveyed and obligations incurred at the time of signing. However, they are not dormant documents. They have a lifespan—the term of the agreement. Throughout the term, the contract itself needs to be monitored for compliance to ensure timely and accurate fulfillment of each party's obligations. If circumstances change for either the licensee or licensor, such as change of corporate ownership through merger or acquisition or devolution into bankruptcy, appropriate formal amendments must be made. A comprehensive database should contain not only the original contract but also records and correspondence related to payment, technology transfer, and other contractual commitments or deviations. Lack of attention to contract management may result in termination if obligations are not met fully and in a timely manner. Similarly, failure to periodically audit the contract may result in significant revenue shortfalls. Periodic audit for payment and other compliance matters requires diligence. For contracts as for the portfolio or business as a whole—if you don't manage it, you won't maximize its value potential.

Summary

The conceptual foundations for defining IP value maximization strategies and the operational infrastructures needed to support them have been presented succinctly. Guidelines have been provided for creating and calibrating an IP inventory that is aligned with the company's business and technology strategies. Means to ensure that this inventory is cost-effectively managed and competitively advantaged have also been highlighted. In order to turn these assets into powerful value generators, the IP disposition strategies of defense, assertion, and leverage have been articulated. For each of these strategic thrusts, suggestions have been made about operational infrastructures that can enhance the efficiency and effectiveness of IAM-based businesses. These integrated infrastructure elements range from the assignment of roles to individual functions and multidisciplinary teams to the use of various processes and databases to deliver results. The separate elements are presented in summary fashion as a consolidated table to facilitate reference and support your efforts at implementation in Exhibit 10.8, Integrated IP Strategy and Operational Infrastructure Matrix.

To drive and protect their aligned technology and business strategies, organizations expend significant financial and human capital on creating intellectual property assets. These assets, however, are only partially utilized in pursuing their traditional business strategies or in defending their portfolios to protect their revenue streams and freedom to operate. To maximize returns on investments in these assets and to enhance their overall competitiveness, the intellectual property portfolio requires both continuous calibration and additional commercialization.

EXHIBIT 10.8 INTEGRATED IP STRATEGY AND OPERATIONAL INFRASTRUCTURE MATRIX

			Operational Infrastructure			
			Assignments	**Processes**	**Deliverables**	**Databases**
IP Strategic Thrusts	IP Inventory Strategies	Create	**Cross-functional Teams** (*Legal, Technical, and Business*) review and score invention disclosures and potential patent applications. **Patent Attorneys** draft and prosecute patent applications on behalf of **Inventors.**	Invention Disclosures Generation Invention Disclosure Review and Scoring Patentability Assessment and Scoring Maintenance Reviews	Invention Disclosures Trade Secret Designations Invention Disclosure Scores Patentability Scores Patent Applications Renewals and Abandonments	Invention Disclosure Scoring Trade Secret Log Patentability Scoring Patent Docket Prosecution History Inventor Reward and Recognition Patent Portfolio Patent Keepers List
IP Strategic Thrusts	IP Inventory Strategies	Calibrate	**Technical and IP Business** conduct maintenance reviews; make renewal or abandonment decisions. **IP Business with Technical** profile competitors' portfolios; assess competitiveness of own and others' portfolios.	Maintenance Reviews Comparative Analyses	Renewals Abandonments Replenishment Recommendations Investment Recommendations Competitive Analyses and Profiles Filing Recommendations	Maintenance Data and Decisions Patent Keeper's List Company Profiles
IP Strategic Thrusts	IP Disposition Strategies	Defend	**Patent Attorneys** review claims and prior art; assess legal merits; coordinate discovery/ negotiate legal portion of settlements. **Technical staff** investigates products; provides data to attorneys. **IP Business** analyzes potential exposures and develops business negotiation strategy; negotiates business portion of settlements.	Infringement Analysis Invalidity Analysis Prior Art Investigation Business Risks and Revenue Exposures	Defense Value Proposition Defense Claims Charts Rebuttals Defense Business Case Defense Disposition Strategy Defense Negotiation Strategy Defense Litigation Strategy Response Correspondence	Defense Archives/Prior Art Repository Defense Investigation Results Defense Proof Packages Defense Correspondence
IP Strategic Thrusts	IP Disposition Strategies	Assert	**Technical** analyzes target products and publicly available documents/conducts teardowns and tests. **Legal** interprets claims and confirms/prepares and presents proof packages utilization. **IP Business** develops business case; issues notice; conducts settlement negotiations.	Target Identification Product Investigations Claims Analysis and Interpretation Business Assessment	Assertion Investigation Results Assertion Proof Packages Assertion Correspondence Assertion Value Propositions	Assertion Investigation Results Assertion Proof Packages Assertion Correspondence Contract Database Encumbrances Database Contract Database
IP Strategic Thrusts	IP Disposition Strategies	Leverage	**IP Business** identifies and qualifies market opportunities for licenses, strategic alliances, or joint venture partners; develops marketing materials, value propositions, and deal structures; conducts negotiations. **Technical** mines portfolio; refines the scope/depth of benefits provided by the IP.	Portfolio Mining to Find and Assess Licensable Technologies, Patents, Copyrights, and Trademarks Business Case Development Target Identification Marketing Programs	Leverage Value Propositions IP Offerings Target Qualification Marketing Collaterals Deal Structures Negotiation Strategies Strategic Alliances	Licensable IP Taxonomies Portfolio Mining Results Lead Generation Contact Records Contract Database Encumbrances Database

CAPABILITIES DEVELOPMENT

Competitive Power through Integrated IP Strategy

Observations & Action Items for Corporate Performance Improvement

A. Observations

1. Dr. Jaferian's chapter is the perfect tutorial for the person who wants to get the company's IP program started. It is worth the study it takes to understand it. She has done this in several Fortune 500 companies, and were there a Hall of Fame for IP strategists, she'd be in there!
2. Dr. Jaferian's strategic thrusts and operational infrastructures offer the perfect template for the comprehensive management and commercialization of IP assets.

B. Action Items

1. Become familiar with IP-related software and databases and develop or acquire the ability to search and sort through the massive patent databases to categorize one's own organization's assets and to characterize competitors' portfolios—create your own IP-focused technology-industry map.
2. Develop analytical capabilities and financial skills to generate value propositions for licenses, litigation settlements, strategic alliances, joint ventures, spin-outs, mergers, acquisitions, licensee audits, and alternative financial structures such as securitization and lease-back arrangements. (This is not a short-term internal development activity. It will require external support and a robust process improvement discipline to acquire these capabilities.)
3. Develop technical analytical skills to investigate possible infringements, identify prior art, develop test methodologies to acquire evidence to support infringement allegations, and find ways to characterize the cost and performance advantages others could realize through the authorized use of the organization's IP. (Use of outside resources is the fastest way to become proficient in these knowledge/skill mixes.)
4. Utilize multidimensional negotiation skills to handle the range of technical, legal, business, and contractual deliberations to create new business deals.

C. Performance Improvement

1. Ensure strategic alignment of business, R&D, and IP units for patent filing and IP deployment.

(continues)

CAPABILITIES DEVELOPMENT

Competitive Power through Integrated IP Strategy

C. Performance Improvement *(Continued)*

2. **Create multidisciplined collaborative teams to execute the processes defined.**
3. **Develop and use a periodic practice and policy report to the CEO and facilitate education of the board.**
4. **Do not be intimidated with the new focus on developing new knowledge, skills, and capabilities. Getting started is the toughest step and you will find yourself up the learning curve very quickly and guiding the company's new focus on wealth creation through IP.**

The Corporate Capabilities analysis is done by Bob Shearer and represents the analysis of the corporate performance behaviors found in the chapter, and supplemented by the Taskforce Subject Matter Experts (see Acknowledgments for a list of SMEs) over the course of related discussions and work sessions. Dr. Jaferian assisted in this capabilities analysis.

CHAPTER 11

Accelerating Wealth Creation through IP Management in the Mid-Market Company

DR. MARK KARASEK

As more and more of corporate value is associated with intangibles like intellectual property and brands, managing the intellectual capital portfolio becomes a necessity, not an option.

KEY POINTS TO LOOK FOR

- **IP must be fully integrated with business strategy to maximize shareholder return.**
- **Corporate structure for IP management will be driven by an IP committee and an intellectual capital team to complement senior management's strategy, direction, and decision making.**
- **Managing IP today requires agility in strategy, teaming to exploit your technologies and IP assets in other industries, and spin-off ventures that can create new wealth in new ventures.**

THE POWER OF IP IN THE EMERGING AND MID-MARKET ENTERPRISE

Most mid-market companies learn about IP only when they receive a letter alleging infringement on some unknown party's intellectual property (IP) or a competitor responds to one of their new product releases with a very similar feature and function to theirs. This is the classic wake-up call for the CEO and executive team to tell them that there are some things that may have been overlooked or underfunded as the company has been responding to market demands. The scramble to find out what just happened might lead to a giant step toward managing the most versatile asset of all, intellectual property.

In a situation where IP is "discovered" through a letter alleging infringement, or the knockoff of your own technology by a competitor, the first impulse is to think: Who should have known? Actually, in the well-managed company, such knowledge and responsibility is distributed across the entire executive team.

IP can have a defining impact for the growing company, but none so great as in the mid-market enterprise, where market and cash position can dramatically turn on prevailing in a lawsuit by a larger enterprise that strategically plays for a dominant position in a negotiated settlement or judgment.

What follows is the experience of an engineering executive who was tasked to lead the development of an effective IP strategy for his company.

The results of a 10-year development program have done much to ensure the market position of the company, expand its markets, improve its technological capabilities, and build its cash flows and shareholder value.

Chamberlain Group is a successful mid-sized company in the consumer durables industry. The company's intellectual property management effort evolved from a narrowly focused, defensive activity to a proactive, business-focused strategic management process. The corporate path from tactical to strategic management of the portfolio began with a commitment by the CEO to drive intellectual property for greater shareholder return. With this top-down focus, the company developed an IP management team.

The responsibilities of the team included the education of the rest of corporate management about intellectual property and then driving this focus throughout the entire company. Intellectual property development and exploitation became an integral part of the company's business. IP is discussed in each and every monthly meeting of senior management and at every quarterly board meeting. The CEO speaks of IP's fundamental value to the company in quarterly employee update meetings. Discussions about IP are as natural as talking about a successful product line, a key manufacturing facility, or a valued customer. Each and all of these topical discussions focus on a corporate asset that must be recognized and managed for shareholder value.

Why IP Requires Active Management

The key characteristic of any successful strategic management of IP is the clear connection to the goals of the enterprise. Intellectual property is a corporate asset, and as such it should be strategically managed to return cash to the shareholders. It is sometimes tempting to focus on having more patents than your competitors, or to lose sight of good business decision making in the heat of infringement litigation. Most IP portfolio managers have experienced these temptations repeatedly. But quantity of patents is no substitute for quality, just as having more factories than your competitors does not guarantee a competitive advantage. And a cool head instead of a quick temper is as important in infringement actions as it is in a business acquisition negotiation. This recognition of IP as a corporate asset is the ultimate justification for expending senior management energy on effective IP portfolio management.

Intellectual property is a corporate asset, and it can be managed for shareholder return in a variety of ways. Intellectual property can protect a unique selling proposition in the marketplace and generate incremental (or marginal) profit dollars for products that your competitor cannot match because he lacks the protections you hold. IP can be used to force competitors to expend precious resources in "working around" key patents, leaving fewer investment dollars available for their innovations and development. IP allows the company to generate additional revenue streams using carrot-and-stick licensing avenues, which fall directly to the bottom line. Carrot licensing is a negotiated royalty rate, whereas stick licensing indicates that the threat of litigation lies behind the patent holder's contentions. The most powerful and effective approach to intellectual property management is to weave all of these aspects together into the fabric of the company's business tactics and strategy, combining them with other more traditionally recognized corporate assets.

Structure to Manage the Day-to-Day IP Operations

The daily management of IP assets is broken into three managerial elements: (1) the intellectual property committee; (2) the intellectual capital team, and (3) senior management's role. Exhibit 11.1, Intellectual Capital Management Organization, presents a cross section represented by the dotted lines that provide integration at the EVP level and focus on the engineering and technical functions that provide the structure for the intellectual capital committee and the intellectual capital team.

The Intellectual Capital Committee

Chamberlain uses a cross-function–based decision-making approach across many business processes. Intellectual property management is no exception. The governing body for portfolio management is made up of senior executives from engineering, marketing, and legal, as well as senior managers from the design and R&D groups. The intellectual capital committee is the glue between the senior management strategic focus and the functional organization's tactical execution. The team has three roles:

1. Review decisions that fall under the control of the functional management team
2. Make investment and prioritization decisions
3. Recommend legal action and intellectual property purchases to senior staff

The combined membership of senior executives in primarily strategic roles and functional managers in tactical execution roles ensures that strategies turn into actionable IP tactics.

The Intellectual Capital Team

The intellectual capital team makes many day-to-day decisions, led by a director with wide experience in engineering and intellectual property. The team is supported by this subject-matter expert group with individuals skilled in patent and technology research, database manipulation, and technical evaluation and testing.

EXHIBIT 11.1 INTELLECTUAL CAPITAL MANAGEMENT ORGANIZATION

CEO

CFO/ Controller
EVP Marketing
EVP Engineering
EVP Administration
EVP Business Administration
EVP Operations

VP Intellectual Capital
Project Manager
IP Technical Support
Project Manager
Intellectual Capital Team

VP Residential Engineering
VP Commercial Engineering
VP Research and Development
Intellectual Capital Committee

It is important to note that the Chamberlain team elected to use a gifted engineer with an interest and enthusiasm for intellectual property as its leader. At the beginning of the company's transition to a strategic intellectual property management process I, as vice president of engineering, served as the team lead. As the team's expertise and portfolio management capabilities grew, we quickly realized that a dedicated IC team leader was justified, based on the potential return on the assets employed.

The team discussed the characteristics needed in a leader of intellectual property activities and concluded that the job should go to either a very strong engineer or a capable young lawyer. The team decided to go with the engineer, because our future intellectual property development would be focused around our controllers and their imbedded logic. Someone who would understand the products intimately and be able to evaluate and explain the sometimes subtle differences between infringement and clearance was determined to be a decisive criterion for consideration for the position. The company enjoyed a strong and reliable relationship with its outside counsel, and figured that the strength of that relationship could support the legal aspects of patent portfolio management. The consideration was heavily influenced by the law firm's understanding of the company. The law firm's exceptional knowledge of Chamberlain and its proficiency in the company's technologies offered strong assurance of legal support and created the opportunity to place the more technically knowledgeable engineer in this sensitive and critical position.

The work breakdown of the IC team is shown according to its corporate responsibilities in Exhibit 11.2, Intellectual Capital Team Responsibilities.

The team has developed simple and disciplined processes to cover most of these activities, and they actively educate the larger organization on how to use them effectively. An example of Chamberlain's approach to portfolio management is shown in a simplified version of the invention disclosure potential value tool. This tool is used to evaluate all invention disclosure generated internally and received from outside sources through our "open" innovation activities. Similar tools have been developed for the deciding where to file internationally in each of our core businesses, as well as if and when to pay maintenance fees in each country of issue. Exhibit 11.3, Invention Disclosure Evaluation, lists many responsibilities; most, if not all, are standard tasks for a group charged with managing an intellectual property portfolio.

Other Considerations

There are several other considerations that might not show up on everyone's IP management list. These might include:

- **Acquisition:** The company makes special efforts in its due diligence process to evaluate patent opportunities and risks very early in the acquisition process. A portfolio assessment and general patent landscape analysis often precedes the first formal contact with a potential acquisition target. We have found that we can learn a great deal about a potential target by combining information from patent databases, the Internet, and government sites (such as the FCC web site). Intellectual capital considerations are an integral part of every acquisition target evaluation and due diligence activity.
- **Competitive intelligence:** The IC team is very effective in its ability to gather information about competitors. There is a significant overlap with the approach to business acquisition due diligence and competitive intelligence gathering that includes patent database mining, Internet and government database search, and the use of a wide variety

EXHIBIT 11.2 INTELLECTUAL CAPITAL TEAM RESPONSIBILITIES

- Invention disclosure evaluation
- Patent acquisition evaluation
- Patent application prosecution
- Portfolio life cycle management
- Business acquisition due diligence
- Potential in and out licensing opportunity evaluation
- Infringement detection
- Competitor intelligence gathering
- Litigation support
- Design clearance

EXHIBIT 11.3 INVENTION DISCLOSURE EVALUATION

Invention Disclosure Potential Ranking

FINANCIAL—Maximum points: 40

Cost to market—Maximum points: 12

Points	*Development time, measured in man-months*
6	If it is less than A man-months
4	If it is between A and B man-months
3	If it is between B and C man-months
2	If it is predicted to be greater than C man-months
Points	*Expense cost in dollars*
3	If the cost is between $ and $$K
2	If the cost is between $$K and $$$K
2	If the cost is between $$$K and $$$$K
1	If the cost is greater than $$$$K
Points	*Capital cost in dollars*
3	If the cost is between $ and $$K
2	If the cost is between $$K and $$$K
2	If the cost is between $$$K and $$$$M
1	If the cost is greater than $$$$K

(continues)

EXHIBIT 11.3 INVENTION DISCLOSURE EVALUATION (CONTINUED)

Invention Disclosure Potential Ranking

FINANCIAL—Maximum points: 40 *(Continued)*

Time to market—Maximum points: 8

Points	*Time to market in years*
8	Takes less than 1 year to get the product to market
6	Takes between 2 years and 1 year to get the product to market
4	Takes between 5 and 2 years to get the product to market
2	Takes more than 5 years to get the product to market

NPV of first 5 years of margin—Maximum points: 16

Points	*NPV of the first 5 years of margin (Sales increase, Sales maintenance, and Price maintenance)*
16	> $M
8	$$$K–$M
2	$–$$$K

License out potential (10 years)—Maximum points: 4

Points	*Potential outside the Chamberlain markets*
4	High potential
3	
2	
1	Low potential

STRATEGIC—Maximum points: 40

Protect core business and market—Maximum points: 40

Points	*Business Unit A*
16	Being designed into product presently
10	Potential for future use

Points	*Business Unit B*
6	Being designed into product presently
4	Potential for future use

Points	*Business Unit C*
12	Being designed into product presently
8	Potential for future use

EXHIBIT 11.3 INVENTION DISCLOSURE EVALUATION (CONTINUED)

	Invention Disclosure Potential Ranking
STRATEGIC—Maximum points: 40 *(Continued)*	
Points	*Business Unit D*
4	Being designed into product presently
2	Potential for future use
Points	*Business Unit E*
2	Potential for future use
In sandbox but outside core—Maximum points: 16	
	Total maximum points: 24 = Potential for future combined
Points	*Potential of the non-core patent*
16	Potential to start new high-volume product area potential of new core product
10	Potential to start medium-volume product area
4	Potential to start small-volume product area
	Maximum points: 8
Points	*How strong is the core?*
4	The original patent is presently the only way known to create the technology
2	The core can be worked around, with difficulty and/or cost
Points	*How good is the support?*
4	Company is the sole provider of the technology
2	A competitor has the technology but this patent would allow Company to use this technology
Out of sandbox and outside core—Maximum points: 10	
	Total maximum points: 16
Points	*Potential of the non-core patent*
10	Potential to start new high-volume product area potential of new core product
6	Potential to start medium-volume product area
3	Potential to start small-volume product area

(continues)

EXHIBIT 11.3 INVENTION DISCLOSURE EVALUATION (CONTINUED)

	Invention Disclosure Potential Ranking
	Maximum points: 6
Points	*How strong is the core?*
3	The original patent is presently the only way known to create the technology
1	The core can be worked around with difficulty and/or cost
Points	*How good is the support?*
3	Company is the sole provider of the technology
1	A competitor has the technology, but this patent would allow company to use this technology

NOVELTY—Maximum points: 20

Fundamental vs. incremental technology—Maximum points: 10

Points	*Type of technology*
10	New fundamental change
9	Incremental improvement of a fundamental
6	New feature
4	Feature improvement

How crowded is the space?—Maximum points: 5

Points	*Number of patents crowding*
5	No patents of similar technology
3	1 or 2 patents of similar technology
2	3 or more patents of similar technology

How broad is the coverage?—Maximum points: 5

Points	*Potential claim language*
5	Broad
4	
3	
1	Narrow

Total—Potential Action by Ranking

55 or Greater	File
46–54	Discuss
45 or Less	No Action

of proprietary business and technical databases. When combining these sources, the team is able to provide a relatively complete picture of how a company does business, where they are investing their innovation resources, who their key innovators are, and who else in their industry or related industries might be aiming to gain market share at their expense. It is common to create this kind of profile on a variety of current and potential future competitors. The team reviews these profiles with the intellectual capital committee and, when appropriate, with the larger senior management team.

- **Product clearances:** Product clearances are another area where Chamberlain may focus more attention than other companies of similar size and sophistication. The company has taken a very aggressive position on defending its intellectual property assets and has not hesitated to resort to the courts for enforcement. While this posture has increased the value of the IP portfolio and made future litigation less likely, it has had the effect of sensitizing our industry to the value of intellectual property and has made careful product clearances a necessity. The company begins the product clearance process when a product or feature is still in the R&D stage. At this point, product clearance and evaluation for potential patentable ideas are natural partner activities. Doing homework on patentable ideas naturally leads to questions of patent clearance and vice versa. As the company progresses through the R&D stage to the product design and development stage, work continues on product clearance throughout the entire process. Chamberlain employs a formal design review process at multiple points during product conceptualization and detailed design development to ensure design quality and regulatory compliance. The IC team is an integral part of these design reviews, and the director of intellectual capital is a required attendee at all of these meetings. Catching and avoiding potential infringement situations are common activities during these design reviews.

Managerial Anecdotes

Several examples of the value of the inclusion of intellectual property review in the design review process offer a stronger sense about the effectiveness and savings that are created by the combined review process. The two anecdotes that follow illustrate the typically unrecognized value of IP in the mid-level enterprise.

Liability Limitation

We were developing an accessory to our core product for sale primarily at "big box" retailers. Very early in the product-development process, the engineers reviewed the approaches they were considering in a formal design review. One of the preferred approaches was identified by the intellectual property team member as potentially infringing an existing patent owned by an individual inventor. In the ensuing debate, it became apparent that this was the best approach to designing the product. A decision was made based on this design review to pursue acquisition of the patent, which was accomplished well (this timing is important) prior to product introduction at a cost that met the company's criteria for return. Prior to the inclusion of intellectual property experts in the design review process, the potential infringement would likely not have been identified until very late in the product-development project when the outside attorneys performed the final clearance review.

Innovation Stimuli

The development team for a new design of a critical core accessory line brought their preferred design approach to the design review meeting. The intellectual property representative identified that a relatively strong competitor already had a series of patents covering this technology. This led to a brainstorming session on alternative approaches, which resulted in the development of a superior design. This design was then patented, providing a cost-effective and secure future for the product line.

Senior Management's Role

The senior management team plays a key oversight role in the company's intellectual property management activity. The CEO holds monthly staff meetings for his senior management team. At each of these meetings a review of the financial results for the various businesses is conducted, including a separate breakout of intellectual property–related revenues and expenses. The management team follows this financial review with discussion of key strategic issues and action plans that invariably touch on intellectual property issues multiple times and many ways. While many companies would describe their senior management meetings in a similar way, it is important to note that this team is explicit about intellectual property interactions in each of these discussions. Intellectual property is not a subtone in these meetings but rather a repeating theme. And questions or insights about the intellectual property aspects of a given topic are just as likely to be articulated by our senior executives from finance or marketing as those from engineering or legal. This demonstrates the level to which intellectual property has been taken in the management practices of Chamberlain.

How IP Management Has Impacted Our Business

At this point, it might be helpful to provide an example of how we have used our approach to intellectual property management to support our strategic goals.

The overriding strategic goal of the company is to build a growing business that produces superior returns for our shareholders over the long term. Management has an enviable track record in realizing these goals. One important aspect of our growth and superior shareholder return has been the licensing royalties received on various individual pieces of intellectual property. Chamberlain's view extends far beyond it own industry in the pursuit of ways to exploit its technologies and IP assets.

One particular patent involves a key piece of technology that is licensed to a partner in another industry. This patent is well written with strong, defensible claims. But the true value of that patent can be realized only when it is combined with other key business assets, in this case, market share and market penetration. (An analogous effect is described by Dr. James Conley in his article "Patents Come and Go—Trademarks Are Forever" (*Executive Counsel,* Vol. 2, No. 2, March/April 2005), where his focus is on the synergy that can be developed between patents and trademarks in consumer products.) The licensee of this patent has built a thriving business in an unrelated field and is creating new value for both companies.

One distinctive feature about Chamberlain is that it typically keeps one eye focused on the long term while the other watches the near term. In one recent situation, the company recognized that one particular patent would expire in less than a decade. Ten years may seem like a long time in business terms, but that is not always the case. The realities of market share and installed base along with a somewhat long lead time for product changes at our licensee make this a relatively short-term issue to be addressed in one specific case. Consequently, the IC committee began work immediately to create the next patentable technology improvement that will replace the current technology well before the patent expires. The IP strategic execution calls for having the next-generation patents in place and productized in the marketplace to support a continued revenue stream. This foresight was the result of the committee's evaluation and its plans to secure the revenue stream when the patent expired. The IC team and committee proposed the solution to the senior management team for approval. Each part of the company's intellectual capital management activity worked as intended in identifying, evaluating, and addressing a business issue related to intellectual property.

Closing the Loop

Intellectual property is a corporate asset and should be strategically managed to return cash to the shareholders. There are many ways to structure an organization to achieve this end, but all of them start with a commitment and vision at the very top of the company. The CEO must recognize the value of intellectual property and be willing to drive this focus throughout all levels of the organization. The more corporate value is associated with such intangibles as intellectual property and brands, the more managing the intellectual capital portfolio becomes a necessity, not an option.

CAPABILITIES DEVELOPMENT

Accelerating Wealth Creation Through IP Management in the Mid-Market Company

A. Observations

Dr. Mark Karasek offers an insightful and detailed explanation about how his company (Chamberlain Group) reshaped IP management practices in its industry. It is a rare and generous set of guidelines about how to bring one's company into a competitive position in IP management.

B. Action Items

1. Develop a contingency plan for responding to a letter "suggesting a license" (a/k/a alleging infringement).
2. Find proficient legal counsel (internal or external) that can manage IP in an operational context as well as litigation (may not be the same one) who is immediately accessible to guide IP communications of defense or assertion.
3. Create and use a technology map of the company relative to the remainder of the industry to show who is pursuing what technologies that might create IP advantages and identify vulnerabilities.
4. Coach your CEO in the criticality of recognizing the influence of IP on the business—take an active role in making IP a key part of the company's operations.
5. Develop training programs to help employees recognize the importance of IP so as to drive IP-related knowledge and practices throughout the enterprise.
6. Be aggressive in defining what constitutes a business asset as opposed to a financial asset.
7. Develop the capability to identify potential infringements and design around the technologies of specific competitors in the industry.

C. Performance Improvement

The article is so descriptive that it can serve as a blueprint for IP performance—use it to help get organized.

The Corporate Capabilities analysis is done by Bob Shearer and represents the analysis of the corporate performance behaviors found in the chapter, and supplemented by the Taskforce Subject Matter Experts (see Acknowledgments for a list of SMEs) over the course of related discussions and work sessions.

CHAPTER 12

Intellectual Property's Impact on Corporate Financial Management

CHRISTOPHER J. LEISNER,
CPA, CMC

As a result of a robust IP management initiative, the CFO and the company will recognize that if IP is better managed, the balance sheet improves and profits are increased.

KEY POINTS TO LOOK FOR

- **SFAS 141 and 142 standards are driving changes that require the CFO to make determinations about the value of IP and other intangible assets annually.**
- **The analyst and investment communities are demanding more insight into IP value impact.**
- **The CFO already has much of the information needed to develop an IP-financial management capability readily accessible from traditional business documentation.**
- **The value of the company's IP assets can be developed systematically by determining what the company's assets consist of in terms of their value to the owner as well as their value to other companies.**
- **Those companies that do communicate IP value to the investment community will likely find favor, but those that lag in developing and reporting will more likely be punished as "laggards."**

Combining IP Asset Management with Traditional Tangible Asset Management Standards

The landscape of IP management is shifting dramatically, especially as it relates to the new responsibilities required of the CFO. Recent AICPA pronouncements regarding intangible assets are one concern the CFO must take into account, but the focus here is more intently on the positive and pragmatic approaches to generate greater earnings per share and shareholder value. The practices presented are already in place in some of America's leading companies. Consequently, the emphasis is on the robust integration of the existing corporate IP management systems and data that can be used by the CFO to provide the same level of financial management and disclosure reporting provided for tangible assets. By clearly establishing the IP–financial linkage, the CFO can acquire and develop practices, procedures, and measures to elevate the company's financial performance.

Shifting Expectations for the Company's Senior IP Executives

Although business historians will debate when IP management emerged as a critical component of a well-run company, we know that from at least the 1980s, IP management became integrated with the exchange of corporate IP within the technology transfer industry. Using this general starting point, we can observe how the task of IP management has shifted not only from one discipline to another, but in how most companies traditionally viewed the relative importance of their IP. Certainly, the historical perspective of the legal team was the construction and maintenance of an effective collection of intellectual property rights. The number of issued patents was often used as the barometer of a company's IP prowess.

As the costs of prosecution and maintenance grew, "quality versus quantity" became a central IP management theme. Perhaps in part due to this shift, R&D executives increased their participation in setting (and therefore enforcing) corporate policy surrounding which innovations would receive support and which were to be abandoned. Making money (and saving taxes) from IP innovations became an important focus of the

IP executive. This pragmatic practice lent itself to the exercise of establishing an out-licensing capability, and as the revenues grew in size, this position steadily moved up the corporate organization chart to where many IP holding company presidents were on a par with other established operational and corporate senior executives.

Exhibit 12.1, IP Management's Expanding Landscape, illustrates how, as the technology transfer market has grown over last 25 years from $50 to $175 billion, many corporations have shifted the responsibility for their IP management from the legal department, to the R&D department, and then to the newly formed licensing staff. Today, there is another shift where the focus is on the CFO. IP management and IP value extraction responsibilities are being transitioned (shifted away) from the legal, technical, and licensing teams over to the financial division.

It is important for the CFO to study how his or her predecessors in the company have managed the company's IP. There are many existing databases and procedures that the CFO's predecessors developed that can make the CFO's IP management more efficient and more effective. As discussed subsequently, each of the other departments that were previously managing IP can still provide useful information to the CFO. Such information can be incorporated into sound internal systems of control and value creation that, when properly summarized, can provide useful information for internal decision making and also prove a source of investor insight without disclosing trade secrets to the competition.

FASB Demands for Change

Recent FASB pronouncements require the CFO to identify and value intangible assets acquired in a stock purchase. Under SFAS 141, "Business Combinations," all business combinations must now be accounted for as purchases—pooling accounting is no longer permitted. The pooling approach allowed the buyer to merely add the account balances of the acquired entity to the buyer's own balances, thereby using "historical cost" as the value of the company acquired, rather than the market value as of the date acquired. Under the purchase treatment, the acquiring company must record the acquired assets at market value and further account for any excess purchase price that exceeds market value under the pronouncements set forth in SFAS 141. SFAS 141 provides initial measurement and

EXHIBIT 12.1 IP MANAGEMENT'S EXPANDING LANDSCAPE

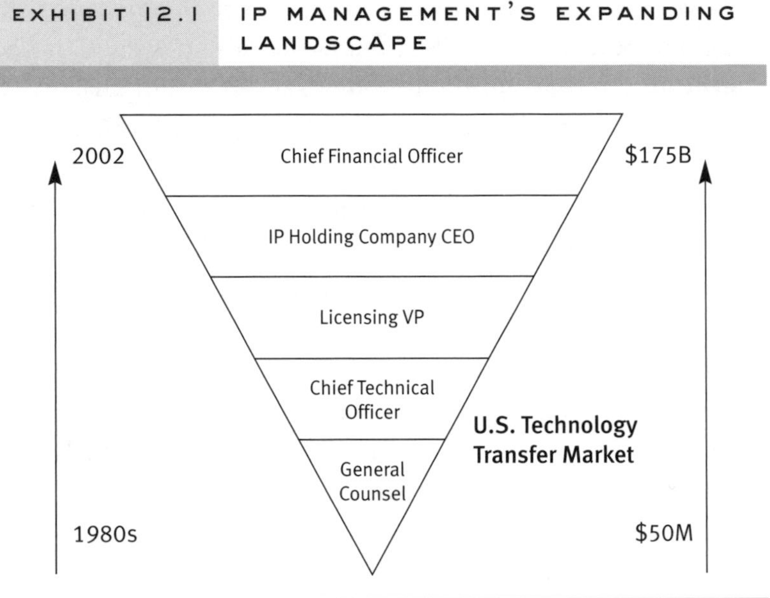

recognition guidance for intangible assets and goodwill acquired in a business combination, including mandates as to the recognition of intangible assets apart from goodwill. (See Exhibit 12.2, SFAS 141 Business Combinations.)

SFAS 141 was a significant departure from previous accounting rules and now requires the CFO to specify, in certain situations, what acquired intangibles benefit which business unit, as well as the carrying value (meaning the amounts reflected in the specific asset accounts) of those intangibles!

The volume of new accounting pronouncements relating to intangible assets has been greater during the past four years than during the prior

EXHIBIT 12.2 SFAS 141 BUSINESS COMBINATIONS

- Sets forth rules on purchase price allocation
- Requires companies to establish fair value of all identifiable assets
- Requires that asset values be allocated to individual reporting units
- Goodwill is no longer amortized
- Sets values to be tested annually for impairment

fifteen. The rate of issuing new requirements is so fast that this 2001 cornerstone pronouncement—SFAS 141—was revised (SFAS 141-R) within four years of its effective date.

Although not currently required, there is great anticipation that CFOs will soon be required to apply these departmental IP measurement and reporting standards to *internally developed IP,* and not just to *acquired IP.*

Accounting for acquired intangibles, including goodwill, in years following the acquisition is provided in SFAS 142, Goodwill and Other Intangible Assets. SFAS 142 provides that goodwill should not be amortized; it mandates that impairment tests of goodwill be conducted annually or, in some circumstances, more frequently; in addition, it provides guidance on recognizing impairments. (See Exhibit 12.3, SFAS 142: Goodwill and Other Intangible Assets.) In contrast with earlier GAAP, which required amortization of all intangibles, SFAS 142 addresses whether intangible assets other than goodwill have *indefinite* useful lives and therefore should not be amortized but instead tested at least annually for impairment, or *finite* useful lives and therefore should be amortized over their estimated useful life.

Intangible assets with finite useful lives are tested for impairment under SFAS 144, Accounting for the Impairment or Disposal of Long-Lived Assets. Intangibles having finite lives and thus being amortized must also be reviewed for recoverability of carrying amounts in a process similar to that under SFAS 142. Auditors examine useful lives and review management's reassessment, which are altered when warranted by circumstances (e.g., technological obsolescence making the useful life of a patent much shorter than the legal term).

EXHIBIT 12.3 SFAS 142: GOODWILL AND OTHER INTANGIBLE ASSETS

- Establishes requirement to test the book value of goodwill on an annual basis
- Carrying value of reporting unit
- The fair value of assets assigned to each reporting unit, including tangible and intangible assets plus goodwill, will constitute carrying value
- Compare carrying value of reporting unit to fair value in subsequent impairment tests

Wall Street's Demand for Change

Wall Street and the SEC are demanding more transparent reporting as well as a more open policy of reporting intangible asset performance and balance sheet values. The majority of today's investing community, especially institutional investors, understand that effective IP management can influence their stock ownership strategies. Interfacing with the investors is a primary responsibility of the CFO. Investors and analysts are increasingly asking the CFO about IP and its effects on corporate performance.

Surprisingly, Wall Street and the SEC continue to thwart the CFO's efforts to appropriately report IP by making them use outdated, historical cost–based tools. The capital market community remains addicted to its dependency on the single unit of measure it knows how to handle, namely, "cash." Unless the CFO converts non-cash, IP value expressions into cash equivalents, such as net present value or EBITDA, Wall Street representatives and rating agency analysts seem inclined to declare that the CFO has fallen short in his performance. Most of the intangibles that contribute to a company's market value do not throw off free cash flows that can be uniquely attributed to specific forms of IP. Rather than expand the array of acceptable value expressions, the capital markets are forcing the CFO to stay within a measurement construct that requires data not available to the CFO.

However, there are other measures currently in force. For example, the U.S. federal courts have been resolving disputes over IP for decades, and in particular, the courts must resolve issues relating to the "value" of the IP at the center of the lawsuit. Three typical measures are: (1) the value the defendant generated as a result of its "ill-gotten gain," (2) the profits the plaintiff would have recognized "but for" the actions of the defendant, and (3) an estimated "reasonable royalty" that otherwise would have been recognized by a hypothetical license agreement. Ill-gotten gain and lost profits can each include such measures as market share, pull-through sales (follow-on sales of related but separate goods and services), improved credit rating, and increased market cap. Hypothetical license agreements used as a foundation for a reasonable royalty reflect *potential* rather than just *historical* royalty revenues.

To date, most CFOs have expressed reluctance to disclose internal "estimates of value," citing their fiduciary duty to the shareholders to protect company trade secrets and avoid improper revelations to the company's competitors. Prior to SFAS 141 and 142, as well as Sarbanes-Oxley, CFOs had been successful in using the "less is more" disclosure strategies. However, Sarbanes-Oxley has tipped the scales in favor of the investors, who can now require the CFO to quantify the company's success in its IP value identification and its IP value extraction initiatives! More on this will follow.

Getting Ahead of Sarbanes-Oxley's Impact

Ever since it was published in 1995 that approximately 74 percent of the total value of the Standard & Poor's 500 Stock Index was composed of "intangible assets," the investment community, the Securities and Exchange Commission (SEC), and the Financial Accounting Standards Board (FASB) have increasingly pushed for more insight into what exactly constitutes this value. These three communities demand more meaningful, reliable, and timely financial information regarding intangible assets—in particular, regarding intellectual property (IP).

Meanwhile, most companies are reluctant to respond to these pressures for fear of disclosing competitive information or reporting on something as amorphous as intangible assets. In the wake of the Enron, Global Crossing, and other financial reporting abuses, companies are even more exposed to the enforcement demands from the Sarbanes-Oxley Act of 2002. The company must develop and implement stronger systems of internal control or risk possible exposure to criminal proceedings. The CFO is now *personally* liable under the Act, and under Section 807, the CFO's exposure now includes possible imprisonment. With the exception of the CEO, no other senior executive has been forced into this position. Certification language now reaches further and typically includes such declarations as:

> The registrant's other certifying officer and I have disclosed, based on our most recent evaluation of internal control over financial reporting, to the registrant's auditors and the audit committee of the registrant's board of directors (or persons performing the equivalent functions):
>
> > a) all significant deficiencies and material weaknesses in the design or operation of internal control over financial reporting which are reasonably likely to adversely affect the registrant's ability to record, process, summarize and report financial information; . . . .

These statements clearly impose responsibility and accountability at the highest levels of management, but the thrust of the statements also calls for a shift in thinking at the executive and board levels. The widely respected Jim O'Shaughnessy, former chief IP counsel at Rockwell Automation, summed up the situation for the CFO quite succinctly:

> If one accepts that the goal of Sarbanes-Oxley is a well-informed investor, then intangible assets require the same degree of attention as tangibles. . . . Investors are more interested in what is being done with intangible assets than in receiving an abstract report hedged with qualifications to fend off litigators.

Creating a Financial–IP Map for Data Management and Financial Reporting

Exhibit 12.4, Developing the Financial–IP Map, presents the kind of data, documents, and procedures frequently found within the company that the CFO can turn to for the information necessary to incorporate into IP accounting and reporting procedures. The specific kinds of IP management procedures and available data will vary from one corporation to another, however. As a starting point, this table can help support the CFO's current IP-related internal controls review procedures.

The table aligns a typical IP creation and protection life cycle with information and documentation commonly used in most companies. That documentation, although prepared for a very different purpose, can be the source of data that the CFO would need in order to quantify the carrying value of the intangible asset(s) in question. The table groups (column headings) this information into four categories:

1. **Market Definition:** An important determination of market value is the determination of primary and alternative markets where the IP may bring benefits. The larger the defined markets become, the more robust the value examination will be, and consequently, the total value expected to be extracted from that IP.
2. **Product or Product-Line Attributes:** One layer below the market analyses is the identification of specific product lines and/or products impacted by the IP. In addition to the definition of potential markets and submarkets, this information allows the refinement of

EXHIBIT 12.4 DEVELOPING THE FINANCIAL—IP MAP

Internal IP Management		CFO's IP Accounting and Valuation Data			
IP Life Cycle	Source Documents Generated	Market Definition Analysis	Product/ Product-Line	Customer/ Licensee Identified	Revenue/ Profit Projections
R&D director assigns research project	Research work program and budget	Yes	Likely	Possible	Possible
Researcher status reports	Actual versus planned results	Yes	Likely	Possible	Possible
Inventor submits request to patent committee	Technical disclosures; competitive research; budgets and ROI estimate	Yes	Yes	Yes	Likely
Patent committee ranks and approves/denies funding	Meeting minutes; committee member notes	Yes	Yes	Yes	Likely
Inventor meets with IP counsel	Validity research; prior art analysis; inventor/assignee report	Likely	Likely	Yes	Possible
Inventor meets with development team	Manufacturing prototype; cost projections; market/product analyses	Yes	Yes	Yes	Yes
IP licensing team meets with R&D and marketing staffs	Licensing strategies; triage/ rank targets; revenue forecasts	Yes	Yes	Yes	Yes

market research so that actual quantities and values per unit can be assembled.

3. **Customer/Licensee Identifiers:** Product purchases and sales lend themselves to the identification of potential users of the IP. This information can provide significant data that further supports the determination of the IP's value.

4. **Previous Estimates of Revenues:** As part of the justification provided by innovators and product commercialization decisions, the innovation life cycle will often generate preliminary estimates of value. Although these studies may not be current, the methodologies and the data sources used by R&D, patent committees, and licensing personnel will provide meaningful assistance to the CFO staff as they prepare their IP value analyses.

The responses shown in this table reflect how likely it is that the kind of data that the CFO will need for items (1) through (4) above, can be found in the steps of the life cycle and/or the documents noted in the row descriptors. For example, in the first row, executive management within the R&D division initially assigns a research project to a specific researcher or inventor. As a part of that process, certain initial documents will be prepared that, in part, set forth the justifications and anticipated benefits of the project. That justification would typically identify markets and key players in those markets. It is likely that specific competing products or product lines are discussed. As part of that market discussion, it is possible that representative target consumers/customers are disclosed; these target customers help to define target licensees. Also, as part of the overall discussion of goals for the project, certain economic justifications could possibly be set forth. Such economic justifications would typically include revenue, cost, and profit data.

Integrating IP into Financial Management

As the CFO becomes more involved in IP management, her management considerations will fall into three categories focusing on the key IP management questions:

1. What IP does my company have?
2. What is the value of the IP to our company?
3. What is the value of the IP to other companies?

What IP Does My Company Have?

Many consider "IP" to be just the legal protection, such as a patent or trademark, that attorneys obtain to protect the new invention. Others see

IP primarily as the invention itself. Both are accurate. IP is eclectic—it is a combination of technology and legal protection. But in addition, the distinct intangible asset called a patent along with the distinct intangible asset called "know-how" each have accounting and financial attributes that influence their valuation and financial reporting. (See Exhibit 12.5, IP Is Composed of Three Distinct Intangible Assets.) It is when the technical, legal, and accounting attributes are identified and measured that the CFO has captured the total value attributable to IP.

These features are important to consider as the CFO addresses the basic intangible asset ownership and inventory question, "What IP do we own?" Although the legal department will likely have an inventory of patents, trademarks, and copyrights, it may not have an inventory of trade secrets or of newer innovations that should be patented. To obtain this additional information, there are several procedures that can be implemented, including the following:

1. **Create an Internal Gap Analysis** whereby the CFO maps processes and business operations to the existing IP portfolio; those unprotected business operations are potentially trade secrets and/or items

EXHIBIT 12.5 IP IS COMPOSED OF THREE DISTINCT INTANGIBLE ASSETS

- IP is defined as intellectual assets that have been enhanced with specific legal rights.
- IP is composed of three categories of intangible assets, each with unique and powerful value drivers.

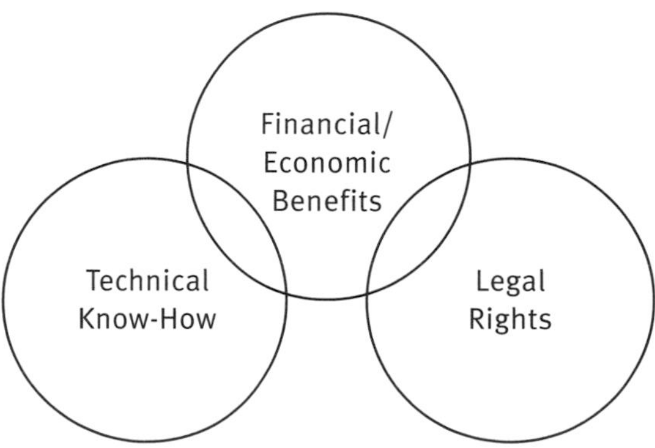

worthy of legal protection. It is quite likely that in addition to CTO departmental records, the CFO's own internal auditing staff has field inspection reports that discuss departmental compliance with internal control procedures.

2. **Review Inventor Assignments and Technical Disclosure Documents** as maintained by the R&D director and the IP legal staff. In this review, the CFO will become familiar with the process by which new innovations migrate from pure research into product development and into legally protected intangible assets. Again, the majority of the information that the CFO is seeking already exists in other departments. However, by incorporating the Sarbanes-Oxley component to this exercise, it is likely that the existing procedures will be improved and interdepartmental communications enhanced.
3. **Review IP as Cataloged in the Legal Department's Patent Registry;** this task will render not only an inventory of IP but also an aging of that inventory. As with a depreciation schedule of fixed assets, the CFO's staff can employ existing procedures and systems to more robustly manage intangibles. Further, by studying the kind of data maintained in the registry, the CFO staff will be better equipped to evaluate the carrying values of the intangibles, as is the case with SFAS 142.
4. **Obtain Competitive Intelligence Research** as maintained by the marketing department, the licensing staff, the IP legal staff, and the R&D directors. Each of these corporate representatives maintains distinct, yet related databases of competitive intelligence relating to research, product development, patent prosecution, and market penetration that the CFO can use to catalog the company's intangible assets.

What Is the Value of the IP to Our Company?

As noted previously, IP is perceived differently by various executives of the company. Is it a technical asset or a legal asset or a financial asset? Exhibit 12.6, IP Now Seen as a Financial Asset, shows how the same assets are perceived very differently by executives from different disciplines. As value extraction choices are evaluated, the financial implications of one

EXHIBIT 12.6 IP NOW SEEN AS A FINANCIAL ASSET

IP executives and corporate finance professionals see the same basket of IP as two very different types of assets:

IP Executive	VP Corporate Finance
Technical Disclosures	Promise to Pay
Improved Technology	Time Value of Money
Competitive Edge	Credit Ratings
Legal Protection	Risk/Reward Evaluation
Assets Are "Unique"	Interchangeable = Strength

structure versus another can be material to the point where the company may choose to alter its value extraction game plan. For example, the presence of expiring capital loss carry-forwards that can be harvested only if the IP is sold may shift an out-licensing strategy to one of an IP sale. Considering the financial and accounting value drivers is, in many situations, just as important as considering the technical and patent claim value drivers.

Once the CFO has established procedures to identify and inventory current and emerging intangibles, he or she can develop procedures by which internal values can be quantified, managed, and reported. The CFO already measures the value of IP associated with acquired companies under SFAS 141 rules. Often, the "141" analysis determines the incremental increase in value to a business unit that the intangibles bring as a result of the acquisition, often by way of an analysis known as a "Relief from Royalty." Those "141" processes, in addition to the steps outlined subsequently, provide the CFO with IP values that can be managed, commercialized, and ultimately reported to stockholders. Additional procedures that allow for this internal value determination include the following:

1. **Summarize Historical Expenditures** as reflected in the cash disbursement and tax deduction/R&D credit files. However, rather than just assigning them to a general ledger account, this summary should also be coded to reflect internal business units, market sectors, product lines, and USPTO patent identification codes.
2. **Study Previous SFAS 141 IP Valuation Analyses** and determine the kinds of data relied upon by outside appraisers. Then, with assistance

from the IT department, compare this list of information with available internal information so that internal management reporting systems can have better access to this data. The CFO may also want to incorporate this information into the goodwill impairment testing as required under SFAS 142.

3. **Prepare R&D/IP-to-Product Mapping** whereby research is categorized by products and product lines offered by the company. Ultimately, incremental changes in related product sales and enhancements in relevant market shares can be tied to R&D expenditures. As a result, internal trending data can be accumulated that measures, on a "before-and-after" basis, the anticipated revenues being attributed to in-process R&D.
4. **Inventory Existing and Forecasted Licensing Agreements** that are known to the licensing and the legal departments. The inventory needs to be expanded to include not only financial information, but market, product, and patent classification codes. This inventory lays the foundation for the initial estimate of free cash flows directly associated with specific IP.
5. **Incorporate Preliminary IP Values into Rating Agency Models** and then compute an updated credit rating for the company. In this procedure, the CFO is able to track the potential reduction in the company's cost of capital as a result of its expanded inventory of intangible asset values. It is worth noting that there is a growing sector in the financial services industry that have dedicated products based on IP; they are often referred to as "credit enhancement" programs.

What Is the Value of the Company's IP to Other Companies?

After the CFO is able to report on the company's intangibles and after procedures are established to estimate the value those assets bring to the company, analyses can be constructed that present an estimated value these intangibles could provide to other companies. One way to construct such an analysis is to separate "IP Value" into two categories: Strategic Value and Financial Value. Strategic Value relates to the innovation(s) behind the IP; the licensee is primarily interested in the technology and not just the legal protections established by the patent or other legal protection. Financial values are derived primarily from the legal intellectual property rights as reflected in the patent claims or copyright protection afforded by the issuing government.

As an initial step, the CFO can review the existing and anticipated licensing agreements and classify them into strategic versus financial categories. Although some will have attributes of both, the identification of IP by these classifications will affect the type of valuation model used in the quantification step. The CFO should confer with the director of the licensing department, as this grouping may likely follow that department's licensing triage procedures. The licensing department typically has more IP to license out than it has staff to do the work, and therefore it should have procedures and analyses that identify the patent clusters that have a greater likelihood of successful out-licensing (the "low-hanging-fruit" analysis). Exhibit 12.7, Key IP Value Considerations, lists a set of criteria that frequently appear on the licensing department's checklist of attributes by which to locate low-hanging fruit. Remember, in order for a license to be issued, the licensor must agree to share the IP and the licensee must be willing to pay for that IP.

This review of licensing agreements will also yield a list of actual and potential licensees. With the assistance of the licensing department, the CFO can then investigate those licensees' patenting policies and track records. If, for example, a specific licensing target has maintained a steady release of "new and improved" products but has not filed many patent

EXHIBIT 12.7 KEY IP VALUE CONSIDERATIONS

Must Be Licensable IP!

1. Strong Technology—Base and Alternative
2. Balanced Patent Claims
3. Robust Patent Clusters
4. International Filings
5. Three to Five Years of Product Implementation
6. Active or Growing Market Sectors
7. Comparable License Agreements

applications recently, then that target may be more receptive to a strategic license agreement. If the opposite is true (few products but lots of patent applications), then the target may be more interested in acquiring specific patent rights to round out its portfolio. The CFO should then consider meeting with internal IP counsel to discuss the company's own policies regarding these indicators. Because the costs of patent prosecution must be justified, the internal requests for patent prosecution will likely have information that the CFO can incorporate into this research.

From there the CFO can direct research into the patent portfolios of its primary competitors. As the CFO initiates and refines these procedures to measure external IP values, three benefits arise:

1. Corporate IP value measurement procedures will be significantly improved.
2. The CFO will have a more robust working relationship with the other members of the IP Management Team.
3. IP monetization and commercialization initiatives will become a more common event.

Knowing the Value of the IP Is Not Enough

Identifying IP held by the company is an important component of IP management, but the CFO will need to determine ways in which to extract that value for the benefit of the shareholders. Quoting Jim O'Shaughnessy's article again:

> Those assets not held for future purposes ought to monetize, which can be done in many ways, investors will begin to expect it, then demand it, and eventually punish the laggards.[1]

The CFO has several specific value extraction approaches to choose from; some contribute to IP-based earnings, and others merely improve liquidity. Generally speaking, these options can be expressed along a continuum of Risk/Reward as well as Cash/Earnings financial goals (see Exhibit 12.8, IP Value Extraction Options). At the lower end of the risk continuum, enhanced borrowings are common; at the higher end, Gain on Sale

EXHIBIT 12.8 IP VALUE EXTRACTION OPTIONS

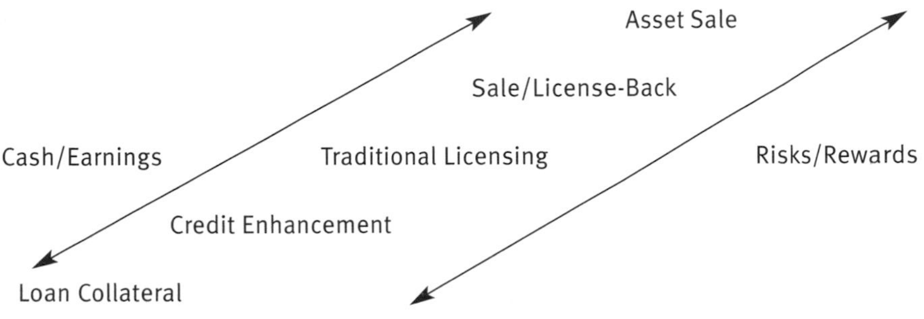

profits can be recognized if the company is willing to part with the ownership and control of the IP. Interim hybrids, such as Sale/License-backs exist where risks are reduced while profits from asset sales are recognized.

Summary

The landscape of IP management has dramatically shifted such that the CFO is now *required* to take a leadership role. In meeting those new roles and responsibilities, the successful CFO will integrate into his or her department the skills, data, and insights of those departments that have been creating, protecting, commercializing, and licensing IP for decades. As a result of a robust IP management initiative, the CFO and the company will recognize that if IP is better managed, the balance sheet improves and profits are increased. This initiative also supports the CFO's design and maintenance of expanded internal controls and management reporting that now includes intangibles. Ultimately, the CEO and CFO will be able to demonstrate compliance with Sarbanes-Oxley in regard to intellectual property.

Note

1. Jim O'Shaughnessy, Esq., "Sarbanes-Oxley Will Drive Reporting of Intangibles," *Executive Journal,* Nov./Dec. 2005.

CAPABILITIES DEVELOPMENT

Intellectual Property's Impact on Corporate Financial Management

A. Observations

1. Mr. Leisner has produced a CFO starter's kit for effective utilization and value management for IP-based assets.
2. This chapter also represents a sophisticated state-of-the-art checklist for the CFO where value recognition and reporting about IP assets are concerned.
3. One major aspect of this commentary reveals how pervasive IP reaches into the enterprise and where one can go to identify and define the value linkages.

B. Action Items

1. The company must develop ways to map IP asset value to revenues, cash flows, market share, and earnings.
2. The CFO needs to integrate IP asset accounting, tax implications and alternatives for IP assets into the normal financial operations of the company.
3. There are some unique requirements for the company's annual impairments tests of IP assets required by complying with SFAS 141 and 142 that must become a corporate capability.
4. The CFO and CEO need to orient the board of directors about the complexities and unique considerations of communicating IP value and IP management capabilities to the investment community.

C. Performance Improvement

1. The capabilities of the company can best be accelerated by bringing the General Counsel, IP Counsel, CFO, and Controller into daily contact regarding IP asset value and revenue generation.
2. Design your action plan along the lines Mr. Leisner has suggested by retrieving the related documents used for other purposes (as noted) and begin to define your information needs to better manage this process inside your company.

The Corporate Capabilities analysis is done by Bob Shearer and represents the analysis of the corporate performance behaviors found in the chapter, and supplemented by the Taskforce Subject Matter Experts (see Acknowledgments for a list of SMEs) over the course of related discussions and work sessions.

SECTION FIVE

Creating New Wealth

The satisfaction that comes from realizing your earnings forecasts to create value for your shareholders is virtually unmatched in business. The idea that you can now determine the value of your brand and its reputation and its contribution to shareholder value is simply revolutionary. The authors of Chapter 13, Dr. Pam Cohen and Jonathan Low, tell you how this is possible—and possible after only a few months of research. Most CEOs do not think about reputational value and communication strategies in quantitative terms, but now it is possible and would go a long way toward benchmarking your position relative to where your shareholders' interests lie and where the competition really lives. This brand and reputational value is where much of the approximately 70% of intangible value cited in earlier sections resides. Cohen and Low can define that intangible value and they tell you how in Chapter 13.

Value recognition and value extraction are the concerns of one of America's leading forensic accountants and corporate governance consultants. Dr. Steve Henning uses his experience with the FASB Intangibles Task Force and the SEC to focus in on corporate value extraction considerations and techniques. Chapter 14 offers some insightful narrative and a much stronger version of capabilities benchmarked to proficiencies. Every company should measure its proficiency in value extraction based on the level defined by the Taskforce SMEs and included in Dr. Henning's chapter, Internal Operations to Leverage IP Assets.

Sue the bastards! Karl Fink offers insight into how businesses are using the courts to gain competitive advantage. During the current period of IP consolidation and shakeout, the ability to use the courts and manage litigation now simply assumes a project status. Businesspeople make the decisions to sue. Mr. Fink's tutorial in Chapter 15 will help get you grounded in this new business process.

Mr. Fink's commentary is the perfect conclusion to a book dedicated to helping you increase your company's competitive capabilities and create new wealth for your employees and shareholders. The shock of IP suits and increased litigation might call for this to be chapter number 1. But today we are scrapping for every asset we can keep, not just for commercial gain; but the push for IP conversion to cash has opened a small door to the nation's technological interests wherein an unknown buyer may purchase (or merely infringe on) some of America's most sensitive technologies without anyone being aware of the technology transfer and intellectual property rights that occurred with an IP transaction.

CHAPTER 13

Defining Brand and Reputational Value

JONATHAN LOW AND
DR. PAM COHEN

Intangible asset valuation analysis is already being conducted by the financial markets and could become a regulatory (governmental) requirement in the not-too-distant future; that means it will be up to each company to develop its own priorities, procedures, and measures for brand value and other forms of intangible value management.

KEY POINTS TO LOOK FOR

- **Brand and reputational value may be more highly valued than market cap in many large, public companies.**
- **Multinational corporations are being required to report on their intangible asset values, especially in Europe; measurement now can attract investment.**
- **Management needs to measure and understand the value of brand and reputation to manage those assets more effectively before making them part of the financial reporting process.**
- **Brand value is best measured over time. It starts with a snapshot, but is best managed day in, day out, year in, year out.**

(continues)

KEY POINTS TO LOOK FOR (CONTINUED)

- **The ability to define reputational and brand value is available today. It is not something that remains in an abstract or theoretical realm of business performance.**

Competitiveness Overview

The impact of intangibles such as intellectual property, reputation, and brand on financial outcomes is frequently overlooked in traditional assessments of organizational value. Advances in business and academic research as well as new approaches to valuation have now given executives the ability to more accurately evaluate—and quantify—the effect on financial and operational outcomes of investments in intellectual capital.

In service-oriented economies, value is increasingly being created by ideas rather than things. The manufacture of share assets has become subject to commodity-pricing regimens (although sales of raw materials such as oil or steel may increase from time to time due to shortages) while products based on intellectual property enjoy consistently higher margins. Even in a manufacturing-based export economy, higher margins may be derived from the sale of maintenance service, financing, and supply chain support than from the sale of core manufactured products.

Intangibles such as reputation, research and development, communications, brand, and IP may account for 50 to 80 percent of corporate market value in an increasingly service-based economy. Institutional investors have reported in surveys that more than 35 percent of their portfolio allocation decisions are based on intangibles. *Forbes* magazine's report on the 25 Most Valuable Corporate Brands demonstrates that some corporate brand values are greater than the parent company's market value. Related research has established causal relationships between inputs such as IP and outcomes such as sales growth, market share, and stock price performance. Extensions of this research have further demonstrated the impact that communications about these intangibles have on financial and operational results.

The implications of this methodological approach are significant. The demands of global markets, with their emphasis on comparability, higher standards, and greater transparency, are requiring institutions in the private, public, and not-for-profit sectors to provide more data about their allocations of people and capital. The markets are further demanding that the efficacy of these investments be demonstrated. In this acutely competitive environment where knowledge is capital, perceptions matter. The sustainability of an organization—its very license to operate—may depend on how financial, reputational, and human capital markets value the impact of such investments.

Global Competitiveness

Prior to the late nineteenth century and the widespread adoption of conventional accounting methods, a person's reputation—the ultimate intangible—was the basic building block of business success. Global U.S. competitiveness will increasingly depend on the development of intellectual capital–intensive services as supply chain value strategies and improving developing economy logistics drive production to low-cost locations. In the near term, as seen in late 2006, U.S. competitiveness is eroding because of the nation's inability to deal effectively with intangible assets. In Europe and parts of Asia, companies, academicians, and governments are ahead of the United States in their thinking about the management and disclosure of intangible value as a strategic point of differentiation.

There are several developments in Europe that are potentially significant in their effect on the United States and any major corporation operating there.

- The U.K. passed legislation referred to as the OFR, which stands for "operating and financial review." In effect, this legislation mandates that these types of data—"intangibles data"—must be captured for the next two years and presented in the management disclosure and analysis section of the annual report. It looks as though the ultimate goal of the U.K. is to ultimately require mandatory disclosure of this sort of information.
- The French have passed legislation governing the management of their pension funds requiring the pension funds to gather much more

> information about the companies in which they're investing. It is anticipated that this kind of mandated disclosure will be accelerated across the developed world since similar uneasiness about pension fund commitments and financial capabilities to administer the benefits are being felt in all major economies.

To illustrate the global impact of all this, the 2005 OECD conference on intellectual asset management in Italy was sponsored by the Japanese government. The 2006 OECD intellectual asset management conference is being hosted in Tokyo by the Japanese government. So, other countries are quite active in the area of intangible asset recognition; the Japanese are quietly and effectively moving to start global standard setting and information gathering on this issue of intangibles reporting.

As with GAAP versus International Accounting Standards, intellectual property law, and the alleged impact of Sarbanes-Oxley disclosure requirements on securities listings, harmonization of U.S. policies with the demands of the global market may well affect the U.S. attitude towards disclosure of information about intangibles. Current U.S. policy is driven by a combination of concerns about tax consequences and an overarching predisposition against any sort of government participation in the policy formulation process. However, the cost of maintaining separate sets of books and the instantaneous flow of information make it increasingly likely that U.S. corporations will begin to measure and manage intangibles simply because it is the competitively intelligent course to take.

The harsh reality of global sourcing means that no company can afford to waste time or resources. In particular, no business can safely underestimate the potential impact of an asset in which it has invested or in which value may be accruing in spite of the fact that it might not yet meet GAAP standard criteria. Intangibles must be recognized and managed as business assets even if they do not qualify as financial assets. In fact, it is not clear that the so-called GAAP standard is even particularly meaningful any more; companies continue to search for beneficial ways to disclose information about themselves (more than 400 now produce supplements to their annual reports on such issues as sustainability, child labor, and various others). As use of the Internet becomes more universal, sustainable competitive advantage decreases because competitors, lenders, shareholders, suppliers, and customers all have access to more information and can make better judgments about what is in their own best interest. To achieve first-mover advantage for even a short period of time, effective application of every corporate asset becomes a crucial competitive differentiator. That means that training, process improvements, knowledge support, and other such intellectual capital are critical to global success.

Ultimately, to become part of the global supply chain, a business must convince its corporate customers that it is reliable. To achieve that goal, companies must implement and communicate information about their intellectual property, their processes, their governance, their ability to innovate, the quality of the training their employees receive, and the quality of their products based on recognized international standards. Chinese and Indian companies have begun to realize their potential and, though infamous for ignoring intellectual property rights of others, have begun to protect their own intellectual capital. (We do mean intellectual capital, the broader category.)

Corporate Innovations

Intangibles provide a new source of value for the company, one in which the company has already invested and yet may not have thought about in terms of reaping a return. The cost basis may be low in accounting terms, but the return may be quite high. In addition, having fewer fixed "tangible" assets and more intangibles gives an enterprise more agility (i.e., the ability to move operations to whichever regions in the world or products and services that offer the highest potential return).

Furthermore, intangibles make money for the company in four ways. First, they make a company more effective at what it does—for instance, making products cheaper and quicker to market. Second, they can be sold as intellectual property as in selling a patent. Third, they can be sold as a service, such as providing consulting advice to other companies (i.e., as a process improvement). Fourth, they can enhance the long-term value of the enterprise if it is to be sold to another company.

Most U.S. and European companies already capture data on approximately 70 percent of their intellectual capital. Typically, this information resides not in corporate management information systems, but in operating unit databases. Frequently, the biggest challenge is not in measuring the value or impact of these intangibles, but in getting business units to share that knowledge with each other.

Corporations measure intellectual capital for a variety of reasons, but the most common are (1) to assess a value for transactional purposes if one is selling or acquiring an asset through licensing, merger, or acquisition; (2) to determine a range of values for financing purposes, such as securing a loan based on the value of an intangible; and (3) to measure the impact of intangibles such as brand on financial outcomes such as sales or price/earnings ratio.

One of the recent studies based on a survey of financial executives at Global 500 corporations asked these executives to tell the researchers:

- The most important drivers of value for their businesses
- How good was the information they were receiving from inside their own companies

There was a sizable gap. What was particularly interesting about this was that the researchers discovered that if you could close the gap between the importance of the information and the quality of the information, there were significant statistical correlations with financial performance measures such as return on equity, stock price performance, and sales growth.

But the most elusive issue is to be able to create the quality of comparable data necessary to use information about intangibles as a management asset. This is a process that has already begun. In fact, it's not even revolutionary any more within corporate America, as many companies are now developing their own approaches to measuring intangibles. What has been lacking is an overarching theme or regulatory hand. Perhaps that's for the best, because what is clear is that a lot of creativity and innovation is being brought to bear by Ford, AT&T, and the hundreds of other corporations around the world that are focusing on this need to define intangible value.

National and International Infrastructures

From a financial, regulatory, and managerial standpoint, we, as an economy, are unable to define values that are clearly impacting our ability to allocate capital, to make smart internal investment decisions, or to communicate value to the capital markets. This kind of valuation analysis is not going to become a regulatory (governmental) function, and that means it will be up to each company to develop its own priorities, procedures, and measures for brand value and other intangible value management. The governing bodies such as the SEC and the FASB are not going to move until they see more evidence of this kind of quantification. It also reinforces the Taskforce position that these methodologies, measures, and metrics are best developed, refined, and perfected as useful business management tools before advancing them to the public policy arena. This is one of the efforts that the Taskforce is working to facilitate—an economic infrastructure that can recognize the value of these assets and bring the investment and regulatory communities into concert with the corporate business methodologies so that value can be recognized, capitalized, and leveraged.

Communications and Brand Value Analysis

The growth of the Internet as an entertainment and advertising channel combined with the disintegration of the mass television market are together driving companies to more effectively measure the impact of their communications strategies. Advertising, public relations, and promotions are all being reevaluated in light of these developments. Examples follow of the types of communications and brand analyses currently being utilized by U.S. and European companies. Exhibit 13.1, Intangibles—The Measures That Matter, provides two sets of factors that contribute to intangible assets and their communications component.

Evaluation of the impact corporate communications have on financial results frequently employs statistical methods to quantify the causal relationships between communications about a company's products, services, or other attributes and the resulting financial implications of change to any of those factors. Exhibit 13.2, Drivers of Client Market Value, reveals that 69 percent of the company value is driven by tangible financial drivers and 31 percent is derived from external communications.

To get the input data, analysts use either media analysis data provided to companies by outside vendors who specialize in that sort of analysis,

EXHIBIT 13.1 INTANGIBLES—THE MEASURES THAT MATTER

Factors that contribute to Intangibles include, but are not limited to:

- Leadership
- Human Capital
- Technology and Processes
- Communications

Factors that contribute to Communications include:

- Analyst Relations
- Customer Relations
- Employee Relations
- Shareholder Relations
- Supplier Relations
- Capital Structure
- Cost Control
- Profitability
- Revenue Growth
- Stock Performance
- Better than Competition
- Market Share
- Environmental Responsibility
- Legal and Ethical
- EO Strength
- Fosters Entrepreneurship
- Overall Management
- Brand
- Reputation

PREDICTIV

---

or proxy surveys of a company's customers, competitors, suppliers, and/or financiers asking them to rank the company on a range of 1–10 on certain "drivers" such as communications about image, price, functionality, and the like. Once this information has been gathered, the results are aggregated and tabulated to a scaled score with a range of 0–100 for each driver.

Once each driver has received its score, simple linear regression is used to determine the correlation between the drivers. A predictive (causal) model is then created to determine the statistical relationships between the drivers, including how the drivers are linked causally to each other and how they are linked causally with respect to other performance measures. These analyses can be focused on a particular topic or public relations message and how those messages impact increases or decreases in the company's revenue. Exhibit 13.3, Impact on Revenue, organizes the statistical impact of communications based on specific message content and enables management to quickly analyze and plan for future communications to influence market value.

EXHIBIT 13.2 DRIVERS OF CLIENT MARKET VALUE

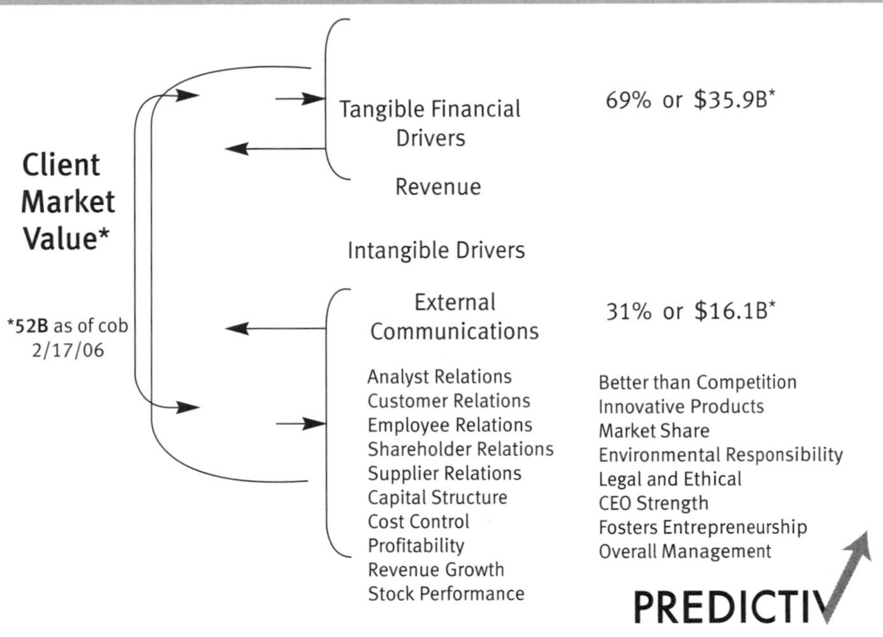

EXHIBIT 13.3 IMPACT ON REVENUE

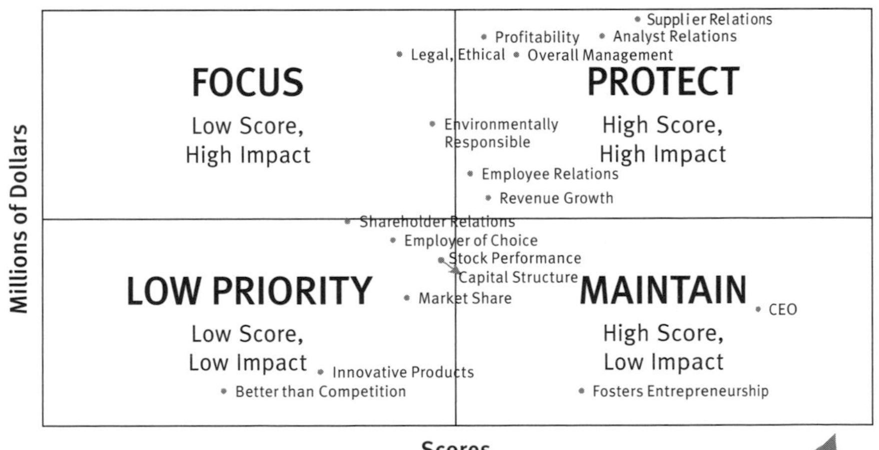

Use of longitudinal or time-series data in these analyses, spanning quarters or years, permits corporations to look at trends over the long term rather than relying on one-time "snapshots."

This type of analysis permits executives to make informed decisions about how a particular change could affect other financial outcomes, and it can also mitigate damage caused by unavoidable or unforeseeable changes (product recalls, environmental mishaps) by increasing the company's focus on other, positive drivers of equal strength (by issuing positive press, for example, on earnings), creating, in effect, communications arbitrage.

Forbes magazine asked Predictiv LLC to rank the top 25 U.S. corporate brands. The intriguing part of this assignment is not so much that a value could be assigned to these brands, which has been done before, but that because of research advances, four specific drivers of brand could be identified.

The drivers of brand uncovered in this analysis were (1) reputation, (2) management, (3) human capital, and (4) innovation. There were numerous others, but these were of greatest importance.

The AT&T valuation approaches that appear elsewhere in this book illustrate the increased levels of sophistication employed inside U.S. companies and their ability to adapt to their own recognized need for better internal measures and metrics about such intangibles as brand value. Make no mistake, however; brand value is no longer intangible! Companies can now determine their brand means using these methodologies. Brand value must be defined in context. Exhibit 13.4, Contextual Considerations of Brand Value Determination, provides the checklist for focusing your brand value communications.

EXHIBIT 13.4 CONTEXTUAL CONSIDERATIONS OF BRAND VALUE DETERMINATION

- **a.** To whom does the company want it to mean something?
- **b.** Are they talking about investors?
- **c.** Are they talking about lenders?
- **d.** Are they talking about potential employees or current employees?
- **e.** Are the talking about suppliers?

This measurement process allows companies to begin defining what and why managing brand value is important. During the process of defining the top brands for *Forbes,* Predictiv found five companies whose brand value exceeded their market value—an amazing realization for the companies involved.

Current methodologies pioneered by Predictiv take a combination of publicly available and proprietary information provided by client companies to compare the company's performance against both internal hurdle rates and competitors' benchmarks to achieve critical data for strategy, planning, and execution.

The CEO's reputation and corporate reputation, among other intangible communications measures, has a tremendous impact on stock price performance, in some cases as much as or more than earnings. Analysis can quantify that impact. This process is iterative in nature, but the model is causal rather than correlative, meaning that results can be predicted with as much as a 95 percent degree of confidence. Anything less is unacceptably subjective. The market wants and insists on quantitative linkages and explanations of performance. That capability is one that will dramatically serve the interests of management and shareholders and will build a formidable presence in the global market. Most importantly, it is an asset that can be recognized and valued immediately.

CAPABILITIES DEVELOPMENT

Defining Brand and Reputational Value

A. Observations

Cohen and Low have developed a reliable system to recognize brand value and perhaps, more importantly, they can tell you (in quantitative terms) how your communications strategy can shape your market cap.

B. Action Items

1. Establish a capability to identify and define the value of intangible assets as these assets are being used in Europe to create an advantage in its capital markets.
2. Develop the capability to stay abreast of international as well as national developments in accounting and financial reporting, and take appropriate actions to create better business methods to gain a competitive advantage.
3. Establish the practices that recognize and eventually value IP assets as business assets until they can qualify as financial assets.
4. Identify key business drivers for your company and your industry in capital markets; track and strategize how a flow of communications based on these drivers influences your company's market value.

C. Performance Improvement

1. Reexamine your communications strategies to help build market cap and relational and reputational value.
2. Begin the work to define value for the company to support decision making at the board and executive levels in the enterprise.

The Corporate Capabilities analysis is done by Bob Shearer and represents the analysis of the corporate performance behaviors found in the chapter, and supplemented by the Taskforce Subject Matter Experts (see Acknowledgments for a list of SMEs) over the course of related discussions and work sessions.

CHAPTER 14

Internal Operations to Leverage IP Assets

DR. STEVE HENNING

Most companies do not gather information about their IP internally that would lend itself to the external disclosure to the investment community. Neither do they have IP-related information available. And still more, they do not have the measures and metrics that might provide some clue to management or outsiders as to the value that they possess.

KEY POINTS TO LOOK FOR

- IP is the primary source of corporate earnings.
- Fewer than 3 percent of all patents are used to generate royalty income.
- Most companies do not (and perhaps do not know how to) report the value contributions of their IP and IA on their financial statements.
- The new corporate challenge is to the CEO and CFO, who should be active in developing the answers rather than leaving valuation metrics to the external forces that drive reporting and make the accounting rules.
- It is the corporate executive team that must take the lead in this activity, to drive this new business innovation that can result in de facto valuation standards before a legislative or regulatory solution is imposed.

Intangible Value

IP measurement and its reporting is of critical importance in the capital markets. The implications of SARBOX compliance and living with the standards and regulatory bodies that are monitoring the Taskforce work to establish value protocols and determinants set the stage for a more practical and essential first step—understanding the value internally so that management has more reliable and relevant information on which to base its investment and operational decisions. The focus is on maximizing the corporate capabilities to create new wealth—that is, by analyzing and leveraging IP assets. These are the *internal IP operations.* Chapter 4, The Economic Infrastructure, Standards, Regulations, and Capital Markets, revealed that during the past decade the vast majority (75%) of value in the top 500 largest firms (based on market capitalization value) comes from intangible assets.

That conclusion was arrived at by simply looking at the value invested in tangible assets, computing the return generated by that investment, comparing that number to market value, and finding that the majority of all value is attributable to the unrecorded assets. Additional research established that intellectual property is a primary driver of the reported corporate earnings.

What this means is that, given all of the cumulative efforts that a company goes through to create the assets, products, and processes, *intellectual property is the primary source of corporate earnings.*

What is amazing about this is the next number: *fewer than 3 percent of all patents are used to generate royalty income.* This statistic shifts the "value focus" to the patents that are really an intellectual or "soft product," whereby licensing of the IP—the knowledge asset (patents)—is sold on terms that are quite different from ordinary products. Significantly, licensing revenues can be in addition to productized revenues to create additional revenue streams. In spite of the efforts to differentiate, there are many occasions and arguments to support the licensing of core technologies that many companies have traditionally held as untouchable; but are they really untouchable in this era of intangible assets and knowledge-driven, innovative organizations?

Patent licensing in 2000 generated about $110 billion in the U.S. economy. Ernst & Young reports that by 2015 that number is expected to be $500 billion. There are two ways to look at this:

1. Growth of 400 percent over the 15 years is significant, but
2. The potential value that patents could generate is still largely untapped and unrecognized.

External Infrastructure

It is now a business imperative to know how organizations actively track the value generated by the IP portfolio, in terms of the market capitalization or of additional revenue streams. What remains to be done is to successfully find (and develop) the linkages and methodologies, measures, and metrics to define the financial impact of IP on total corporate value.

Most companies actively track the value generated by the IP portfolio. Our Taskforce sample showed 86 percent track IP value. This suggests that our companies are maturing in their internal use of IP-related data. But, if tracking is widespread, then financial reporting of that value has been problematic. It's not that companies do not measure performance, but that in our economy only three percent of the patents are generating revenue.

I do not suggest that every patent has monetary value or that it ought to be licensed, because clearly the patents that aren't licensed out are being used in some fashion, perhaps defensively or through productization to generate earnings. The point is that we need to think aggressively about whether or not the value inherent in our portfolios is being maximized.

The economic evidence indicates that most businesses do not know the value of their IP portfolios. From the perspective of the SEC, the FASB, or the International Accounting Standards Board, here in the United States of America, there is little knowledge about, and perhaps even less desire or even a responsible notion about, reporting IP value.

Whatever the factors might be that play on this absence of disclosure to the investment community, we can and must proactively develop the protocols and define the measures and metrics for our knowledge economy. The standard setters and regulators have been reluctant to impose a reporting paradigm simply because they are not sure themselves what exactly ought to be reported. But at this point, I ask you to ask yourself: "What is it that my company does to actively track this value; how could that information be structured to say something meaningful to the market about our ability to create and extract value?" *This process is an innovation and would create positive corporate differentiation in the capital markets ostensibly inviting investor favor.*

Some observers may suggest problems that are inherent in the disclosure process, but most objections are based on fears of revelation of strategies and company secrets about where scarce resources are being applied. The encouragement of increased disclosures is not a question of "tipping off the market," but rather of creating an economic infrastructure that can allow our companies and our economy to grow and prosper. Please understand that the best source of the wealth creation for most companies is the employment of their intangible assets. The fact is that most companies do not (and perhaps do not know how to) report the value contributions of their IP and IA on their financial statements. It is very difficult from a public investment perspective to understand that there may be untapped and unrecognized value in the absence of any method or means to quantify and communicate this huge intangible value. But to ignore (or avoid) this component of value creates inequities in the capital markets with the net effect of suppressing corporate value.

Shareholder interest is the guiding principle in our capital markets, and the questions that arise out of these considerations are powerful: "*How do I hold managers accountable for creating and realizing intangible value; and how do I evaluate performance and progress with the utilization of my IP assets?*"

The Internal Operations

Although there is a lot of debate about what information should be provided to strengthen the nation's economic capability to recognize IP and intangible value, the operations inside the enterprise are evolving too. Valuing IP and intangible value is a science and practice that is beginning to find traction as executives adjust their decision dynamics to accommodate and account for the intangible element of their investments. The successful enterprise will find ways to solve these problems and communicate its internal successes to the external world.

This is the new challenge to the CEO or CFO and the boards of directors. It is the CEO and CFO who should be active in developing the answers rather than leaving its solution to the external forces that drive reporting and make the accounting rules. Isn't one Sarbanes-Oxley enough for a generation or two?

Perhaps the major impediment to this business innovation to create value and report success with IP is that today this is a soft process; this will not be so in the near future. But today's regulatory community is merciless about these soft issues. Reluctance to talk publicly about IP valuation or the importance of the portfolio is rooted in the potential liabilities of a misstatement or shift in the market. The Taskforce is advocating a safe harbor for reporting of IP value for a period of three to five years in order to overcome this negative influence on reporting. Such a safe harbor protocol is not a new idea, and it seems to be gaining some traction within the regulatory community.

Managing IP assets has traditionally been the responsibility of in-house legal departments. Most corporations still hold to a functional or departmental focus. This organizational structure has served us well for generations and is anchored in the university system of schools for each discipline within the university. The legal group has its own particular issues or demands on intellectual property, and the technology and operations people have their own beliefs about the value that is inherent in this portfolio. And, of course, the corporate finance people have their own objectives with regard to liquidity, credit ratings, meeting quarterly earnings, estimates, and other data used to support an upward movement in market cap and shareholder value.

Corporate executives are expected to monitize the intellectual property that their units produce. It is no longer good enough just to produce intellectual property; that property must have an ROI value to justify the investment. The capital markets, the financial users, and every company's stakeholders are becoming increasingly aware of this process. As they become more informed and sophisticated, they are requiring greater information and greater accountability as it relates to the management of intellectual property.

In recent cases some companies have been frightened by the threat of litigation, because the plaintiff has alleged that management has been ineffective or negligent in the way it creates value from its intellectual property. So, increasingly these stakeholders are focusing on what management does in the IP process.

It is important for the senior executives to come together, coordinate, and develop a plan to better manage their IP and intangible assets. IP monetization will not happen unless it is understood and driven by the CEO.

IP attorneys and research directors play a role in this. They have to educate the rest of the organization as to the pervasive and critical role IP plays in the creation of sustainable performance.

The IP attorneys are the hub in the "spoked wheel" of this new demand on corporate and executive performance. The accountants and the attorneys alike must become conversant with the valuation models. At the point where the investment bankers begin to understand the monetization opportunities, the company will find its sources and costs of capital reduced, but that condition will only follow the more disciplined application of acceptable valuation methodologies. Consequently, it is the corporate executive team that must take the lead in this activity—to drive this new business innovation that can result in de facto valuation standards before a legislative or regulatory solution is imposed.

Implicit in this movement toward a more effective internal operational capability is the creation of a concurrent capability to establish IP value recognition in the external economic infrastructure. This can be accomplished only through increasingly common IP-based valuation and related transactions and a supporting education and standards system for the investment community. This support system is going to focus tightly on the communication of definitive performance factors, their relationships, measures, and metrics. How can a company best convey this information to the market? Are our executives (are we) to be content letting people try to guess the value of the assets that we sit on based on our earnings results without us helping them make the direct link?

Most companies do not gather information about the IP internally that would lend itself to the external disclosure to the investment community. Neither do they have IP-related information available. And still more: they do not have the measures and metrics that might provide some clue to management or outsiders as to the value that they possess.

Value Extraction Strategies

In 2004, the Taskforce Subject Matter Experts (SMEs) developed a scorecard for monetization options. Everyone is well aware of the carrot-and-stick licensing opportunities, sale, or spin-off, and the Taskforce's own "extended licensing program" that uses a financier and strategic alliances to generate immediate cash and long-term royalties.

The use of IP as loan collateral or as asset-backed securities generally has the result that people have to "way overcollateralize," and that is not a good option for monetization for many firms. Way overcollateralization means that the amount of benefit is simply not commensurate with borrowed money. IP assets used as collateral typically are treated in total—that is, the entire portfolio is used as security to preempt the use of derivative IP should the borrower default. IP assets are, to date, also treated as having less value than tangible ones.

The venture capital community has an almost inverse relationship. This community invests in the idea and the market position. This was the fuel for the "dot-com" run-up, of course, and that experience has set us back a decade or more in our willingness to even look at intangible value.

Finally, donations of IP are under attack by the tax courts. Discussions about whether the credit should be based on a fair value valuation or on a cost basis continue. Look for donations to be an increasingly difficult technique for generating tax credits, and expect that such tax credits will soon become totally unacceptable.

Exhibit 14.1, Taskforce Value Extraction Strategy Scorecard, developed by the Taskforce Subject Matter Experts, provides the performance measures and proficiency levels for value extraction strategies that can be used

EXHIBIT 14.1 TASKFORCE VALUE EXTRACTION STRATEGY SCORECARD

IP Value Extraction Mechanisms *(NOT presented in any order of potential impact)*	**Organizational Capability Statements** Generally speaking, the scaling is structured as **1** is not competitive; **2** is competitive; and **3** is advanced competitiveness
1. Donation The act of obtaining tax credit for giving IP to an educational institution	(1) Portfolio is not organized. (Donations should not be considered as a value extraction mechanism if the portfolio is not organized.)
	(2) Portfolio is organized, periodically reviewed, and can support competitiveness and tax-based decisions.
	(3) Portfolio is organized and regularly assessed regarding strategy, value, tax, market share, and earnings impact.

(continues)

EXHIBIT 14.1 TASKFORCE VALUE EXTRACTION STRATEGY SCORECARD (CONTINUED)

IP Value Extraction Mechanisms *(NOT presented in any order of potential impact)*	**Organizational Capability Statements** Generally speaking, the scaling is structured as **1** is not competitive; **2** is competitive; and **3** is advanced competitiveness
2. Licensing In The act of obtaining IP rights to improve technology, processes, or market share	(1) Company has no IP or technology strategy. (2) Company has integrated IP and technology strategy; identifies patent(s) blocking access to a potentially valuable market and seeks to license to facilitate access to the market; further has relationships with universities, customers, and suppliers in core technologies. (3) Company actively monitors and searches for technologies to create market opportunities.
3. Licensing Out The act of making one's IP available to others to create revenues	(1) Company has no dedicated licensing activity. (2) Company engages in licensing activity that extends beyond obvious application and into other industries. (3) Company uses an active licensing function aligned with strategy according to technology and operates to protect IP and expand market share and earnings, preferably through a profit center structure.
4. Cross Licensing The act of providing IP rights to improve revenues or market share to access critical technology in exchange for making one's own IP available to another party	(1) Company has no cross-licensing activity, except in a reactionary or expedient mode to reach a settlement or capture an opportunity. (Company is active in reaching out to maintain its technological base through employee education and publications, events, etc.) (2) Company develops and maintains alternative and supporting IP to make cross-licensing opportunities available in critical technologies; cross-licenses are used to enhance brand identity in traditional markets. (3) Company employs a formal communication and incentive system to support strategy and technology for invention, innovation, and identification of potential infringement.

EXHIBIT 14.1 TASKFORCE VALUE EXTRACTION STRATEGY SCORECARD

IP Value Extraction Mechanisms *(NOT presented in any order of potential impact)*	Organizational Capability Statements Generally speaking, the scaling is structured as **1** is not competitive; **2** is competitive; and **3** is advanced competitiveness
5. **Sale—Extended License-Back** The act of selling a selected portion of one's IP portfolio for cash, licensing it back from the buyer, and jointly participating in a more aggressive "out-licensing" activity	(1) Company's licensing activity resides as a function of IP management. (2) Company's IP value extraction strategy and operations include tax, revenue, and earnings considerations. (3) Company's IP value extraction strategy and operations are integrated among finance, IP, marketing, tax, and investor relations with full confidence in Sarbanes-Oxley compliance.
6. **Abandonment** The act of stopping payment of maintenance fees for IP that is considered not economical to the company's business purposes	(1) Company's portfolio is not organized and requires basic review to distinguish among IP value classifications; is a major project to impute value of portfolio. (2) Company's portfolio is organized into classifications of value with some notion of value to business. (3) Company's portfolio is dynamic and the process provides ongoing accountability and review of IP classification and value extraction or cost containment decisions.
7. **Spin-Out** The act of creating a new venture based on IP and its perceived value in the marketplace	(1) Company can identify critical and potentially marketable technology, but is dependent on other party to develop the business model. (2) Company can identify critical technology and develop business scheme to exploit it with other parties. (3) Company systematically reviews its technology and innovative business practices and has relationships to develop and roll out a "new Co" or other venture structure. (Company can set up its own business with an integrated financial and technology strategy, IP, and R&D capability serving as its own incubator.)

(continues)

EXHIBIT 14.1 TASKFORCE VALUE EXTRACTION STRATEGY SCORECARD (CONTINUED)

IP Value Extraction Mechanisms *(NOT presented in any order of potential impact)*	**Organizational Capability Statements** Generally speaking, the scaling is structured as **1** is not competitive; **2** is competitive; and **3** is advanced competitiveness
8. IP for Equity The act of placing one's IP rights into a new or existing venture for a share of ownership in the enterprise	(1) The company places its IP into the hands of another entity for a portion of the ownership. (2) The company integrates its IP in a full business context with other organizations. (3) The company systematically reviews IP for its value in many varied structures to realize optimum value with other known entities.
9. Litigation The notification of infringement, threatening or filing suit for the purpose of extracting money or protecting technology or market share	(1) Company is disrupted and has to find external infrastructure to assess validity of claims against it. (Company does not systematically review its technology for infringement liabilities or competitive advantage.) (2) Company knows industry, competition, and nuisance players and can employ cross-licensing or coexistence agreements while assessing potential impact of litigation on operations and market position. (Company may rely on litigation as one means to maintain or enhance value.) (3) Company tracks new technologies and trends and is able to anticipate actions of others as they might affect operations and IPR.

Taskforce Proposed Value Rating Scale: Capabilities Statements (1–3) are used to rate (scale) the company's capability. Generally speaking, the capabilities statements are as follows:

(1) *Statements that signify early stages of capability development*

(2) *Statements that signify where most competitive companies function*

(3) *Statements that signify advanced competitive capability*

for internal assessments, training needs analysis, or benchmarking of departmental capabilities.

Finally, such factors as technology creation, patent applications, patent grants, and the capital markets are tied. This is an opportunity to monetize. It is an opportunity to get capital—to have access to capital that a company might not otherwise find accessible.

The capital markets are waking up. There is a growing realization that IP represents sources of strategic advantage, and there is great strategic advantage to capitalizing it. The question is: "What are you doing internally in order to realize that value?" Finally, patents when viewed as a financial asset, greatly impact the earnings and market value. We know that companies that do monetize their IP assets realize the benefit of trading at higher earnings multiples (the figure is 30% higher), have greater valuation, and are perceived to be less risky.

Conclusion

The corporation has the opportunity to shape how IP and intangible value will be defined and recognized in the knowledge economy. It is a task that is essential to corporate competitiveness, but it needs the consensus and supporting infrastructure from the financial, investment, regulatory, and standards communities.

If corporate America and its individual CEOs and CFOs and boards of directors do not step up to this challenge, the likelihood of legislative intervention is inevitable and not too far off. Please join with us to take charge of our destiny by defining the economics of our future.

CAPABILITIES DEVELOPMENT

Internal Operations to Leverage IP Assets

Observations & Action Items for Corporate Performance Improvement

A. Observations

Dr. Henning provides some specific proficiency statements for value extraction based on the Taskforce SME's criteria.

1. The internal ability to measure IP value is uniquely a corporate interest. Research to define the measures and metrics of IP in a situational, contextual, and specific industry is a key part of the current Taskforce program.
2. There is no shortcut, you need to begin developing your own internal measures and metrics to benefit your own company's decision making, and use that experience and data to drive the framework for the new economy.

B. Action Items

1. Develop the systems to track IP assets to revenues, cash flows, market share, and earnings.
2. Develop utilization and financial performance criteria for the IP portfolio.
3. Develop the board of directors and the executive team so they can make judgments about internal IP-related performance and reporting.
4. Develop managerial performance criteria and accountabilities for IP management in non-IP functions.
5. Develop a management process to evaluate IP-based assets to support value extraction strategies and execution capabilities.

C. Performance Improvement

The capabilities proficiency table that appears in the previous few pages is the result of the Taskforce SME's analysis and proficiency statements. This analysis employs the same Taskforce methodology used in Chapter 8, Intellectual Property Drives Corporate Changes to Create New Wealth. Dr. Henning's presentation of this capabilities/proficiency table enables you to develop a base line analysis of your firm's present capabilities to extract value from IP assets. Use it.

The Corporate Capabilities analysis is done by Bob Shearer and represents the analysis of the corporate performance behaviors found in the chapter, and supplemented by the Taskforce Subject Matter Experts (see Acknowledgments for a list of SMEs) over the course of related discussions and work sessions.

CHAPTER 15

Value-Added Litigation

KARL R. FINK

Sophisticated shareholders would, in fact, expect the corporate executives to use the litigation tool to add value to the enterprise and their investment.

KEY POINTS TO LOOK FOR

- **Patent litigation decisions have evolved into normal business decisions.**
- **Market share, reputation, lost revenues and profits, and the stomach for a fight are just a few of the quantitative and qualitative factors used to support the decision to litigate.**
- **Patent litigation can dramatically strengthen and protect a company's market position in the industry.**
- **Patent litigation is not a layman's game or something to be done on the cheap.**
- **Companies need an internal procedure to measure their IP business assets in order to make effective litigation decisions.**

VALUE ADDED

One of the shifts in contemporary thinking taking place today is the realization that patent litigation can add significant value to the enterprise. This is something that breaks with the usual perceptions of the business executive, but when a company successfully fights a lawsuit over patent rights, its value is significantly improved—the "value added"—and it can be quite significant.

Most executives normally think of litigation not as a value-added exercise, but as a value-"subtracted" exercise, flushing money and profits away. But today smart litigation is not a waste of money, is not an ego trip for the corporation or its lawyers, is not a primal urge toward fight rather than flight. Instead, it is simply another part of good business, if done right and for the right reasons. Sophisticated shareholders would, in fact, expect the corporate executives to use the litigation tool to add value to the enterprise and their investment.

"Best Goods'" Experience

A company, named "Best Goods,"[1] like more and more companies these days, learned that patent litigation can add tremendous value. Best Goods sold a product used in many, if not most, households in America today. The product was reliable and of excellent quality and it became a preferred feature in most households. The company enjoyed a strong market position and above-average growth. Best Goods had a strong orientation toward customer satisfaction, and its culture constantly worked to improve its product line so that the customers wanted to buy. The company developed a large market share and a high profit margin, and it made a lot of money. Those were the good times.

Best Goods knew about patents during the good times. Sure, it had a few patents. It hired patent lawyers with long, green eyeshades to write up some technical descriptions and file them in the United States Patent and Trademark Office. Best Goods received some patents with fancy ribbons and the official seal of the United States of America, but had no need to do anything with them. After all, Best Goods was in a niche market; it was a market leader and had no serious competition. Nonetheless, some pesky "engineer types" in the company kept on having the patent lawyers get patents on what they were making and selling. This behavior raised eyebrows with management, but management didn't object; the patents were not costing a whole lot, and they provided some value in advertising, didn't they? Otherwise, was there any real value in them?

Best Goods was doing so well that other companies wanted to get in on the action—good old-fashioned competition. So several other companies started making a competing product.

Well, Best Goods knew how to compete with the best of them, and it successfully continued to sell its products alongside several competitors. However, Best Goods had to shave its price and margins a little bit in an effort to hold market share. It lost a few accounts with distributors, dealers, and retail outlets. It lost some market share. Profits dropped a little bit, but the company continued to prosper. But the competition began the performance erosion, and that was the end of the good old days for Best Goods.

The good old times officially came to an end when one competitor, known for the purposes of this story as "Competing Goods," began copying Best Goods' latest product innovation. Best Goods wasn't happy, but it was used to competition. However, it did notice that it had a patent that might cover its latest innovation, now being used by Competing Goods. Best Goods scurried to its law firm to see what it should do. Based on counsel, it decided to send a stern letter informing Competing Goods about the patent and suggesting that Competing Goods take a license.

The letter said nothing said about "ceasing and desisting." Best Goods didn't want to stir up trouble and start a lawsuit. Best Goods knew how expensive lawsuits were and didn't want to "waste" its money and take the risk with the courts. It had few expectations from any legal recourse. What expectations it did have were characteristic of the times: high-priced lawyers, huge legal fees, little confidence in the outcome, and a huge distraction from operations.

Competing Goods, by contrast, was aggressive. They were after the market leader, copying their product, taking customers, taking market share, and generally taking the offensive while taking huge profits from the market. Competing Goods responded to Best Goods' sternness with a nice letter to Best Goods suggesting that Competing Goods take a license. Simultaneously, Competing Goods brought a declaratory judgment lawsuit against Best Goods. In the lawsuit, Competing Goods asked the court to declare that Competing Goods was not infringing Best Goods' patent and further to declare Best Goods' patent to be invalid. So Best Goods counterclaimed for patent infringement.

During the lawsuit, Best Goods at first didn't think much about a damage claim because, after all, it was still the market leader and it really hadn't lost any significant market share because of Competing Goods' infringement. Best Goods thought that it just wasn't gaining as much market share as fast as it would have liked. But the patent lawyers had a damage expert look at the claim and conjure a fancy theory about price erosion and lost sales in certain markets. The experts calculated damages in the hundreds of millions of dollars, much to the pleasant surprise of Best Goods' executive team.

Fast forward several years, through preparation for trial and legal fees of $1 million (this was when billing rates for IP lawyers were lower). Competing Goods then settled on the courthouse steps for many millions.

Not a bad return on a $1 million expense. Factor into this return the preservation of Best Goods' patent, the right to assert it against others, the competitive advantage of having a dominating patent that permits Best Goods to be the sole supplier of an innovation that provides a competitive advantage over all competitors!

In addition to netting millions, Best Goods now had learned the value of managing and asserting its intellectual property rights. It saw opportunity everywhere. It sued other competitors, obtained payments for past infringement many times its legal fees, and either forced the other competitors to stop copying or pay a license. Ultimately, it netted many millions more.

Finally, Best Goods became known as the "big dog" in the field, a competitor to be reckoned with.

Best Goods decided that patents were valuable and patent litigation paid a nice return on investment. Further, management likes its patent lawyers and likes paying its patent lawyers' bills. After all, paying the patent lawyers is not flushing money away; it is an investment well worth making!

Valuing Patent Litigation

How do you measure the potential value of bringing a lawsuit? That evaluation begins with the obvious calculations, specifically:

- Lost-profit damages based on lost sales

- Lost-profit damages based on having to lower prices because of a competitor's sale of an infringing alternative (usually referred to as "price erosion")
- Computation of a reasonable royalty

The reasonable royalty is calculated as a percentage of the infringer's sales. The damages experts, usually accountants and economists, can be creative and conjure up some big numbers. For the purposes of planning on what you can bank on, you might want to discount the calculations of the damage experts somewhat substantially (but not too much).

Next, add the value of obtaining an injunction to stop the infringer in his tracks. If the injunction holds, the competitor has to stop using the infringing innovation. If that innovation were significant, then the injunction would eliminate significant competition. What is that worth to your bottom line? Can you raise prices, raise margins, increase market share, expand customer relationships, expand product lines, add new customers, increase stock value, or attract investors? Any corporation can measure these benefits. Why not do so before you decide whether litigation is worthwhile?

Calculating the Risks

Your calculations may show that the potential bottom line gain from a patent infringement lawsuit could substantially exceed the legal and other costs. Now you want to measure the risks. There are four key elements of consideration. Exhibit 15.1, Key Considerations Pertaining to a Decision to Litigate, lists these four groupings of interest.

Each of these considerations is defined in more detail in the following outline, and each one is based on Taskforce research and review by its SMEs.[2]

1. Analysis of the nature of the patent
   a. Scope: Determine the scope of asserted patent claims (do the claims cover the alleged infringer?). To answer that, you need to understand the meaning of the claims as they would be construed by a court.
   b. Claim construction: Study the patent claims.

EXHIBIT 15.1 KEY CONSIDERATIONS PERTAINING TO A DECISION TO LITIGATE

1. Analysis of the nature of the patent
2. Implications for the business
3. Nature of the relief (remedies) sought
4. Analysis of the risk versus the reward

---

i. The claims must be analyzed under the rules of claim construction as set out by the Court of Appeals for the Federal Circuit.

ii. Claim construction requires analysis of:

A. The ordinary meaning of the terms to one of skill in the art (which may be gleaned from review of the patent, from study of the prior art, or possibly from experts in the field)

B. The use of the claim terms in the specification

C. The use of the claim terms in the prosecution history

D. Any disclaimers or special definitions set out by the patentee in the specification or prosecution history

E. Relevant dictionary definitions including technical dictionary definitions

c. Patent validity. The patent must be checked for its validity.

i. Are there any legitimate arguments for invalidity of the patent? The considerations regarding validity are many. The more significant considerations are listed as follows:

A. Prior art: patents, printed publications, and prior inventions known or used by others

B. Adequacy of description of invention in patent: written description, best mode, enablement

C. Adequacy of claim language: specificity of invention, support in the specification

2. Study of the implicated business of the company
   a. Extent of internal or other company use of allegedly covered subject matter
   b. The profitability of the affected products and/or business
   c. Future marketing and strategic plans of the company
   d. Extent of sales and/or profits of allegedly covered subject matter

3. Nature of relief sought
   a. Injunction—an injunction will cause the infringer to cease operations
   b. Amount of compensation requested
      i. Payment for past infringement (Some companies want past compensation to cover all losses.)
      ii. License going forward (Some companies will also want royalties from future use of their patents.)
   c. Exclusive versus nonexclusive license (One of the greatest attributes of IP is that you can enjoy revenues for the same asset from multiple users.)
   d. Willingness to cross-license (The cross-license is an old form of avoiding conflicts and litigation.)
   e. Form of compensation
      i. Cash, notes, payment plans, and the like
      ii. Royalties on sales, usage, and the like
      iii. Purchase of product from or by patentee
      iv. Buying the company or a portion of it
      v. Covenant not to sue on the infringer's patent(s)
      vi. Assignability of agreement, fields of use, and the like

4. Considerations of risk versus reward, cost–benefit
   a. Analyze cost of litigating
   b. Analyze potential reward
      i. Damages, treble damages, attorney fees
      ii. Gain of sales and market share from injunction
      iii. Effect on profit margins

c. Analyze chances of winning or losing
d. What is the worst-case scenario, best-case scenario, likely scenario?
e. What are the guiding principles of the company that inform the analysis?
    i. Does the company have any policies regarding litigation generally?
    ii. Does the company have any licensing policies? Does it want to license competitors?
f. What effects on the relationships of the company's customers, vendors, and other partners would likely result from litigating?
g. What is the likely effect on the stock value and market perception from litigating?
h. Does this case present the possibility of eroding or bolstering goodwill?
i. What opportunities for expansion of the business open up as a result of litigating?
j. What is the likely impact on other competitors from litigating?
k. How much stomach does the company have for a prolonged fight? (How much of a distraction and erosion of company time and resources is likely to result from a prolonged fight?)
l. Does the company see any advantage in buying time?
m. What are the possibilities that the alleged infringer will be able to design around the patent?

You should consider the factors in the foregoing list, along with the many other factors unique to your business, in determining whether litigation is worthwhile from a cost–benefit standpoint.

Do We Really Want to Litigate?

This is the toughest question for the CEO, especially when there is both high risk and high potential reward. It forces you to ask certain questions about you and your company. *Are you or your company willing to take on risk?* Does your company focus on tangible, measurable indications of costs and benefits only, or does it also look at intangibles? Is your company looking at valuation of IP generally? Are individual decision makers willing to stick their necks out on the matter? Do you have the stomach for a fight? Are you ready to spend millions of dollars for an uncertain outcome? Is your company willing to live with the results, positive or negative?

Conclusion

The decision as to whether to litigate is a gut check as well as an important business decision. It ought to be made by looking not only at the costs but also the benefits in terms of value added to the business after a thorough analysis.

NOTES

1. Best Goods is a fictitious company. Any resemblance to a real-life company is purely coincidental.
2. Taskforce presentation (Nov. 9, 2005) based on SME work sessions on defense and assertion of IP rights.

CAPABILITIES DEVELOPMENT

Value-Added Litigation

Observations & Action Items for Corporate Performance Improvement

A. Observations

1. Litigation is not always your decision. Your company must "muscle up" financially and competency-wise to be ready for another's assertion on what you believe to be your IP rights.
2. Mr. Fink, an experienced and exceptional litigator, sees IP litigation becoming ingrained in the normal course of business processes.

B. Action Items

1. Develop the capability to track IP assets to revenues, cash flows, market share. and earnings from products, technologies, and IP categories.
2. Develop the capability to use these data to make business decisions regarding litigation.
3. Develop and include the capability to include quantitative evaluations regarding damages, punitive damages, risk assessment, market share, and market position.
4. Develop and include the capability to include qualitative evaluations regarding IP value, reputational value, and impact on industry position/share.
5. Obtain the most competent representation in IP litigation matters. (It's sometimes life or death as TI once stated in a Taskforce seminar.)
6. Ensure access to the quantitative and qualitative evaluations to effectively communicate among decision makers at the highest levels of corporate management.

C. Performance Improvement

Begin thinking about your litigation decision process to ensure cost, benefit, and risk are not just concepts but structures for thinking about IP litigation decisions.

The Corporate Capabilities analysis is done by Bob Shearer and represents the analysis of the corporate performance behaviors found in the chapter, and supplemented by the Taskforce Subject Matter Experts (see Acknowledgments for a list of SMEs) over the course of related discussions and work sessions.

Glossary

abandonment—the forfeiture (real or implied) of a potential patent right as a result of an action or failure to act within a certain time frame; the decision to relinquish patent rights by nonpayment of maintenance fees.

AICPA—American Institute of Certified Public Accountants.

assert—formal allegation of patent infringement.

assertion—to accuse another entity of infringement.

barrier to market entry—something that prevents entry of a competitive good or service into a market space. Barriers to market entry are generally economic barriers even if in the form of IP. For example, the cost to acquire IP rights to enter a market may be relatively uneconomical; therefore, the IP is a barrier to market entry.

carrot mining—mining a portfolio for valuable technologies that can be combined with related patents to generate revenue (*see also* **portfolio mining**).

carrot-and-stick mining—mining an intellectual asset portfolio to reveal both "carrots" (valuable patents or technologies that are commercially attractive for another company to generate revenue) and "sticks" (patents that the user is infringing and as a result have value to be licensed or sold to the infringers under the threat of injunctive relief in litigation).

carrying value—the value of an asset as recorded in the balance sheet/general ledger account.

CFO—chief financial officer.

claim chart—a tool used when looking for agreement between the words of a claim and the features of another product or process that allegedly infringes that claim.

claims—numbered paragraphs at the end of a patent application that define what the patent-seeker considers the invention to be and therefore the monopoly rights the applicant seeks. The claims define the legal scope of that patent, and an exclusionary right is granted within the claim definition.

cluster analysis—research and computer analysis of a group of patents to reveal any opportunities for licensing and overall revenue generation.

clustering—procedure to sort a patent portfolio into various affinity groups or clusters (*see also* **sorting**).

commodification—a directed process by which goods or services lose their distinction over competing products or services.

commodity—an undifferentiated good or service; fungible goods or services.

commoditization—a process by which a good or service becomes a commodity.

context-based valuation—assignment of value to a good or service based on the context in which the product or service is used. In a system in which value is context based, the value of goods and services will vary from situation to situation.

copyright—protection provided to the authors of literary, dramatic, musical, artistic, and other intellectual works, protecting the form of expression rather than the subject matter.

CTO—chief technology officer.

counter claim—a competing claim raised by a litigant, typically by the defendant in a lawsuit.

declatory judgement—the declaration by a court that a particular fact is true (for example, that a patent is valid).

EBITDA—earnings before interest taxes depreciation and amortization.

enablement—in practice, one must be able to describe, in words and pictures, *some viable way* of practicing the invention.

encumbrances—limitations or obligations that impose restrictions or present hindrances (e.g., field of use restrictions or previous license grants that limit the scope of rights that could be granted to others).

FASB—Financial Accounting Standards Board.

freedom to operate—being able to make, sell, or offer to sell products with the knowledge that doing so would not infringe others' patents; being able to conduct business without encumbrances or limitations imposed by the rights of others.

goodwill—the excess of purchase price over book value.

human capital—the collective amount of creativity, skills, and productivity of an organization's employees. One of the two major elements that constitute intellectual capital, the other being intellectual assets.

impairment—the condition whereby fair value falls below carrying value.

industrial property—the subcategory of intellectual property with industrial applications—specifically, patents, trademarks, trade secrets, servicemarks, designs, circuit layout rights, and plant breeder's rights.

infringement—use of an intellectual property without the legal consent of the property owner.

injunctive relief—the infringed party may ask the court for injunctive relief, which could be granted and result in an order to stop the infringement (i.e., to stop making any products or services associated with the infringement on another's IP rights).

innovation—something new; a new or improved good or service; a way to perform a task better, faster, smarter, or more economically.

intellectual asset management—increasing the flow of innovations that can be considered for patenting and for commercialization, whether legally protected or not.

intellectual assets—the codified, tangible, or physical descriptions of specific knowledge to which an organization may assert ownership rights. Intellectual assets are one of the two major elements that constitute intellectual capital, the other of which is human capital.

intellectual capital—knowledge that can be converted into profit. This capital is composed of two major elements: human capital and intellectual assets; it is also known as knowledge capital.

intellectual property (IP)—patents, trademarks, trade secrets, and copyrights, either individually or collectively.

intellectual property management—developing a portfolio of defined intellectual properties, then devising the broadest number of avenues for commercializing the properties in the portfolio.

international patent classification (IPC)—an assignment of a classification by the patent office upon issuance.

invalid patent—a patent that has been found by a court to be improperly issued.

invention—an original idea that allows for the solution of a specific problem in a technological field. To qualify for legal protection in most countries, the invention must be novel, nonobvious (or involve an inventive step), and capable of industrial application (industrial manufacture or use).

invention disclosure—description of the invention provided to an internal organization review process for consideration for patenting, with confidentiality being maintained so that patentability is not forfeited.

invention disclosure criteria—see items 1–5 in the following list:

1. Definition of the business problem solved by the invention
2. Definition of how the problem was solved before
3. Description of the shortcomings of earlier solutions
4. Statement of what makes the invention better than earlier solutions
5. Determination of whether the invention is of value to our company or a competitor.

inventor—anyone who contributes to one or more claims of the patent. Inventors are not technicians who perform directed work or managers who state a general goal or problem to be solved; incorrect listing of inventors can invalidate a patent.

keeper list—a record or list of patents that must be maintained because they are under license to others or may have other valuable uses (e.g., for defense against assertion or use in litigation).

know-how—unpatented technical information that is useful and important.

license—the privilege granted to a licensee to use an invention; it does not constitute an assignment. It can be either exclusive or nonexclusive and does not give the licensee the legal title to the patent.Licenses are commonly referred to as "carrot" or "stick" depending on the tactics to extract value from the user. The carrot license is dependent upon making a strong commercial appeal for the user to license your patent. The stick license is the result of a discovered infringement and the IP owner has the "stick" to take the user to court under threat of injunctive relief.

life of the patent—the maximum number of years that the monopoly rights conferred by the grant of a patent will last. In the United States, a patent lasts 20 years from the filing date; it is also known as the term of the patent.

maintenance reviews—(*see* **portfolio maintenance analysis**).

patent—a right granted by a national government for a limited time (usually 20 years from the application date) for a new, useful, and nonobvious invention, allowing the patent owner to exclude others from making, using, selling, offering to sell, or importing the good or service that is claimed in the patent.

patent policy—companies need patents to protect investment in technology, to support cross-licensing, to support licensing revenue generation, and to maintain technological leadership.

patentability—a determination of whether or not an invention should receive a patent, determined by its novelty, nonobviousness, and utility, and also based on a review of the U.S. Patent and Trademark Office's publications and reviews. Generally, patentable objects are any device, apparatus, system, or method that provides a commercial or engineering advantage. For example:

- better quality
- better yield
- better profits
- combines functions
- uses cheaper materials.

portfolio analysis—examining a portfolio to detect valuable, revenue-generating IP.

portfolio maintenance analysis—an analysis that involves sorting through a patent portfolio and examining the fees associated with each group of patents to identify patents that should be discontinued (abandoned) by failure to maintain them because of their low revenue potential.

portfolio mining—performing a portfolio analysis that leads to portfolio development and revenue generation.

prior art—previously used, published, or patented technology that was available before a patent application and may support the rejection or limiting of a claim due to lack of novelty can also be used to invalidate an asserted patent.

product differentiation—a means by which a good or service is distinguished from competing goods or services

profile/profiling—a profile is a characterization or representation of the portfolio by various criteria, such as technology coverage or age.

proof package—the collection of claim charts and related evidentiary support used to confirm allegations of infringement.

prosecution—the process a patent attorney goes through before the U.S. Patent and Trademark Office.

qualitative metric—a measure of the qualitative value of intellectual property. Quite often, qualitative measures of IP value are made by assigning a numeric value to a qualitative aspect of the good or service using a scorecard or other process.

qualitative valuation—assigning a value to a good or service based on qualitative criteria, such as the relationship of the good or service to a key market or product.

quantitative metric—a measure of the quantitative value of intellectual property such as cost, market value, value of an economic benefit, percent utilization of the IP portfolio, or economic return on investment.

quantitative valuation—assigning a value to a good or service based on the cost to create, the market value (by comparison with the value of other similarly situated goods or services), or the economic benefit derived from the good or service.

securitization—the act of committing cash flows from IP works into a debt or equity market to obtain capital.

SFAS—Statement of Financial Accounting Standards.

SFP—subject, format, product system used to classify trade secrets.

specification—the written description of an invention that includes enough detail to ensure that another person skilled in that field could recreate it.

stick mining—examining an intellectual property portfolio to find any patents that are currently infringed, with a plan to sell or license those patents to infringers.

trademark—the right to use a particular word, phrase, or artwork used in commerce to distinguish the goods and services of the trademark owner from those of competitors. A trademark is legally protected and can be in many forms; examples include letters, phrases, words, symbols, and logos.

trade secret—information that has economic value or potential economic value from not being generally known and that is the subject of reasonable efforts to maintain its secrecy.

unpatentable—characterizing an invention that does not significantly depart from what was previously known in the area or that does not relate to the proper subject matter for the patent for any other reason.

valid—a valid patent is an issued patent that is not invalid for one of several reasons, the most common reason being that one or more of its claims read on prior art that was not considered by the patent office during patent prosecution.

validity—patent claim requirements of statutory subject matter, novelty, utility, and nonobviousness.

white space—a "gap" in the array of business, legal and IP relationships that form the corporate assets that can be asserted; that if a gap exists in the array creates a white space that will enable another inventor to legally capture that space. White spaces create vulnerabilities to your company that can be exploited in sometimes messy and costly litigation and can ultimately threaten your business.

workaround—intentionally creating and using distinctions in product design that deviate from aspects covered by others' patents to protect against allegations of infringement.

Index

D

N

O

P

Q

R

T